Self-Sacrifice

SELF-SACRIFICE

Life with the
Iranian Mojahedin

Struan Stevenson

'For anything worth having one must pay the price; and
the price is always work, patience, love, self-sacrifice.'

John Burroughs

BIRLINN

First published in 2015 by
Birlinn Limited
West Newington House
10 Newington Road
Edinburgh
EH9 1QS

www.birlinn.co.uk

ISBN: 978 1 78027 288 7

British Library Cataloguing-in-Publication Data
A catalogue record for this book is available from the British
Library

Set in Sabon at Birlinn

Printed and bound by
Gutenberg Press Ltd, Malta

Dedication

This book is dedicated to Maryam Rajavi and countless other sisters and brothers of the People's Mojahedin Organisation of Iran with whom I have had the privilege to work and campaign. Their self-sacrifice and the self-sacrifice of the PMOI over decades has been an inspiration.

Contents

Illustrations

Struan Stevenson meeting Prime Minister Nechirvan Barzani of Kurdistan

Struan with PMOI protesters outside the UN headquarters in Geneva

More than 100,000 people attending the 2013 PMOI rally at Villepinte, Paris

Struan with PMOI protesters outside the White House, Washington D.C., 2006

Alejo Vidal-Quadras and Struan welcome Mrs Rajavi to the European Parliament, Brussels

Struan hosts a press conference in Brussels for Iraqi Vice-President, Dr Tariq al-Hashemi, in 2013

Struan and Sheikh Dr Rafie al-Rafaee, the Grand Mufti of Iraq, in 2014

Struan with Patrick Kennedy at an NCRI rally at Villepinte, Paris

Struan addressing the 'illegal' PMOI rally in Berlin, 2005

Friends of a Free Iran meeting in the European Parliament, Strasbourg

Struan meeting President Massoud Barzani of Kurdistan

Struan with President Talabani of Iraq, Baghdad, 2011

Struan at the PMOI's International Women's Day Rally in Berlin, March 2015

The landscaped grounds and gardens of Camp Ashraf

Mud and rock-strewn ground surround flimsy portacabins at Camp Liberty

Acknowledgements

My great thanks to my many friends in the PMOI and the Iranian re-sistance for their encouragement in persuading me to write this book, and for the many hours they spent editing and correcting facts, dates, times and places; and in particular, for their friendship and kindness over many years.

Foreword
by
Patrick J. Kennedy
Former Member of the US Congress for Rhode Island

Struan Stevenson's remarkable book details the horrors of repression, torture and execution in Iran and the strange acquiescence of the West in the face of irrefutable evidence of the Mullahs' desire to deploy nuclear weapons and to sponsor terror across the Middle East and worldwide. In *Self-Sacrifice: Life with the Iranian Mojahedin*, the author outlines his own role as an elected member of the European Parliament, standing shoulder-to-shoulder with the main Iranian opposition movement at a time when they were listed as a foreign terrorist organization. More than three decades ago, my father – the late Senator Ted Kennedy – stood alongside Nelson Mandela and the ANC when they were listed as terrorists. Like Stevenson, he was prepared to put his reputation on the line in his fight for freedom, democracy and human rights.

Self-Sacrifice: Life with the Iranian Mojahedin is perhaps the first such book in which the author takes the reader through his personal experiences to show how, as a British Conservative MEP, he ended up getting to know, engaging with, trusting and supporting the People's Mojahedin of Iran (PMOI), despite all the allegations levelled against the organisation. In the course of an interesting and sometimes difficult journey, he even heard the allegations repeated by government officials who sought to discourage him from supporting the movement. He had to conduct his own research and investigations, studying the merits of each allegation and concluding that they were false and originated from Iran's Ministry of Intelligence and Security, to be distributed by Tehran's lobby and unintentionally repeated by others. Stevenson further demonstrates how these allegations have been used by governments to justify their policy of appeasing the Iranian regime.

Struan Stevenson faced threats and smears from the Iranian Mullahs and even from countries closer to home. His vivid chronicle berates Western countries that were prepared to follow a policy of appeasement so that they could continue to do business with one of the world's most evil regimes. His harrowing account of the abject betrayal by the West of 3,400 Iranian refugees trapped in Iraq should stand as a shocking indictment of US, EU and UN policy in that country. In his role as President of the European Parliament's Delegation for Relations with Iraq he courageously exposed the corruption and brutal sectarianism of the Iraqi Government, encouraged and endorsed by the Iranian Mullahs, and warned that it would lead to civil war. In repeated visits to Iraq he met with political leaders and warned that the Iranian regime was exploiting the insurgency to extend its toxic influence across the region.

Stevenson intersperses each chapter in his book with harrowing interviews conducted with survivors of Iran's medieval prisons, detailing the cruelty, torture and executions that continue to this day. His brilliant narrative and in-depth research have laid bare the stark choice we face between the past and the future. He demonstrates clearly that the theocratic dictatorship in Iran is the key problem in the Middle East and should never be regarded as part of any solution. He argues forcibly that Iran's future as a just and stable democracy can only be achieved through support for the main opposition movement, the PMOI.

Stevenson's exposé of Western ineptitude will leave readers horrified. This is a book that should be read carefully by opinion-formers and decision-makers around the world and by students of foreign policy. There is much we can learn from Stevenson's disturbing account of mistakes, duplicities and blunders that have led directly to the rise of ISIS (Islamic State) and the catastrophic events that now engulf the Middle East.

1

Brussels

When does a person reach their tipping point? For me it was the hanging of a 16-year-old girl in Iran for 'acts incompatible with chastity'. Atefeh Rajabi Sahaaleh was hanged in public from a crane in the city of Neka in August 2004. She had been raped and tortured for three years by a 51-year-old former Islamic Revolutionary Guard member turned taxi-driver. He was sentenced to 100 lashes and she was arrested, tortured and then hauled before Neka's local chief religious judge Haji Rezai. Atefeh was so outraged at the injustice of her treatment that she tore off her headscarf and threw one of her shoes at the judge, committing the ultimate offence of contempt of court. The judge not only sentenced her to death but acted as her executioner as well, placing the rope around her neck before the crane dragged the child, choking, into the air. Judge Rezai stated that this would 'teach her a lesson and silence her sharp tongue.'

I was sitting in my office at the European Parliament in Brussels when my senior Parliamentary Assistant at that time, Ingrid Kelling, came in to tell me that the Ambassador to the EU from the Islamic Republic of Iran had arrived for our pre-arranged meeting. Ingrid showed him in and I asked him to sit. He thanked me warmly for agreeing to meet him and launched into a lengthy discourse on the achievements of the Islamic Revolution in Iran. I held up my hand to silence him. 'Mr Ambassador,' I said, 'last week your country hanged a 16-year-old girl in public. This was an outrage against all of our core European values of human rights, the rights of women and the rights of children. I am utterly appalled at this barbarous crime. I have watched in dismay as your country has condoned torture, stoning, amputations and public executions. I can no longer stand on the sidelines. I do not want any explanation or attempts to justify this crime from you. I would ask you now kindly to leave my office and I can assure you that you will not be welcome here again.'

The Ambassador looked stunned. He started to speak and I interrupted him, calling to Ingrid to show him out. I was shaking with rage.

Atefeh was a child. Her crime was to have been the victim of a sexual attack by an older man. To be tortured and hanged in such circumstances was barbarous. Students of Hitler's SS would be familiar with such savagery, but for the vastly cultured and civilised people of Iran, this case, the tenth child to be hanged in the Islamic Republic since 1990, marked another grim milestone on their country's regression to the Stone Age.

I asked Ingrid if she could put me through to the Iranian opposition activist, Firouz Mahvi, who had been to see me on quite a few occasions over the past two years, but with whom I had only made a slightly reluctant acquaintance. Ingrid put through the call. 'Firouz, it's Struan Stevenson.' I explained what had happened and said that I was now so angry that I wanted to do anything I could to help his opposition movement. Firouz asked if he could come straight round to see me. It was to be the start of a long, exciting and often highly emotional journey.

Firouz was overjoyed at my offer of assistance. He briefly reminded me how he represented the People's Mojahedin of Iran (PMOI), also known as the Mujahedin-e-Khalq (MEK), a dissident group which had fought to overthrow the Shah, but then had been seen by the Ayatollahs as a threat to their supremacy. In the 1980s, tens of thousands of PMOI supporters had been arrested, tortured and executed. Many had fled to the West and were now engaged in building international opposition to the turbaned tyrants in Tehran. Firouz asked if he could arrange for me to meet the PMOI's Foreign Affairs Spokesman, Mohammad Mohaddessin, who had written an authoritative book on Islamic fundamentalism. I readily agreed and a date was fixed.

Several days later, Mohammad came to my Brussels office. It was hard to believe that this small, well-groomed man was at the top of Iran's 'Most Wanted' list and had been sentenced to death in absentia. Mohammad explained how Iran had become a rogue state playing a malign role in the Middle East. He showed me a report on the 9/11 Twin Towers terrorist attack, published by the US in July 2004, which detailed how the hardline Mullahs' regime in Iran had direct links with Osama Bin Laden and had sponsored numerous terrorist attacks on Western targets. Intelligence reports stated that the regime was moving towards the development of a nuclear bomb, threatening to plunge the Middle East into apocalyptic conflict.

Mohammad explained how it had been the PMOI which had revealed the Mullahs' top-secret nuclear programme to the West, whose intelligence services had failed to discover it. He explained that PMOI supporters inside Iran were risking their lives to provide this type of intelligence to the West and yet, bizarrely, he described how the PMOI was listed as a terrorist organisation in the EU and US, resulting in the freezing of their assets and making it difficult for them to operate. Mohammad said that this blacklisting was part of the West's mistaken appeasement policy towards the Mullahs in Tehran and had no justification in fact.

Mohammad told me that attempts at reform within Iran had been met with repression. In February of that year (2004), he said, the moderates lost control of Parliament when thousands of their supporters were banned from standing for election. Attempts by UK Foreign Secretary Jack Straw to suck up to Tehran in the pursuit of lucrative oil contracts had also hit the buffers, underlining the failure of the Blair government's policy of appeasement. Earlier in the summer of 2004, the Islamic Revolutionary Guard Corps (IRGC) had seized three British navy patrol boats, on false charges of straying into Iranian waters. The eight British crewmen who had been kidnapped by the Iranian security forces were blindfolded and forced into a ditch, where they thought they would be executed. The Iranians only released the eight men following a grovelling apology from Straw.

The only real hope of regime-change, to avoid another disastrous US intervention, explained Mohammad, lay in the hands of the Iranian resistance. The Mojahedin and the National Council of Resistance of Iran (NCRI), under the leadership of its President-elect Mrs Maryam Rajavi, had led the war against the fundamentalist fascists for the past 25 years, he said. The overthrow of a regime that had executed over 120,000 political prisoners, hanged children in public, endorsed the stoning to death of women and had links with Al Qaeda, was now a matter of urgency.

3

Mohammad said the EU and the US must be urged to remove the terror tag from the PMOI and instead offer their support to this movement, in the fight to rid the world of one of its most evil regimes. He finished our discussion by inviting me to travel to Auvers-sur-Oise on the outskirts of Paris, to the PMOI headquarters, where I would meet with their leader, Mrs Maryam Rajavi. With a little hesitation, thinking that perhaps I was getting into this issue more deeply than I had at first intended, I agreed.

So it was that some weeks later I found myself on the TGV from Brussels to Charles de Gaulle Airport near Paris, where Firouz and his young and energetic colleague Hanif met me. I was a little nervous. I had dug around into the background of the PMOI and discovered that President Chirac had ordered a raid on their Auvers-sur-Oise headquarters in June 2003, arresting Mrs Rajavi and hundreds of her colleagues and seizing vehicles, computers and cash. Protests from respected US Senators and Congressmen accusing Chirac of doing Iran's dirty work for them, together with mass protests by PMOI supporters around the world, quickly led to their release. But, I wondered, what would happen if another raid took place today, while I was there?

As a Conservative Euro MP, I was beginning to wonder why I had agreed to visit the headquarters of a group that I had seen variously described as Marxist and an evil sect, and that I knew was blacklisted as a terrorist organisation. I had read how the PMOI had been accused of waging a terror campaign in Iran in the 1970s, during which they had allegedly assassinated six Americans and bombed many Western targets. Was this something that I should be getting involved in? My nervousness increased as we began negotiating a series of narrow backstreets in the village of Auvers-sur-Oise. My PMOI companions were making repeated calls on their mobile phones, yattering away in Farsi. Soon we entered a long cul-de-sac, with a high security wall running down one side and a tall hedge on the other.

Our car drew up in front of a huge iron gate and immediately Mohammad Mohaddessin and several other men emerged to hold open my door and offer warm handshakes in welcome. I was ushered through the gate and was met with a roar of applause and cries of welcome from a double line of men and women who had gathered

4

to greet me in the courtyard of the PMOI headquarters. I noticed the women were all veiled, and each proffered a freshly plucked rose as I walked slowly down the line, shaking hands with the men and accepting the flowers from the women. Cradling a, by now, large bunch of roses, I was led on to the steps of the main building in the compound, where Maryam Rajavi, the President-elect of the National Council of Resistance of Iran and the effective leader of the PMOI, stood waiting to greet me.

Mrs Rajavi is an elegant woman, with a presence that can captivate a crowd. She also was veiled; she welcomed me in French, her English being poor. She soon switched to Farsi, and with the help of an interpreter, she welcomed me to the PMOI headquarters and invited me inside, where a large meeting room had been specially prepared for our discussion, with two formal-looking wooden thrones, separated by a small table on which had been placed cups of tea and bowls of nuts.

Mrs Rajavi is a lady who displays great humility and who clearly feels the pain and suffering that has been inflicted by the Iranian regime on her people for more than three decades. As such, she feels an enormous sense of responsibility towards her people, but also she longs for peace and stability in the Middle East and the wider world. Despite the difficulties she has encountered, she is courageous, energetic, tenacious and inspiring. She is a Muslim woman who stands for a free, democratic and secular Iran. She represents the rights of the oppressed people in Iran, from women and students to ethnic and religious minorities. Moreover, her modern and progressive interpretation of Islam is an important and necessary example to others. It is for these reasons that she enjoys the support of thousands of democrats around the world, and it was for these same reasons that I quickly recognised Maryam Rajavi as a future President of a free Iran.

Mrs Rajavi told me about the French security police raid on her compound in the previous year, explaining that computers, mobile phones, vehicles and millions of dollars had been seized and had still not been returned.[1] She herself had been held in a prison cell in Paris

---

1. The case was finally resolved in September 2014, ten years after the raid, when French judges ruled that there was no case to answer and that the PMOI/NCRI were innocent of all charges.

for several days. She said that it was vital now to put all of our efforts into removing the terror tag from the PMOI. She said that they had teams of eminent lawyers working on this in the UK, the EU and US and she hoped that I might be able to help. She then went on to describe how 3,400 PMOI fighters were living in a place called Camp Ashraf, north-east of Baghdad. As enemies of the Mullahs, they had gone to Iraq in the early 80s and had been provided with a large area of land in Diyala Province, which, through hard work and sheer endeavour, they had transformed into a small city, with living accommodation, workshops, parks, hospitals, a mosque and teaching facilities.

Mrs Rajavi said that these 3,400 people were the frontline fighters of the PMOI, but they had been bombed and harassed by the US military during the 2003 invasion of Iraq. She reminded me that the previous year I had written an urgent letter to President George W. Bush, pleading with him not to bomb Camp Ashraf, as these people posed no threat to the US. She thanked me for this, but said it was regrettable that the US military had nevertheless bombed the camp, killing several of the PMOI residents.

An article in the *Wall Street Journal* on 17 April 2003 revealed what had been behind the attack:

> The dismantling of the Iranian opposition force in Iraq, known as the Mujahedin-e-Khalq, or MEK, fulfils a private U.S. assurance conveyed to Iranian officials before the start of hostilities that the group would be targeted by British and American forces if Iran stayed out of the fight, according to U.S. officials . . .
>
> But National Security Adviser Condoleezza Rice and Secretary of State Colin Powell contended that Tehran could be persuaded to remain neutral toward the U.S. invasion next door, especially if it knew the MEK would be attacked and prevented from harassing Iran in the future, the official said.
>
> That message was conveyed by British officials before hostilities began. Foreign Minister Jack Straw informed his Iranian counterpart Foreign Minister Kamal Kharrazi in a meeting in London in February.

Britain's Iranian Ambassador Richard Dalton repeated the message in March in a meeting with Hassan Rouhani, the cleric who heads the Supreme National Security Council, Iran's chief foreign policy-making body.[1]

The *Washington Post* wrote on 18 April 2003:

> Two senior U.S. officials met secretly in January with Iranian officials to discuss potential cooperation. The U.S. officials asked that Iran seal its border to prevent the escape of Iraqi officials, among other requests, and suggested that the United States would target the Iraq-based camps of the Mujahedin-e-Khalq Organization, or People's Mujahedin, a U.S. official said.
>
> We told them they would find it advantageous if the United States struck the Mujahedin camps, the official said. A more concrete commitment to attack the camps was later relayed to Tehran through British officials. The Mujahedin-e-Khalq, which has been a source of information on Iran's nuclear programs, has protested angrily about the attacks, saying they were unprovoked.[2]

Now, Mrs Rajavi explained, the residents had voluntarily given up their weapons in exchange for a guarantee of protection by the US army, who were now stationed around the camp perimeter. She suggested that I would be most welcome to visit Camp Ashraf at any time.

As I made ready to leave, Mrs Rajavi presented me with an elegant, heavy, leather-bound volume that she explained was the PMOI *Book of Martyrs*. I leafed through the pages and saw that each page contained the photos and descriptions of PMOI supporters who had been executed by the Mullahs. There were thousands of pages. It was a shocking reminder of how these people were suffering for the cause of freedom and democracy in Iran. This was sacrifice on a scale I had never before encountered.

1. http://online.wsj.com/news/articles/SB105053141922836600
2. http://pqasb.pqarchiver.com/washingtonpost/doc/409532967.html

As I was driven back down the narrow lanes of Auvers-sur-Oise, I no longer had those worries of earlier. I felt comfortable that I had made the right choice. After meeting Mrs Rajavi, I realised that I was dealing with sincere people who were fighting for a good cause and were personally prepared to pay any price. A decade later, looking back, after many meetings and encounters with Maryam Rajavi and her colleagues, my confidence then is confirmed.

2

Interviews with Political Prisoners
Refugee Camp, Tirana, Albania, May 2014

Hengameh Haj Hassan

'My name is Hengameh Haj Hassan. When I was in a prison cell alone and waiting to be sentenced to death, I always thought, "Will anyone ever hear about me? Will I die in secret and be forgotten?"

Almost all of my classmates were executed by Khomeini. In 1981, I was working in the Sina Hospital in Tehran as a nurse. We were supporters of the PMOI because of the repression of women and we were forced to wear the mandatory veil etc. Many women who came to our hospital had had bits of their face sliced off by Khomeini's torturers. I was horrified and said so and soon was identified as a possible PMOI supporter by spies of the regime (the Islamic Association) and was placed under constant surveillance.

My friends and I were threatened; then the Revolutionary Guards attacked the hospital. By this time we had run away, because our colleagues had warned us that the IRGC (Iranian Revolutionary Guard Corps) were coming. But in two or three months, several of our friends, including Dr Sadeq Agmashe and Dr Fahimeh Mirahmadi (who was pregnant) were arrested and executed. Two of the nurses, Shakar Mohammedzadeh and nurse Tuba Rajavi Sani were also executed.

When I was arrested in the street, I was blindfolded. It was a major roundup by the Revolutionary Guards. Every young person in the street would be rounded up and accused of being PMOI supporters and the onus was on you to prove they were wrong. I was tied to a bed in the police station and tortured by being hit on the soles of my feet with electric cables of various diameters. If you resisted, heavier cables would be used. Lajevardi, the Iranian prison chief at that time, would go to every torture room to supervise and participate in the torture sessions in person.

They wanted me to repent and reveal my friends' names and appear on TV to denounce the PMOI. I could hear my friends' screams. On the first night of our interrogation, there were dozens of wounded, tortured people on beds in our cells. My friend Tahmineh Rastegar said that under torture she had taken all the blame on herself, which suddenly explained why they had stopped torturing me. Eventually we were moved to Ward 209 in Evin Prison. We were blindfolded and put in a queue, each with a hand on the shoulder of the person in front. The person in front of me was my friend Tahmineh and she put her hand on my hand. This was the last time I ever touched her. She was executed by a firing squad two months later. We used to hear the roar of machine guns at night when the executions took place. The first time I heard it, I thought it was a lorry tipping out a load of gravel. That's what it sounded like. But then we could hear the single pistol shots as each person was given the *coup de grâce*. We could count the number of our colleagues who had been executed by the number of single pistol shots. Sometimes there were hundreds of shots.

I wasn't aware that Tahmineh had been shot until I was interrogated for the last time and they lied to me and said Tahmineh had given evidence against me. I knew she would never do such a thing. I demanded to see her. They said they would just bring her handwriting. When they brought the papers that Tahmineh had signed, I saw that she had deliberately written misleading information and that she had only repeated the story that we had previously agreed to tell them. She had said, "Yes, these are my friends, but they are innocent." Then she had made a false confession to shift all the blame onto herself.

There is no justice in Iran. After 11 months, they said they were taking me to court to deliver the final verdict. So, I said goodbye to everyone, being certain that I would be sentenced to death and executed. But when we got to the so-called court we could see all the revolutionary guards were laughing and joking. There was a room with a single mullah, Hassan Nayyeri, sitting behind a table. He was flanked by two of my torturers. They asked me if I was a PMOI supporter. I said I was only a naive admirer and had done nothing against the regime. So they could prove nothing, but then they demanded to know why I had never got married . . . which to them was a crime and apparently possible proof that I supported the PMOI! I told them to mind their own business. So the mullah told me that I could go and that he would show mercy. Mullahs act as lawyer, judge, jury and prosecutor all in one. They argue that their sentences are the will of God and they even justify torture and the death penalty on this basis.

However, although I was lucky not to face imminent death, I was returned to Evin Prison, where I quickly realised that all the other members of our movement with whom I had shared a cell had been killed on that day . . . that's why the Revolutionary Guards had been laughing, joking and jubilant.

At Evin, six people were crammed into each cell built under the Shah to hold a single person. After I was arrested, my parents made frantic efforts to discover what had happened to me, and when they heard about the mass execution of my friends, they assumed the same thing had happened to me and held a ceremony to honour my death. This was two months after I was abducted.

I was sentenced to three years in prison, but I was still tortured regularly, not with the intention of forcing me to reveal information, but simply because they claimed that I still supported the PMOI in my heart and mind. During the second year, when I was moved to Qezel Hesar Prison, I was taken to a cage, only half a metre wide. Prisoners couldn't sit down. No movement or noise was allowed; even if we sneezed, we would be beaten with a cable. Many people in the prison, both male and female, were tortured in these coffin-like cages. I spent seven or eight months in one of these cages.

My parents, who by this time had discovered I was still alive, went to Ayatollah Montazeri, one of the allegedly moderate mullahs in the leadership, and bitterly complained about our mistreatment. Montazeri, together with other senior officials of the regime, then made a lot of noise in the Iranian media. This caused a division amongst the Mullahs and some of the prisoners like myself were freed. I started to work in a private hospital, because, as a former prisoner, I could no longer work in a public hospital. One year later, a colleague told me that there were two people from Evin Prison looking for me. I contacted my two closest PMOI friends who had also been released from jail and they said they knew they were also being sought. So we all decided to flee. We got money from our friends, or jewellery, bracelets and earrings to sell in order to get money, with which we paid smugglers to help get us out of the country.

We fled to Iraq and then on to Camp Ashraf. We were lucky. Many of my friends who tried to flee were captured at the border, then taken back to Evin and executed. Many were executed during the 1988 prison massacres. I survived to fight for those people who gave their lives. I only took a small and modest step in the PMOI. But their blood is incredibly strong!'

3

The People's Mojahedin Organisation of Iran

Following my election to the European Parliament in June 1999, I frequently met individuals and organisations in Brussels and Strasbourg, keen to meet and lobby politicians for countless causes. These ranged from local to global issues and each sought to secure the support of European parliamentarians for their cause. As I have explained, one such group was the People's Mojahedin Organisation of Iran. I first met a representative of this organisation in Brussels in 2002, two years before my meetings with Mohammad Mohaddessin and Mrs Rajavi. As someone interested in foreign affairs and the Middle East, this meeting was to shape my understanding and knowledge of Iran and the political situation in that country. But I was also to be introduced to the ideology that is now known as Islamic fundamentalism. Emanating from the Islamic Republic of Iran since its inception in 1979, it is now prevalent in the wider Middle East and beyond, with tragic and far-reaching consequences.

After this initial meeting, it was important for me to get to know the PMOI and to verify and research what I had been told. I needed to find out what the organisation stood for, its political ethos, its views and above all else its practices. This was to be no easy task. When I first met representatives of the organisation, the PMOI was on the EU list of designated terrorist organisations. It was incredibly challenging to separate fact from fiction in the labyrinth of misinformation about the PMOI. I had rarely come across an organisation that created such extremes of opinion and feeling, from staunch and passionate supporters to devout and ardent critics, all vying for support and for people to listen to them.

The overthrow of Dr Mohammad Mossadegh (Iran's democratically elected Prime Minister) in 1953[1] caused political unrest throughout the 1950s and 1960s. Together with oppression and the

---

1. Dr Mossadegh was overthrown in a *coup d'état* orchestrated by Britain and the United States.

eventual banning of all political opposition groups by Shah Pahlavi, this created disillusionment and disenchantment amongst Iran's then 25 million population. Against this backdrop, in the autumn of 1965, three university students, Mohammad Hanifnejad, Saied Mohsen and Ali-Asghar Badizadegan, set up the People's Mojahedin Organisation of Iran,[1] a political organisation originally formed to oppose the corrupt and oppressive dictatorship of Shah Pahlavi and the absolute rule of the monarch. The PMOI would grow to become by far the largest and most active political movement in Iranian history.

In the 1970s, however, a brutal crackdown on the organisation and its members by the Shah's notorious secret service (the Savak) resulted in the execution of the PMOI's original founders, almost the entirety of its leadership and the imprisonment of the vast majority of its members and supporters, including Massoud Rajavi, then Secretary General of the PMOI. Massoud was a graduate of political law from Tehran University and had joined the PMOI when he was 20. He was only spared execution because of the efforts of his elder brother Professor Kazem Rajavi,[2] a renowned human rights advocate who spearheaded an international campaign in the West, which included securing the support of Francois Mitterrand and a number of other international leaders and human rights organisations, including Amnesty International and the Red Cross.

While Massoud Rajavi and the rest of the PMOI's leading cadres were in prison, the organisation suffered an internal set-back. In the years 1972-1975, a number of individuals, including a member who had escaped prison and gained some notoriety among the opposition, took advantage of the absence of the PMOI's leadership and attempted to change the organisation's ideology and direction along Marxist lines.

The remaining members outside prison, who strongly rejected the betrayal of the PMOI's founders and their vision for a future Iran, vigorously opposed this Marxist coup within the organisation. But

1. The organisation is variously referred to as the PMOI, Mujahedin-e-Khalq, MEK, MKO and other versions of its name.
2. In 1990 Dr Rajavi, Iran's first Ambassador to the United Nations after the 1979 revolution, was assassinated in Geneva by agents of the Iranian regime.

suppressing the members opposed to them, the Marxist faction engaged in several armed attacks against American personnel stationed in Iran and their interests.

According to international experts who have closely examined the events of the 1970s, these armed activities were aimed at gaining the upper hand and silencing any opposition to the change in ideology and strategy of the organisation. Massoud Rajavi, although in prison, strongly condemned these individuals and their actions and he went on to play a vital role in returning the organisation to its true and original founding principles and ideology.[1] Thus the PMOI cannot be held responsible for actions by the Marxist faction in which it played no part.

Once released from prison in 1979, Massoud Rajavi and other senior PMOI members set about restructuring the organisation. Because of the group's nationalist outlook, democratic values and modern and progressive view of Islam, they were the natural frontrunners in the 1979 revolution. It was because of this tolerant and progressive interpretation of Islam that the 'PMOI provided ideological inspiration to the millions of Iranians whose nationwide protests ultimately brought down the Shah of Iran in 1979.'[2]

The PMOI wanted a secular government, elections and universal suffrage to be the basis of political legitimacy. Their interpretation of Islam and what they aspired to for a future Iran was, however, in stark contrast to the intentions of Ayatollah Khomeini, a Shiia cleric who had recently returned to Iran from exile. The Shah had imposed Khomeini's exile in 1964 due to his increasing prominence as a religious leader, his denouncing of the Shah's rule and of the influence of the United States and Britain in Iran.

After widespread demonstrations against his rule in 1979, the Shah fled, never to return. Khomeini took advantage of the vacuum created by the Shah's lengthy dictatorship and the elimination of all democratic opposition groups such as the PMOI, whose leaders had

1. For more information see *The Mujahedin-e-Khalq, MEK, Shackled by a Twisted History*, by Lincoln P. Bloomfield Jr, published by University of Baltimore, 2013.

2. 'People's Mojahedin of Iran – Mission Report', Friends of a Free Iran, p. 7.

either been executed or imprisoned, and seized the leadership of the revolution. Lack of democratic institutions and public knowledge about the true nature of Khomeini contributed to his position going unchallenged at the time. He was seen as a spiritual leader who had no interest in material life or in engaging in the day-to-day affairs of the country. Indeed, he promised that this was the case.

However, having secured the support of the people by taking advantage of their religious feelings, he reneged on his promises, and instead of setting up a parliament representing the people to write the new constitution, he set up an Assembly of Experts, which was essentially made up of clerics. This assembly introduced a constitution based on the 'Velayat-e-faqih' (the absolute rule of the clergy). He gave himself the title of the Supreme Leader and established the Guardians' Council, which holds absolute power and controls everything, including all legislative acts, to ensure they are in accordance with their strict interpretation of the *Koran*. Khomeini appointed himself God's representative on earth, changing Iranian society overnight and giving birth to what is now known as Islamic fundamentalism.

The PMOI fiercely opposed this undemocratic seizure of power and refused to take part in the referendum on the 'Velayat-e-faqih' constitution. However, if the PMOI had been eager for power for itself, it would have been more to its advantage to have gone with the tide and not boycotted the referendum.

A report prepared by the British Foreign Office describes this period:

> The MKO [PMOI] played a major part in the revolution and for two years thereafter was an important element in the internal power struggle. It boycotted the referendum on the Islamic Republic's constitution and Rajavi was forced to withdraw his candidacy for the post of President of the Republic when Khomeini said that only those who voted for the constitution could be candidates. Rajavi stood for election to the Majlis [Iranian Parliament] in 1980, but was not elected – almost certainly because of ballot rigging.[1]

1. 'The Mujahedin-e-Khalq', report by the British Foreign Office prepared in March 2001.

Infuriated by the PMOI's stance against him, Ayatollah Khomeini ordered a brutal and bloody crackdown on members, supporters and sympathisers of the PMOI in what has been described as the 'reign of terror'.[1] According to a decree by Khomeini, 'the Mojahedin of Iran are infidels and worse than blasphemers . . . They have no right to life.'[2] Since then, the PMOI have been the principal victims of human rights violations in Iran.

Over the past three decades, 120,000 of its members and supporters have been executed. Dozens more have been assassinated outside of Iran. The execution, imprisonment and torture of PMOI members, supporters and their families continue unabated to this day. As I write, several members and supporters of the organisation are currently on death row in Iran, their only crime being membership and support of the PMOI. In June 2014, Gholamreza Khosravi was executed for making donations to a satellite opposition TV affiliated to the PMOI. After I complained bitterly about his execution to Baroness Ashton, the EU's High Representative for Foreign Affairs, she wrote to me on 14 July 2014 stating: 'As you well know, the EU holds a strong and principled position against the death penalty and continues to call on Iran to halt all pending executions and to introduce a moratorium on the death penalty. This also applies to the situation of Mr Gholamreza Khosravi, who should not have been executed. I had issued a public statement to this end in 2012 – to which you make reference in your letter – calling upon Iran to commute his death sentence. It is indeed very sad that Iran in the end did not do so.' The fact that Iran simply chose to ignore Baroness Ashton's entreaties was symptomatic of all of their future dealings with the EU.

In the summer of 1988 alone, some 30,000 PMOI political prisoners were executed in prisons throughout Iran. They were led to the gallows in their thousands and buried in mass graves in secret locations. In a final act of barbarity, the Iranian regime has for the past 26 years deprived the families of the victims with the knowledge of the final resting place of their loved ones. To this day, families meet in secret throughout Iran, in search of the remains of their loved ones.

1. Ervand Abrahamian, *The Iranian Mojahedin*, pp. 218-219.
2. Mohammad Mohaddessin, *Enemies of the Ayatollahs*, p. 55-56.

Members and supporters of the PMOI who were not executed or imprisoned in Iran, were forced into exile, moving to Paris and other European and North American cities. Despite their political differences with Khomeini, the PMOI did everything to avoid confrontation with him and his regime. Instead it sought change through peaceful means. But when the PMOI had exhausted all possible paths to political participation, as a measure of last resort the organisation took up arms against the Iranian regime. Massoud Rajavi has said: 'The Islam that we profess does not condone bloodshed. We have never sought, nor do we welcome, confrontation and violence. If Khomeini is prepared to hold truly free elections, I will return to my homeland immediately. The Mojahedin will lay down their arms to participate in such elections. We do not fear election results, whatever they may be. Before the start of the armed struggle, we tried to utilise all legal means of political activity, but suppression compelled us to take up arms. If Khomeini had allowed half or even a quarter of freedoms presently enjoyed in France, we would certainly have achieved a democratic victory.'[1]

In my view, the PMOI during this period is best described as an armed resistance movement, fighting tyranny and oppression in their homeland. What the PMOI has never been in its history (past or present) is a terrorist organisation. The PMOI has never sought to achieve its goals using terror. It has never targeted civilians, nor have civilians ever been injured or killed as a result of PMOI campaigns against the Iranian regime. My belief in the unjust, illegal and immoral terrorist designation of the PMOI was why I, and other politicians from around the world, agreed to challenge the designation in successive courts of law. We were vindicated when the verdicts of courts in the United Kingdom, the United States and the European Union ruled that the PMOI was not a terrorist organisation.

Forced into exile, Massoud Rajavi moved to Paris in 1981. He, along with the PMOI leadership, members and supporters of the organisation, continued their opposition to Khomeini and his tyrannical rule from exile, while the movement's underground network was operating in Iran. However in 1986 the PMOI relocated to Iraq, after they came under increasing pressure from the government of Jacques

1. Massoud Rajavi interview with *L'Unité*, Paris, 1 January 1984.

18

Chirac to leave France. Attempting to secure the release of French hostages held by agents of the Iranian regime in Lebanon, the French Government was engaged in negotiations with the Iranian regime, a concession being the expulsion of the PMOI from French soil.

Much has been made of this relocation to Iraq by the organisation's critics, who question the wisdom of the decision at a time when Iran was at war with Iraq. Mohammad Mohaddessin, Chairman of the Foreign Affairs Committee of the NCRI has said of this move:

> Although the French Government's pressures on the Iranian Resistance to leave France had been going on for over a year, Rajavi decided to move to Iraq only when he was assured of the Resistance's independence in Iraq and the non-interference of the Iraqi Government in its affairs. In return, the Resistance would not intervene in Iraq's internal affairs under any circumstances . . .
>
> The Resistance's move to Iraq in 1986 was taking place at a time when regional alignments were vastly different from the situation after Iraq's invasion of Kuwait and the 1991 Gulf War. At the time, all European countries and the United States had warm relations with the Iraqi Government . . . With the very real spectre of the Iranian regime militarily defeating Iraq and occupying that country, Arab countries in the region and Western powers were doing their utmost to prevent such a disastrous outcome to the war, which clearly would have led to the rapid rise of Islamic fundamentalism and extremism across the Middle East and North Africa.[1]

I have often heard it argued that the PMOI somehow lost its legitimacy or popular support because of its relocation to Iraq. My own view is vastly different. I believe the move, while the result of circumstances beyond the organisation's control, showed great courage and political foresight. When Iraq invaded Iran in September 1980, the PMOI fought alongside their countrymen against Iraq. There can be no question of the organisation's loyalty to the Iranian people or to their country.

1. Mohammad Mohaddessin, *Enemies of the Ayatollahs*, p. 114.

Senator Robert Torricelli has said, 'I think that simply because the People's Mojahedin has forces located in Iraq does not make it less legitimate or effective. The People's Mojahedin is based in Iraq because there is no place else for it to go and it needs to be in the proximity of Iran . . . It is a simple reflection of geographic and political realities.'[1]

The PMOI, while fighting against Iraq in the Iran-Iraq war, was also very critical of Khomeini's attempts to create a satellite 'Islamic Republic' in Iraq and the export of Islamic fundamentalism to Iraq and the wider Middle East. After Iraq had withdrawn from Iranian territory and stated its intention to compensate Iran for the war, the PMOI advocated peace with Iraq and an end to the war. The war could and should have ended in 1982, but instead it continued for a further six years until August 1988. Most of the casualties on the Iranian side occurred during this period, deaths which could have been avoided had Khomeini accepted Iraq's offer of peace in 1982. Instead, Khomeini proclaimed that he would not stop until an Islamic Republic, at the cost of over a million dead Iranians and Iraqis, replaced the government of Iraq. Khomeini's slogan at the time, which summed up his ambition, was to 'liberate Jerusalem via Karbala'. According to this plan, Iran should have first captured and liberated the holy Shiite city of Karbala in Iraq and then moved towards Jerusalem.

The PMOI was faced with a difficult dilemma. On one hand the war still continued and the PMOI leadership was fully aware that its call for peace could be misinterpreted by Khomeini to make propaganda, claiming the organisation was working with the enemy. On the other hand, hundreds of thousands of lives of Iranians were at stake. Schoolchildren were being sent to clear mines. The PMOI had to make a choice: either to be silent and let Khomeini send hundreds of thousands of people to their deaths, or to raise the flag of peace. Finally, it was the PMOI nationwide peace campaign, and its presence in Iraq, which broke the back of Khomeini's war-mongering policy. As far as I am concerned, the PMOI position and conduct during the Iran-Iraq war was the most patriotic act imaginable by a political organisation. As a politician I can barely contemplate the

1. Statement made at a press conference on Capitol Hill, 8 June 1995.

difficulty and the political price involved. However, years later, the PMOI has been vindicated.

The PMOI is one of five member organisations of the National Council of Resistance of Iran, a coalition of democratic Iranian opposition groups and prominent individuals, established by Massoud Rajavi in 1981 while he was in Tehran, to oppose the theocratic regime of Ayatollah Khomeini. Now in exile and headquartered in Paris, it is a political coalition made up of approximately 500 members representing all religious and ethnic minorities in Iran, including Kurds, Baluchis, Armenians, Jews and Zoroastrians.

The NCRI is comprised of 25 committees that act as shadow ministries, and are responsible for expert research and planning for a future Iran.[1] Fifty per cent of the NCRI's members are women, and as we have seen, a woman leads the entire coalition. Maryam Rajavi is the President-elect of the NCRI for the six-month provisional period following the fall of the Mullahs, when there would be an orderly transfer of power to the people. Her Presidential term would end following the election of a new President for Iran and the ratification of a new constitution in the Constitutional Assembly.

When I first met PMOI representatives I was also very keen to meet this coalition of organisations that they belonged to. Often referred to as a 'Parliament in exile', the NCRI have representative offices throughout the world and function exactly as one might expect. They have country representatives and staff in each country, dedicated to informing politicians and the public on issues pertaining to Iran and the Middle East. As the organisation is comprised of experts in numerous fields, NCRI members and officials are often invited to provide comment on Iran, as their information and evidence is second to none. For example, it was the NCRI who first exposed the Iranian regime's nuclear weapons programme by announcing the existence of a uranium enrichment facility in Natanz in 2002. These revelations were based on information provided to the NCRI by the PMOI's network inside Iran.

The American government, who had no love for the PMOI, confirmed the role of the PMOI in this, although they were careful not to mention the organisation by name: 'Iran admitted the existence of

1. www.ncr-iran.org.

these facilities only after it had no choice, only because they had been made public by an Iranian opposition group.' (White House briefing, White House spokesman, 10 March 2003.)

'Iran has concealed its nuclear program. That became discovered, not because of their compliance with the IAEA or NPT, but because a dissident group pointed it out to the world, which raised suspicions about the intentions of the program.' (White House Press Conference, 16 March 2005.)

'An Iranian opposition group said today that it had evidence of two previously undisclosed uranium enrichment facilities west of Tehran. The group, the National Council of Resistance of Iran, an umbrella for Iranian opposition organizations, said the facilities were discovered by the People's Mujahedeen, a resistance group that brought the Natanz plant to the attention of international weapons inspectors. "This organization has been extremely on the mark in the past," said a senior United Nations official who is familiar with the situation in Iran, adding, "They are a group that seems to be privy to very solid and insider information."' (*New York Times*, 27 May 2003.)

The NCRI organise symposiums, press conferences and exhibitions and are responsible for excellent and well-informed publications. The organisation's members and officials can be seen rushing to and from meetings in parliaments around the world. I have met many of them and have visited their offices in London, Paris, Brussels, Washington DC and elsewhere. What I always find remarkable in all my dealings with this group and their supporters is their dedication and self-sacrifice. They work tirelessly to assist the Iranian people to realise their inalienable rights to freedom, democracy and respect for human rights and fundamental freedoms. Their offices are also interestingly one of the first ports of call for Iranians who manage to escape the clutches of the Ayatollahs in Iran. They view the organisation as the embodiment of their hopes and desires for a free, democratic and secular Iran.

To my mind, one of the most striking features of the PMOI is the role of women within the organisation. This is in stark contrast to the Iranian regime's three-decade war on women and the rights of women. There is a deep belief in gender equality, but more importantly, in observing equality in practice and not just paying lip service to the word. I have witnessed the organisation's democratic and gender equal ethos in practice.

Encouraged, influenced and guided by the example set by Maryam Rajavi, the women within the PMOI are immensely capable. In the internal elections usually held every two years, PMOI members have repeatedly elected women to be their Secretary General in the past 20 years. Having been held back for decades by a misogynist regime that despises women, the women within the PMOI are a hugely influential and powerful force. I believe they are our greatest asset against the Ayatollahs as they represent the source of inspiration and empowerment to the millions of women in Iran. It is this fact that petrifies the Iranian regime and the reason why they have such utter contempt for the organisation and in particular for the women within the organisation.

One of the most horrifying consequences of the inception of the Islamic Republic of Iran in 1979 has been the export of terror and the aggressive export of Islamic fundamentalism. The PMOI, as the oldest and largest anti-fundamentalist Muslim group in the Middle East,[1] has been invaluable to the international community in the fight against Islamic fundamentalism, now a real global threat to peace and security.

Because they advocate a democratic and tolerant Islam, many Middle East experts and political figures in Europe and North America see the organisation as the antithesis to Islamic fundamentalism. The PMOI's modern and progressive interpretation of Islam is the polar opposite to what fundamentalist Islam represents. The PMOI stands for a secular system of government with complete separation of religion and state. In fact, for nearly 50 years, they have sought free and fair elections. The PMOI has always maintained that the ballot box is the only legitimate basis for government, in contrast to the fundamentalists, who believe they are ordained by God.

What is particularly dangerous about the Iranian regime is their policy of expansionist ideology. Not content with inflicting indescribable misery on the Iranian people, they have exported their Islamic fundamentalism to Iraq, Syria, Yemen, Lebanon and beyond.

1. Mohammad Mohaddessin, *Enemies of the Ayatollahs*, p. 14.

Recognising the organisation's impact, 5.2 million Iraqis signed a statement describing the organisation as a bulwark against Islamic fundamentalism. Therefore the PMOI has immense appeal in the Middle East. To my mind, the PMOI and their experiences are pivotal if we are to defeat the onslaught of Islamic fundamentalism, a disease that is sweeping across the world at an alarming rate, threatening to destroy it. The current relentless influx of ISIS across vast tracts of Syria, Iraq and Libya is a case in point.

The PMOI has immense international support. For example at their annual rally in Paris, which I have attended many times, approximately 100,000 Iranians and non-Iranians meet to support the PMOI and the democratic aspirations of the Iranian people. The PMOI enjoys the majority support of parliaments around the world, including in the European Parliament and both chambers of the British Parliament. Their support is bipartisan. I am often stunned by how politicians from extreme ends of the political spectrum can be united in their support of the PMOI, and yet disagree on just about everything else!

4

Interviews with Political Prisoners
Refugee Camp, Tirana, Albania, May 2014

Mahnaz
(Only first name given to protect her family in Iran)

'My name is Mahnaz. I was 16 when I was arrested in Tehran with all of my family, my mother, father, sister and two brothers. Another of my brothers had been executed in 1981. He was 17 and a member of the PMOI. He was a student, arrested, tortured and 20 days later the state-run TV reported the names of 100 people who had been accused of being 'corrupt on earth' and executed. My brother's name was among them. We found out later from sources in prison that he had been strangled under torture, so they never returned the body. All we got was the number of his grave in Behesht-e-Zahra cemetery. For years, my parents refused to believe that he was dead.

I was arrested one year later. We were all taken to Evin. My 15 year-old sister and I were placed in one room. My 11-year-old brother was also taken to Evin. My father and mother were separated. My older brother aged 27 had been arrested earlier in the street. He was a medical student. We were taken to section 7 and we could hear the screams of the tortured, both male and female. But then they took me behind a room and separated me from my sister and suddenly I could hear my brother's screams. A man nicknamed Islami came to me and threatened me, demanding to know details of my brothers' friends and whether they were supporters of the PMOI. I was deeply shocked. I asked to see my brother. They took me to him. He had been tortured and I could see under my blindfold a glimpse of his face. Wounds up to his knees indicated that he had been beaten and was badly swollen and covered in blood. His face was bloody too. They forced him to insist that I cooperate, twisting his arms. He said, "You should tell them that you did nothing . . . they don't know that you did nothing."

Immediately two people named Islami and Fakoor started to beat us both with cables and batons; my brother was hit by the baton on his mouth, which broke his teeth; they accused him of instructing me not to talk. After an hour of this I was taken to a torture chamber and chained hands and feet face down on a bed, beaten on the ends of my feet and a heavy weight was placed on my back . . . so I felt I was suffocating. Fakoor said, "Just raise your hand when you want to talk." I raised my hand to get respite and said, "You know I've done nothing." They began to torture me again until I was unconscious. I think this went on for approximately four hours and it continued like this every day for three days. I was moved to the so-called clinic of Evin Prison, because my feet were infected and were bleeding. I couldn't walk.

Two years later my brother was executed and two weeks after his execution my father, devastated by the news, died of a heart attack in prison. My mother and 11-year-old brother were released after three months in prison; they had both been beaten with cables. My brother was mentally disturbed for years thereafter, because of the screams he heard and because they took him to see my older brother being tortured, to put more pressure on him to reveal information. My mother was harassed for years after her release and also died of a heart attack. So now only myself, my sister and my youngest brother remain of my family. My brother is forbidden to leave Iran and my sister has been in prison for the past twelve years in Iran.

After being sentenced to ten years imprisonment plus four years suspended, four years after my imprisonment in 1986, I was one of the people released but on the understanding that I report weekly to a local police station. I did that three times and then escaped. Each time they asked me who did you meet this week, what have you been reading, why are you not married, what are you thinking? I realised I had to escape from Iran and I joined the resistance army in Iraq.'

5

Berlin

Back in Brussels, I was invited to be a keynote speaker at a massive PMOI Rally they were planning to organise in Paris in February 2005. I readily agreed and was somewhat surprised, a few weeks later, when my Parliamentary Assistant Ingrid took a call from a lady calling herself 'Mrs Felicity Brown', claiming to be a senior official at the Foreign and Commonwealth Office (FCO) in Whitehall, London. I asked Ingrid to put the call through and Mrs Brown said, 'Mr Stevenson, it has come to our attention in the FCO that you are intending to address a PMOI Rally in Paris next February, in your capacity as an MEP. The FCO would like to advise you that we think this is a very bad idea. The PMOI are a listed terrorist organisation and your association with them will be damaging for your own political credibility and will be exploited as a propaganda tool by them.'

I was taken aback by this and replied, 'Mrs Brown, please do not seek to dictate to me as an elected parliamentarian, what I should do, where I should go and whom I should meet!' I spent a few minutes explaining to Mrs Brown why it was unjust for the PMOI to have been placed on the UK, EU and US terrorist lists in the first place and how I was actively working to have them delisted.

When the call ended, I suddenly became suspicious. Why would a senior civil servant in the FCO try to order around an elected MEP? I asked Ingrid to call FCO in London and ask for Mrs Felicity Brown. Needless to say, there was no such person. It was only much, much later that I finally discovered that Mrs Brown was actually working for MI5. It was a salutary lesson. Incredibly, my own British intelligence service was keen to sever my links with the PMOI, which had clearly come to their attention. Their attitude made me all the more determined to speak at the Paris Rally.

The tenth of February had been chosen for the great Paris Rally to mark the twenty-sixth anniversary of the revolution that toppled the Shah of Iran in 1979. The National Council of Resistance of Iran (NCRI) had obtained permission from the French authorities to hold the mass rally in Paris. They estimated that around 40,000 exiled Iranians from around the world would attend. I had purchased my flights to travel to Paris from my home in Scotland, when suddenly, only two days before the event was due to take place, I was informed that the French had pulled the plug on the whole affair. Under heavy pressure from the Iranian Mullahs, bolstered by a strong lobby of French companies holding multi-billion-dollar contracts with Iran, the French government had predictably caved in. Permission had been withdrawn at the eleventh hour.

Determined not to be out-manoeuvred by the Mullahs, and equally determined not to disappoint the hordes of PMOI supporters already making their way to Europe, the NCRI quickly shifted the focus of the Rally to Berlin, where the municipal authorities gave the green light for a demonstration in front of the historic Brandenburg Gate. The phone lines between Tehran, Paris and Berlin must have been red-hot on the eve of the demo, because at 4 am on 10 February, the German Government also pulled the plug on the rally. By dawn, a four-kilometre security cordon had been set up around the Brandenburg Gate to ensure no one was allowed near the area. Charter planes, buses and private cars bringing thousands of Iranians to Berlin were stopped and turned back by German police.

Again, the persistent dissidents refused to give up. Throngs of would-be demonstrators wandered peacefully around the city, waving their placards and flags, and thousands of them gathered in a square, some 5 km from the city centre, to hold a spontaneous rally. So it was that on a cold, drizzly day in early February, I found myself standing on top of a grassy knoll in a frozen Berlin square, trying to be heard through a megaphone, over the clatter of police helicopters hovering overhead and 40,000 cheering, flag-waving PMOI supporters thronging the surrounding streets.

You would have been forgiven for thinking that in a week when key leaders in the West were taking turns to condemn the ruling ayatollahs for their continued sponsorship of terrorism and their determination to construct nuclear weapons, that 40,000 Iranian dissidents calling for democratic change in Iran would have received a friendly welcome. Well, not in Berlin. As I spoke on a makeshift stump, the rows of green-clad German police surrounding the square, standing ten-deep in places, wearing helmets and visors, shields and batons in hand, lines of armoured cars behind them, blue lights flashing and sirens shrieking, and police helicopters buzzing overhead, created a surreal scene.

I was told that the Chief of the Berlin Police had arrived and was demanding to speak to the 'organisers' of the rally. I pressed my way through the cheering, backslapping mass of people to the police lines and asked to see the Chief. Several heavily armed policemen led me through the lines to where an officer, whose uniform and peaked cap were sparkling with silver braid, was issuing orders to a clutch of senior commanders. I thrust myself into their circle and holding my parliamentary pass, announced that I was an elected member of the European Parliament and was conducting a law-abiding and peaceful rally in Berlin. The Chief of Police straightened up until he was staring me in the eye. 'This is an illegal rally and these people are blocking streets and access roads to this square. In the event of an emergency, fire engines and ambulances would be unable to gain access. I will reluctantly permit you to continue the rally only if everyone steps off the streets and congregates on the grass in the centre of the square. If you fail to do this, I will order my men to arrest you all.' I assured the chief that I understood and would do my best to clear the streets.

I struggled back through the chanting crowd and made my way to the top of the mound in the middle of the grassy area. Grabbing the megaphone I yelled for silence, although the roar of the helicopters made it almost impossible for me to be heard. 'I have spoken to the Chief of Police,' I shouted. 'We can continue our rally only if you get off the streets and stand on the grass. You must clear the way for emergency vehicles otherwise the riot police will arrest us all!'

This announcement was met with great roars of approval and the crowds started to surge forward onto the grass. Soon the streets were cleared and the police cordon formed a tight circle around the crowd to ensure no one moved off the grass. I roared my message of freedom and democracy for the oppressed people of Iran through the megaphone to thunderous cheers and applause.

With seven other European parliamentarians, I then held an impromptu press conference on the spot to denounce the unjustified German ban on our intended rally at the Brandenburg Gate. Just as we were winding up, it was announced that a panel of judges in Berlin had ruled in favour of an emergency appeal filed by the PMOI. The court ordered that the demonstration could now go ahead at the Brandenburg Gate after all. German justice had prevailed over the policy of appeasement. The sight of tens of thousands of Iranian demonstrators waving photos of Maryam Rajavi and flashing victory signs as they made their way to the Brandenburg Gate startled Berliners, who readily responded with cheers and applause.

Amazingly, when we arrived at the Brandenburg Gate, surrounded by lines of riot police and still shadowed by armoured military vehicles and helicopters, the PMOI staff had re-erected the podium, which they had begun to dismantle earlier when news of the ban was first made public. Huge banners and flags draped the stage and towering banks of loudspeakers meant that the hand-held megaphones were now redundant. I mounted the stage to ear-shattering cheers and savoured the adrenalin rush from addressing a massive crowd in front of one of Berlin's most famous landmarks. On that grey February afternoon in Berlin, I glanced to my left, as the crowd chanted, 'No to appeasement, No to foreign war. Help the Iranian people and their resistance to bring about democratic change.'

Past the Brandenburg Gate and the famous Adlon Hotel, there was the open ground above the site of Hitler's bunker. It was here in 1945 that the Nazi leader had committed suicide, bringing to an end his murderous regime. It seemed an appropriate place to be calling for an end to another evil dictatorship. While the resilience and courage of the Iranian dissidents turned the Berlin rally into a great success, the knee-jerk decisions taken by Paris and Berlin to ban the demonstration raised serious concerns in my mind. Where on earth was European policy on Iran heading?

When Tony Blair in the first week of February 2005 grudgingly admitted that the Iranian regime was a 'sponsor of international terror', and when the French and German foreign ministers expressed concern at Iran's policies, it was more to do with pressure from the Americans than any wish to criticise Tehran. Tony Blair, Gerhard

Schroeder, the German Chancellor, and Jacques Chirac, the French President, had been at the forefront of a failed 'engagement policy' with Iran that had only strengthened the most radical factions of the theocratic regime. The UK Foreign Minister Jack Straw had shuttled back and forth to Tehran in zealous pursuit of a diplomatic policy that to many was reminiscent of Neville Chamberlain's 'peace in our time' sop to fascism.

For me, it was becoming increasingly obvious how wrong this policy had been. It was already clear that the Mullahs had no intention of halting their accelerating quest to build a nuclear bomb. More than a decade later, we still seem not to have learned that lesson. Back in 2005 the Mullahs had already developed the Shahab-3 missile system, capable of delivering a nuclear payload over a distance of 1,000 miles. The Iranian Deputy Foreign Minister Gholamali Khoshru, during a visit to the European Parliament, had lied that these missiles were purely for defensive purposes, to protect Iran from its immediate neighbours in the Middle East. Why, then, he was asked, was Iran developing a new generation of missiles capable of reaching Berlin, Paris or London?

It seemed glaringly obvious that the policy of appeasement would never succeed. Indeed, the more the EU sought to appease the Mullahs, the more oppressive their regime had become. I pointed this out in speech after speech in the European Parliament. In the 26 years since the overthrow of the Shah, the tyrants in Teheran had executed 120,000 opponents. Women were routinely hanged in public and stoned to death. Offenders were regularly publicly flogged. Convicts had their limbs amputated or eyes gouged out. Democracy, freedom of speech and human rights were clearly alien concepts in Iran, where the Mullahs played host to al-Qaeda and poured unlimited funds and agents into the bloody insurgency now raging in neighbouring Iraq. The West turned a blind eye to all of this. Oil contracts and money were more important than human rights.

Mrs Rajavi and her allies in the NCRI had produced a political platform from which to build a secular democracy in Iran. Their activities were unnerving the Ayatollahs in Tehran. Indeed, when Britain, France and Germany sought a temporary halt to Iran's nuclear programme, the Mullahs' top demand was to keep the PMOI on the

EU terrorist list. By accepting this ludicrous demand, the EU played into the hands of Tehran, effectively handcuffing the only viable opponents of the Islamic fundamentalist regime.

Iran's clandestine nuclear project, exposed to the West by the PMOI, had steadily evolved into a major international challenge; and this challenge had become even more pressing since the 'election' in 2005 of Mahmoud Ahmadinejad as president. The son of a blacksmith, Ahmadinejad was a populist hardliner who called America 'The Great Satan' and took a defiant stance on Iran's right to a nuclear programme. A Holocaust denier who called for Israel to be 'wiped off the map', Ahmadinejad initially enjoyed the full support of Supreme Leader Ayatollah Ali Khamenei, who liked his hardline approach. However, the international community was alarmed at Ahmadinejad's rise to power. It was claimed that he had been one of the hostage-takers during the notorious siege of the American Embassy in Tehran in 1979, although he fiercely denied it. Nevertheless, like most powerful figures in the Iranian elite, he had served his time in the brutal Islamic Revolutionary Guard Corps (IRGC). Despite all of this, Jack Straw and other political leaders in Europe still thought that appeasement was the way to go.

Risking their lives to uncover more intelligence about the Mullahs' nuclear ambitions, PMOI agents were able to tell the West that the programme was no longer in the hands of the scientists, but had been handed over to the control of the military. The IRGC, whose role since 1979 had been to defend the Khomeini revolution, was now in charge of the weapons programme, giving the lie to the assertion by the Mullahs that this was simply a domestic energy programme.

6

Interviews with political prisoners, Refugee Camp, Tirana, Albania, May 2014

Azam Hadj Heydari

My name is Azam Hadj Heydari. I was a teacher because I wanted to serve my people. Their lives were full of pain and my job was to provide life by way of education. My school was in an impoverished area of Southern Tehran. Every morning my students would describe the pain of being deprived of the freedom they had sought by getting rid of the Shah. So I looked for a new direction and found the PMOI.

After four years the regime arrested me, and my whole family were made to turn against each other. We tried to pursue our goal peacefully; by 21, I was arrested four times and taken to secret houses. I was tortured in a new unnamed secret prison opened by Khomeini. Houses previously owned by the Shah had been converted into secret prisons. I was held for 15 days and given only water, no food. We were told that we should get the idea of freedom out of our minds and that the revolution's goal was to institute the absolute rule of the clergy. Eventually I was thrown out onto the street barefoot and walked home.

In the summer of 1981, I was walking in a Tehran street when I saw my brother. I knew he would betray me because he was opposed to the PMOI. I went to my aunt's house at 1.30 am. Fifteen minutes later the doorbell rang. I looked out the window and saw that the square was surrounded by Revolutionary Guards, with my brother among them. Ten minutes later, they started to bang on the door. They broke the glass, entered the house and both my cousin and I were arrested. We were blindfolded and taken away.

They drove us around for hours to prevent us from identifying the destination. I was eventually placed in a 1 x 1 metre-square cell. I got a dirty, broken plate of food pushed in through the door once a day. I was held for 25 days and allowed out only for prayers. One day I heard somebody screaming and realised that it was my older sister. They were threatening and torturing her to put pressure on me. My sister was placed on an electric chair, in hopes of forcing her to reveal more information about me, but neither of us said anything. A month later we were taken out of the cell and mixed in with ordinary prisoners. My sister was held in the cell across from mine. They kept threatening to kill us. After 20 days, my sister and I were gagged and transferred to Evin Prison.

There we were tortured. In 1982, it was freezing cold in winter and we had 500 people in our cellblock. We were given ten minutes each a week for a cold shower. There were women as old as 80, pregnant women, people horribly injured by torture, and children as young as four. The regime wanted total silence as a sort of psychological torture. The prison windows had bars, but did not allow any light to come in. Despite that, however, we were full of energy and were determined to fight on. One day 80 of us were taken out and made to stand in deep snow from 6 am until 9 pm. The cold was unbearable. On another night I realized that Masoumeh Azadanlou, Mrs Maryam Rajavi's sister, who was pregnant, was tapping on the wall of the neighbouring cell to deliver a sort of message. She had been badly tortured. She said, "Be brave; and remember PMOI fighters never get tired of fighting." They had placed live snakes in her cell for four days, but they did not harm her. She was executed shortly thereafter.

We were made to stand all day and every day in the snow for a week. I was moved to another prison and placed in a tiny cage for eight months, where there was total silence. The punishment for making even the slightest sound was severe beating. A guard called Mohammad would beat us with batons and threaten to keep us there until our teeth were black and our hair turned grey. Eventually, after ten years of imprisonment, they released my sister and me. I escaped from Iran, but could not walk properly as a result of being tortured. After leaving Iran, I joined the ranks of the resistance in Iraq.'

7

London

Our campaign to remove the PMOI from the UK and EU terror lists now moved into top gear. Intensive lobbying was taking place in the European Parliament and in parliaments throughout the EU. Eminent lawyers and legal experts were preparing evidence to supply to the courts.

The PMOI/MEK was first registered on the US list of foreign terrorist organisations in 1997, as the result of a direct request by the Iranian Mullahs to President Bill Clinton. On 9 October 1997, the *Los Angeles Times* quoted a senior official as saying that the PMOI was put on the US terrorist list 'as a goodwill gesture to Mohammad Khatami, the new Iranian president.' On 26 September 2002, a senior US official, Martin Indyk, special assistant to President Clinton and the senior director of Near East and South Asian Affairs at the United States National Security Council in 1997, told *Newsweek* that 'The Mojahedin's designation was part of Clinton's policy of rapprochement with Tehran.'

(In October 1999 this listing was amended to include what the US State Department described as the MEK's aliases, namely the PMOI and the NCRI.) Then on 15 August 2003, several months after the invasion of Iraq, the US closed down the offices of the PMOI/MEK and NCRI in Washington. This was a follow-up to America's promise to the Ayatollahs on the eve of the Iraq invasion. Jack Straw, who was the British Home Secretary, added the PMOI to the UK terror list in March 2001. The EU listed the PMOI as a terrorist organisation in May 2002, at the specific request of the UK Government, and its assets were frozen.

In February 2006, the European Court of First Instance took up this case and I, Alejo Vidal-Quadras, Vice President of the European Parliament, and several prominent dignitaries such as France's former First Lady, Danielle Mitterrand, attended the court in Luxembourg.

The lawyers representing the EU did not have much to say, and simply emphasized the authority and competence of the EU. On 12 December 2006 the Court ruled that the EU had not followed the correct legal procedure and had failed to inform the PMOI about the freezing of its assets in Europe. They ordered the money to be unblocked.

In an extraordinary move, the European Council of Ministers decided to ignore this ruling. The Council of Ministers reviewed the list of groups and individuals in the terrorist list every six months. In this way the Council played a dirty game by claiming that the European Court had annulled the decision of the EU during the first half of 2006, but the PMOI was placed on a new list during the second half of 2006! In this seemingly endless cycle the Council continued to preserve the PMOI's terrorist listing.

Meanwhile, in the UK, a complaint by 35 senior MPs and Peers, representing all three major British political parties, had been lodged against the Home Secretary for his refusal to lift the terror ban on the PMOI. The British government made an enormous effort to prevent the Court from making a ruling in favour of the PMOI. In an un-usual move, in August 2007 the government sent a letter to point out the dangers of delisting and the Iranian regime's potential retaliation against British interests, urging the Court that before it informed the PMOI of any delisting, it should inform the government two weeks prior to making such a decision. This was clearly a new ploy to prevent the removal of the PMOI from the UK list. The Court however did not accept this request.

On Friday 30 November 2007, after five days of public hearings, several days of judicial discussions behind closed doors and four months of intensive deliberations, the judges of the UK's Pro-scribed Organisations Appeal Commission (POAC) released a 144-page and 362-point verdict declaring the inclusion of the People's Mojahedin Organisation of Iran (PMOI) on the list of proscribed organisations to be void and unlawful. The Labour Home Secretary – Jacqui Smith – appealed against this judgement, but the Court of Appeal rejected her case and ordered that the blacklisting of the PMOI should be revoked following a debate in both Houses of Parliament. The PMOI was finally removed from the UK terrorist list in June 2008.

During the course of reviewing the case by the Proscribed Organisations Appeal Commission (POAC) and the Court of Appeal, lawyers acting on behalf of the 35 MPs and Peers who had lodged the original appeal with the POAC demanded sight of all the so-called 'classified' evidence on which the UK government had based its claims of terrorism against the PMOI. Hundreds of pages of carefully censored files were duly released to the courts. These included details of the mysterious phone-call from Mrs Felicity Brown, the lady pretending to work for the Foreign Office who turned out to work for British Intelligence. There were even several pages of transcripts of our conversations, with the MI5 officer admitting candidly that I had seemed 'well informed' about the PMOI.

There was also a detailed, almost verbatim, account of a meeting that I had held in Brussels following a request from a senior FCO civil servant. I thought the FCO official was coming to the European Parliament to speak to me about international fisheries agreements, as I was president of the Fisheries Committee at that time. However, it turned out to be another attempt to browbeat me into severing my ties with the PMOI. I really blew my top at this meeting and gave the civil servant a piece of my mind, reminding him that he was a paid official, while I was elected by the UK citizens. I warned him to tell his political masters that I was not going to be intimidated or bullied in this way and that their policy towards Iran and their proscribing of the PMOI was simply wrong. I demanded evidence to substantiate claims that the PMOI were indeed engaged in acts of terrorism and I was bluntly told that such evidence was far too sensitive to divulge to a mere member of the European Parliament and was 'classified'. It was a very ill-tempered exchange, all of which duly appeared in the 'classified' documents released to the POAC.

Equally amazingly, although unsurprisingly, much of the so-called independent evidence on which the UK government based their decision to list the PMOI as a terrorist organisation turned out to have come from two individuals who lived in the UK and were well-known as paid agents of the Mullahs in Tehran! Iranian citizen Massoud Khodabandeh had been recruited by the MOIS, the Iranian Ministry of Intelligence and Security, in the late 1990s, and his British wife, Anne Singleton, had been recruited by the MOIS in 2002.[1] Both had been trained by Iran and were well-known for press articles and propaganda that always sought to trash the PMOI and its leadership and supporters. For the UK government to base their terrorism charges on evidence supplied by two MOIS agents was preposterous. The whole thing was farcical and exposed the appeasement charade in which Blair and Straw had been engaged. No wonder the POAC delivered such a withering judgement.

The POAC's verdict stated: 'This appeal against the refusal of the Secretary of State to de-proscribe the PMOI is allowed' and 'we order that the Secretary of State should lay before parliament the draft of an Order under section 3(3)(b) of the 2000 Act removing the PMOI from the list of proscribed organisations in Schedule 2'. The judgement also noted: 'Having carefully considered all the material before us, we have concluded that the decision at the first stage is properly characterised as perverse. We recognise that a finding of perversity is uncommon. We believe, however, that this Commission is in the (perhaps unusual) position of having before it all of the material that is relevant to this decision. In our view, that is a requirement of the 2000 Act and of the procedures adopted before this commission. The material available to us is, therefore, wider, more extensive and more detailed than the evidence that is commonly before a judge in the Administrative court.'

As the legal battles raged, the European Council of Ministers, in an act of open defiance of the courts, renewed the EU proscription of the PMOI on 15 July 2008. On 4 December that year, the Court of First Instance annulled the renewed proscription of 15 July and once again ordered that the PMOI be delisted and their assets unfrozen. Despite this ruling, there were further attempts by the European Council, stoked up by pressure from Tehran, to defy the courts. But by mid-December, the Court of First Instance rejected, as 'manifestly inadmissible', all attempts by EU governments to delay implementation of their 4 December judgement. As a result, after a war of attrition that had raged for years, the PMOI were finally delisted in the EU on 26 January 2009. Justice had at last prevailed.

1. A Pentagon report of January 2013 identified Massoud Khodabandeh and Anne Singleton as trained MOIS agents.

The willingness of the UK, French and other EU governments to defy the courts was breathtaking. Although British judges in the POAC had gone into the substance and full details of the case and had ruled that the decision of the UK Home Secretary to maintain the PMOI on the UK list of proscribed organisations was 'perverse', the UK Government still trotted out a junior minister to make a fatuous announcement that the government 'did not accept' the court's verdict and had decided to appeal. They tried every legal and political trick to defy the courts.

The entire affair was marked by a long and disgraceful series of blunders by the Blair government at Westminster over its handling of the PMOI and relations with Iran in general. It was common knowledge that, as Foreign Secretary, Jack Straw had visited Tehran more often than any other capital in the world except Brussels and Washington. But the deals he struck with the fascist Mullahs left an indelible stain on Britain's character. Straw had admitted in a BBC Radio interview that he placed the PMOI on the UK terror list at the direct request of the Mullahs, who greatly feared the ability of this popular opposition movement to topple their odious regime. The Mullahs further pressed Straw to place the PMOI on the EU's terror list, threatening commercial penalties for UK interests in Iran if he refused to comply. Displaying characteristic weakness, Jack Straw had readily concurred, despite the fact that he had once been an open supporter of the PMOI as an Opposition Labour MP.

No one would have guessed that EU bureaucrats, entrusted to enact and uphold the rule of law, would scramble to find ways to defy the courts, making a mockery of the rule of law upon which the institutions of the EU and European member states are founded. Violating the rule of law and placing the European Council of Ministers' opinion above that of the EU's highest courts in yet another pathetic attempt to appease Iran was both scandalous and shameful.

In a speech in the European Parliament in Strasbourg I said:

The decision by the Council of Ministers has stepped over recognized red lines in Europe. While the Mullahs' President Mahmoud Ahmadinejad is calling for the annihilation of Israel and, according to Western intelligence reports, Iran is within years of having the nuclear capability to carry out his threat, it ill befalls the European Council to continue its failed policy of appeasement. While Iranian Revolutionary Guards roam freely in Iraq, inflaming the insurgency, killing allied troops and murdering countless innocent civilians, the Council of Ministers should be confronting Tehran from a position of strength, rather than displaying craven weakness. The EU should be offering support to those who oppose the Mullahs, rather than seeking to tarnish them with lies and distortions. The EU and the 500 million citizens it represents are proud of their democracy and its principles. These principles are in danger of being compromised by a few bureaucrats who have made the terror label a bargaining chip to curry favour with the very regime that is one of the world's leading sponsors of terrorism. In the fight against terrorism, we must keep the moral high ground and respect our democratic principles. Otherwise, how different will our democracy be from those tyrannies we so despise? It is time for EU bureaucrats to practise what they preach. Pay heed to the ruling of the European Court of Justice and remove the PMOI from its terror list once and for all.

Terrorism is the greatest threat of our time. Terrorists not only endanger our lives, they also challenge our freedoms and our democratic system of government. The difference between democracy and tyranny is the system of checks and balances. What made it frustratingly difficult for me was the fact that some bureaucrats in the EU were contemplating compromising this sacred principle for the sake of political expediency. What made it even more perplexing was that these political leaders had been given the mandate of safeguarding our democratic system. For them to seek to undermine the system under the guise of combating terrorism was particularly perverse.

Since the late 1990s, the issue of the PMOI was part and parcel of the EU's negotiations with the Iranian regime in a futile attempt to moderate Tehran's behaviour. For instance, on 21 October 2004, the Agence France-Presse agency reported:

> According to the preparatory text for European proposals on the Iranian nuclear programme, the EU 3 underscored that if Iran complies with the EU on the nuclear issue, we would continue to regard the PMOI (Iranian resistance group) as a terrorist organisation.

The official document made it abundantly clear that the issue was finding ways to placate the Mullahs and had nothing to do with the merit and conduct of the Iranian resistance movement.

The continued determination of the PMOI, over many years, to clear its name and remove the unfair and unlawful terrorist designation with which it had been labelled, had become an almost classic example of a David and Goliath struggle. Victory in the British courts and subsequently in the EU courts was a first major taste of success for the PMOI and a severe blow to the Mullahs in Tehran. It was also a clear demonstration that the PMOI and its network of international supporters could achieve the impossible.

8

Interviews with Political Prisoners
Refugee Camp, Tirana, Albania, May 2014

Najmeh Hadj Heydari

'My name is Najmeh Hadj Heydari. I am Azam's sister [see Chapter 6]. I was arrested in the city of Saveh in 1982 and taken to Evin in Tehran. While in the torture chamber I told them I was pregnant. They did not believe me and started to torture me with cables, whipping the soles of my bare feet. In the public ward they asked me what I thought about the Mullahs and Khomeini. I said they deserve to die for usurping the freedom of the people of Iran. A half hour later they took me to Ward 311, the punishment ward.

There were six or seven people in each cell, usually awaiting execution. They would open the cell three times a day for food. Then it fell to once a day. I was placed in solitary confinement for 45 days and only allowed out to go to the washroom. We were not allowed to shower and we were given no bedding. I was freezing. 45 days later I was brought back to the larger cell. A girl called Maryam Yazdi Ostovar, who was only 16 years old, had a bloody mark on her left leg, and her feet were shredded and swollen as a result of torture. Surgeons had removed the skin from her leg to mend her feet. She was from the city of Qazvin and told me that her brother had been executed. "They wanted me to divulge information and whipped me relentlessly on the soles of my feet, shredding them to pieces. Eventually they realised that I could tell them nothing, so they operated on my feet to mend them too."

Later I noticed that Maryam had been taken for interrogation again. Peeking from under her blindfold she recognized one of the people being interrogated. But half an hour later they took her out again and she disappeared for two weeks. When she returned, she could only walk on her knees. She asked for a copy of the *Koran* and lay down next to the wall, put the *Koran* on her chest and told me what had happened. Her feet were shattered. This continued for a whole week. Since she could not stand they tied her in order to hold her upright so they could continue torturing her. After telling us this she said, "leave me alone". At 5 am they opened the door of our cell for prayers and she was unable to get up. We went to prayers, but when we returned we realised she was dead. The Guards forced us to stand next to the wall until her body was taken away.

Another woman named Razieh Ayatollahzadeh Shirazi, a student who had joined the PMOI during the Shah's time, was pregnant and had been tortured. In Ward 311 there used to be a bakery, the heat from which transferred to the floor of the prison. She said the heat would eventually kill her baby. Three weeks later, her baby died. She said the baby's death was the price we pay for freedom. Her husband had already been executed. In 1985 she was executed too.

I got to know a 45-year-old mother named Rezvan Rafipoor in Ward 240. She was tortured every three weeks in order to extract information from her about her daughter. The severe beatings had left horrible bruises on her body. She was then taken to "the dormitory", a special ward for political prisoners. After experiencing that ward, she was so distraught that she said it was impossible for her to re-establish contact with other people. When her cellmates were asleep, she got a rope, placed a bucket under her feet and hanged herself. One of my friends found her and screamed. The guards cut her down but it was too late.

I was pregnant when I was imprisoned. They even forbade me from giving birth at a regular hospital. My baby spent one year in prison with me and then was looked after by my parents. When I was freed after three and a half years, I fled with my baby to Iraq and joined the resistance in Ashraf.'

9

Strasbourg

In the autumn of 2004 we decided to arrange for Mrs Rajavi, in her capacity as President-elect of the NCRI, to come to the European Parliament to address a meeting of the all-party Friends of a Free Iran Intergroup (FoFI), which I co-chaired with Paulo Casaca, a Socialist MEP from Portugal and a close friend. Together we had set up FoFI for the purpose of backing the restoration of democracy, the rule of law, human rights, women's rights, the abolition of the death penalty and the abolition of nuclear weapons in Iran. On behalf of FoFI we had both travelled widely throughout the Middle East, Europe and the US in pursuit of our objective of having the PMOI taken off the various terror lists. Indeed we went to the United States on many occasions, to the Congress and the Senate. Paulo Casaca, Alejo Vidal-Quadras and other colleagues also on several occasions travelled to Iraq to visit Camp Ashraf, where at that time over 3,400 key frontline members of the PMOI were stuck as defenceless refugees under the fragile security of the occupying US military forces. These refugees were under constant threat of attack or eviction.

Paulo and I met many obstacles during our campaign. We were vilified in the media by Iranian intelligence with spurious press articles, accusing us of being 'friends of terrorists'. Obscure advertisements naming the PMOI as a terrorist organisation appeared in parliamentary magazines and news journals in an attempt to smear us. They sometimes provided a website address, but any attempt to make contact was always met with silence. There was never an answer; the web addresses were bogus as these ads were all placed and funded by Iranian Intelligence (MOIS). They are afraid of the PMOI. They know it is the only threat to their stranglehold on Iran. That is why they became hysterical when they heard that meetings with Mrs Rajavi were taking place within the European Parliament.

The Mullahs also threw endless resources into backing bogus NGOs in Europe such as the Nejat (Saviour) Association and the Edalat (Justice) Society. Their task was to spread lies and false news about Camp Ashraf residents and the leadership of the resistance, and to traduce parliamentarians like me, Paulo Casaca, Alejo Vidal-Quadras and other opinion-leaders who backed the PMOI. The lengths the regime was prepared to go to and the resources it was prepared to invest in demonising us demonstrated the PMOI's effectiveness and status in Iran.

The FoFI meeting on 15 December 2004 was held in the European Parliament in Strasbourg, because Mrs Rajavi was still under strict travel restrictions following her arrest by Chirac. We deemed it safer for her to travel internally by car in France from the PMOI headquarters outside Paris, to Strasbourg. (Some months later, in June 2006, a French court cancelled the ludicrous travel restrictions imposed by the Chirac government.) The meeting was attended by more than 150 MEPs and Mrs Rajavi for the first time proposed her Third Option, a clear prospect to resolve the Iranian crisis, which had caused anxiety on a global scale. She said:

> In response to the Iranian crisis, two options are regularly proposed: either compromise with the Mullahs' regime, in a bid to contain or gradually change the regime. Western countries have pursued this policy in the past two decades. Or overthrowing the Mullahs by way of a foreign war, similar to what occurred in Iraq. No one is interested in a repeat of the Iraqi experience in Iran. But, I have come here today to say that there is a third option: change by the Iranian people and the Iranian Resistance. With the removal of foreign obstacles, the Iranian people and Resistance would have the ability and the preparedness to bring about such change. This presents the only way to avert a foreign war. Offering concessions to the Mullahs is not the alternative to a foreign conflict and will not dissuade them from pursuing their ominous intentions.

Encouraged by the success of this visit, in the autumn of 2005 we decided to arrange a meeting for Mrs Rajavi with the majority

45

European People's Party-European Democrats (EPP-ED) Group in the European Parliament. I had been elected 2nd Vice President of the EPP-ED Group following the 2004 European parliamentary elections, and I sent a formal written request to our leader Hans-Gert Poettering. Hans-Gert agreed to place my request on the agenda for a future meeting of the Bureau or Cabinet of the Group, which consisted of all eight Vice Presidents, together with the Group's Treasurer Othmar Karas and President Hans-Gert himself.

At the Bureau meeting in June 2006, controversy raged. I made a strong case for inviting Mrs Rajavi, based on the fact that she was leading a democratic opposition movement who could replace tyranny and the threat of nuclear war with respect for human rights, the rights of women, an end to torture and the death penalty and the eradication of nuclear weapons; my initiative was fiercely opposed by Othmar Karas from Austria. Indeed while I was addressing the meeting, Othmar's mobile phone began to ring and he rather noisily took the call. The blood seemed to drain from his face. 'That was my Chancellor – Wolfgang Schüssel. He has just received a call from Javier Solana [the EU's High Representative for Foreign Affairs] who is in Tehran trying to negotiate a nuclear pact with the Mullahs. They have heard that we are thinking about inviting Mrs Rajavi to the European Parliament and have demanded that we do no such thing, otherwise they will pull out of the nuclear talks!' News of our intended invitation to Mrs Rajavi had clearly leaked, and it had not taken long for the Iranian embassy in Brussels to pick it up and transmit it to Tehran, causing a major flap. Hans-Gert Poettering said that we should adjourn any decision on the invitation until each of us had time to discuss it with our respective political delegations, and if necessary with our party leaders.

Later that day, 29 June, the EPP-ED Group left for a three-day conference in Bordeaux, and that same evening I found myself at the top table with the rest of our Group Bureau at a dinner in the beautiful Château Smith-Haut-Lafitte. During the course of the dinner I left to go to the toilet. Having washed my hands and as I was heading for the exit, I noticed Elmar Brok, the President of the all-powerful Foreign Affairs Committee, having a pee amongst several other men at the urinal. Elmar is a large, rotund and florid German with a shock of blond hair and a beady glass eye. I said, 'Hello, Elmar' on the way past. Glancing over his shoulder, he shouted: 'Stevenson, you must not invite this woman Rajavi to the European Parliament.'

'Why not?' I replied.

'Because Angela Merkel says so,' he shouted.

'Well, I don't take my orders from Angela Merkel,' I said.

Elmar exploded. 'Well I do,' he screamed, spinning to face me and peeing down the leg of the man next to him in the process.

I hurried out of the Gents, leaving behind shouts of exasperation from the man who had been soaked and Elmar's grumbling apologies! Back at the dinner table I recounted the whole sordid tale to Hans-Gert and the other Bureau Members, to hoots of delight and roars of laughter.

The following day, Hans-Gert told me that he had received a telephone call from a very agitated José-Manuel Barroso, the President of the European Commission. He confirmed that Javier Solana, pleading with him to try to stop Mrs Rajavi coming to the European Parliament, had also contacted him. It seemed that I had triggered an international incident. Sure enough, during the course of the day I was told by my good friend Alejo Vidal-Quadras, Senior Vice President of the European Parliament and an MEP from Spain, that he had received a telephone call from his own party leaders ordering him not to support the invitation; even Hans-Gert Poettering had been telephoned by Angela Merkel with the same message. It was beginning to look as if my plans for Mrs Rajavi's visit were about to unravel.

During this hiatus, a colleague in the EPP Group, Michael Gahler MEP, a former German junior diplomat, began what became an almost hysterical and obsessive campaign against Alejo Vidal-Quadras and me, because of our support for Mrs Rajavi and the PMOI. Despite the fact that he was a member of the same political family as us, he courted support from other political groups in the European Parliament, repeating false allegations which originated from the Mullahs and raising petitions and signatures on letters, which sought to denigrate our activities. Gahler continued this obsessive activity for all the years I served as an MEP, making himself appear increasingly irrational in the meantime.

47

The intervention of the many European government leaders who tried to prevent Mrs Rajavi's visit served to underline the clear importance of the PMOI and Mrs Rajavi to the Iranian regime. All this fuss for a 30-minute speech! Since the majority of the EPP Group's bureau was in favour of her visit, the Group chair, Hans-Gert Poettering, had sent her a formal invitation, but we were under tremendous pressure. Mrs Rajavi was supposed to address our group meeting on Tuesday 4 July. She was already in Strasbourg on the Monday evening in preparation for her intended speech, but when she became aware of the situation, she ended the crisis with an amazing initiative.

Hans-Gert received a letter from Mrs Rajavi saying that she would not like to do anything that might jeopardise the nuclear discussions in Tehran and that she was therefore willing to postpone any intended visit to the EPP Group until later. So the pressure on the group was lifted. Mrs Rajavi came to the European Parliament on 5 July and spoke in a press conference organized by FoFI, with me, Alejo and Paulo. She said: 'The situation has been temporarily resolved, but nevertheless once again we are dancing to the Mullahs' tune.' She warned that the likelihood of any meaningful success in the nuclear talks was extremely limited; and so it turned out to be. Despite all the threats and warnings from the Iranian regime, the nuclear talks ended with no agreement. The Mullahs were insisting that their uranium enrichment programme was only for peaceful purposes and would continue without interruption. Solana returned to the EU with his tail between his legs, once again outmanoeuvred by Tehran.

I decided to use this humiliation of our EU appeasement policy to resurrect the controversial invitation to Mrs Rajavi. This time, no credibility could be given to the threats from the Iranian embassy and from the Mullahs in Tehran. The EPP-ED Group's Bureau, under the leadership of Hans-Gert Poettering, bravely agreed to my request and a formal invitation was sent to Mrs Rajavi. A date was set for her address to the entire group of 268 MEPs in Strasbourg.

On the day of her visit, the protocol service of the European Parliament had arranged for her to be met at the VIP entrance. She arrived amid tight security in a convoy of cars. Alejo Vidal-Quadras and I presented her with a bouquet of flowers and we led her along the red carpet to the EU flags, where official photographs were taken, with more than a dozen other senior MEP supporters. Mrs Rajavi's address to the EPP-ED Group was profound. She outlined the Iranian Resistance's viewpoints for the future of Iran in a ten-point plan:

1. In our view, the ballot box is the only criterion for legitimacy. Accordingly, we seek a republic based on universal suffrage.

2. We want a pluralist system, freedom of parties and assembly. We respect all individual freedoms. We underscore complete freedom of expression and of the media and unconditional access by all to the Internet.

3. We support and are committed to the abolition of the death penalty.

4. We are committed to the separation of Religion and State. Any form of discrimination against the followers of any religion and denomination will be prohibited.

5. We believe in complete gender equality in political, social and economic arenas. We are also committed to equal participation of women in political leadership. Any form of discrimination against women will be abolished. They will enjoy the right to freely choose their clothing. They are free in marriage, divorce, education and employment.

6. We believe in the rule of law and justice. We want to set up a modern judicial system based on the principles of presumption of innocence, the right to defence, effective judicial protection and the right to be tried in a public court. We also seek the total independence of judges. The Mullahs' Sharia law will be abolished.

7. We are committed to the Universal Declaration of Human Rights, and international covenants and conventions, including the International Covenant on Civil and Political Rights, the Convention against Torture, and the Convention on the Elimination of all Forms of Discrimination against Women. We are committed to the equality of all nationalities. We underscore the plan for the autonomy of Iranian Kurdistan,

49

adopted by the NCRI. The language and culture of our compatriots from whatever nationality are among our nation's human resources and must spread and be promulgated in tomorrow's Iran.

8. We recognise private property, private investment and the market economy. All Iranian people must enjoy equal opportunity in employment and in business ventures. We will protect and revitalise the environment.

9. Our foreign policy will be based on peaceful coexistence, international and regional peace and cooperation, as well as respect for the United Nations Charter.

10. We want a non-nuclear Iran, free of weapons of mass destruction.

These positions are all meant to herald the establishment of a genuine and enduring democracy in Iran, to which Mrs Rajavi has dedicated her life. She said, 'We are not fighting and making sacrifices to be able to grab power. We have not even set our sights on sharing power and the ability to govern. Our biggest mission is the establishment of the people's sovereignty and democracy . . .'

10

Interviews with Political Prisoners
Refugee Camp, Tirana, Albania, May 2014

Mohammad Hossein Ebrahimi

'My name is Mohammad Hossein Ebrahimi. I was 15 years old when I was arrested in 1981. I was sentenced to three years imprisonment in a kangaroo court, but actually ended up being imprisoned for four years. My main crime was that my heart was beating for Massoud Rajavi, I was told. In the prison, I heard about the death of my brother, Mehdi. He was 19 and I had seen him several times before in the prison. We could see each other from a window at the top of our cells. The last time I saw him he was smiling and very happy. I realised later it was because he had been informed that he was to be executed, and he wanted to show his high morale.

Later I heard the Revolutionary Guards had gone to my parents and they took them to the woods in the north of Iran, where they said they would show them their son. But instead they gave them his body. I also heard that my other brother had been executed as well. Later, my only sister was executed. Her husband's brother is now here in Tirana, after being transferred from Camp Liberty.

In 1988, during the massacre in Iranian prisons, 30,000 PMOI prisoners were executed, including my remaining brother Ali Akbar, who was 29 years old. In fact all of my family members were supporters of the PMOI. My father died. My mother now lives in France. My mother and I are the only ones left from my family. After spending four years in prison, I was released and escaped with the help of human smugglers to Camp Ashraf in Iraq.

I also have a touching memory of my friend Abdal when we were both in prison. I was imprisoned at Gorgan, but was transferred to Gohardasht prison at the time. Gohardasht's construction had begun during the time of the Shah, but was completed during Khomeini's time. It has 1,000 solitary confinement cells. The cells were about

51

1.5 metres by 2 metres wide. There was a window with small holes that I would get a tiny amount of light from every day. Many of the prisoners were mentally tortured. One colleague, Razaq Farkhondeh, was so psychologically damaged that, upon his release, he committed suicide.

We were held in strictest silence. We tried to communicate with the other cells, but it was virtually impossible. If you were caught talking you would be badly beaten. I had heard there was a way to communicate using Morse code, by tapping on the adjoining walls, but I didn't know what it was like and how to use it.

In that three-storey prison, we could hear tapping noises (Morse-code signals) coming from the floor above and the floor below. One day I heard something from the adjacent cell and so brought my mouth very close the wall and tried to speak to the person in that cell. While pretending to sing, I used certain words to ask his name. The prison guards would check on us routinely and if they suspected we were talking to each other they would drag us out of our cells and beat us.

But on this particular day I heard a muffled response from the other side of the wall, so I realised we could talk in this way sort of vaguely. I asked the other guy if he could understand Morse and he said yes. I said, "Could you teach me?" He replied, "Yes, do you know the Morse alphabet?" I said no. He tried to teach me and I managed to learn the Morse alphabet in four days. He then taught me how to use different signs for each letter. I had to memorise all this in my head, because we were not allowed to have papers or pencils.'

11
Tehran

It was Anton Chekhov who said: 'Love, Friendship and respect do not unite people as much as a common hatred for something.' How very true in the case of Iran, where a common hatred towards the tyrannical Mullahs was beginning to unite the people in passionate opposition to their oppressors. But distinguishing friends from enemies was a skill sadly absent in Europe at the beginning of the new millennium, at least in the context of EU policy towards Iran.

Since Iran's President Mahmoud Ahmadinejad took office, the fascist clerical regime in Tehran, under the iron grasp of Supreme Leader Ayatollah Ali Khamenei, had been able to advance its goals by taking advantage of indecision and division among Western allies. Repression had been stepped up, with a rising number of executions, amputations, stoning to death of women and men, mass arrests and closure of media outlets. The increasing incidence of public hangings of political prisoners was designed to terrify and subjugate the restless Iranian people.

On the nuclear issue, the regime had continued the relentless expansion of the project, with over 3,000 centrifuges operating in cascade to enrich weapons-grade uranium. The Mullahs argued that this enrichment process was purely for the generation of electricity, but there is only one nuclear power station in Iran, at Bushehr, and no additional ones were being built. The Bushehr plant had been constructed by the Russians and its fuel was supposed to be provided by them.

In March 2004, the PMOI were able to pinpoint the precise location of the regime's top-secret nuclear command and control centre at Lavizan, where work was well advanced on the manufacture of a neutron generator and a trigger for an atomic bomb. They also identified the extensive top-secret site at Khojir, southeast of Tehran, where nuclear warheads were being produced. In each case, the PMOI were not only able to provide the exact location and activity that was going on, but also even named the scientists and key personnel involved. All of this information was passed to the International Atomic Energy Agency for investigation.

The West meanwhile pretended to back tough sanctions on Iran. Nevertheless, EU companies continued to supply sophisticated drilling equipment, and teams of experts to train the Islamic Revolutionary Guard Corps (IRGC) in their operation. This equipment, ostensibly for use in innocent hydrology projects, was essential for the construction of the massive underground water and bunker infrastructure required for the Mullahs' aggressive nuclear weapons programme. Other EU companies had lucrative contracts to supply the mobile construction-cranes routinely used to hang opponents of the regime in public squares across Iran.

While we in the West filled our pockets with Iranian gold, the Mullahs' regime was busily training and deploying hundreds of suicide bombers and insurgents in Iraq, in a bid to foment civil war and deliver that country into the clutches of Iran. The IRGC provided the sophisticated roadside bombs (EFPs) that were being used to kill and maim allied military personnel on a regular basis. They were also the puppet-masters of Hezbollah during the war with Israel in Lebanon and their support for the militant Palestinian group Hamas led to the rupture with Fatah and the partition of Palestine.

The PMOI, due to its extensive network within Iran, began to expose the Mullahs' meddling in Iraq. They tried to make the US understand that Iran was seeking to impose its hegemony in Iraq, but the Americans, in a continuation of their wrong-headed policy that led to the invasion of Iraq, kept the doors open for Iran. Between 2003 and 2011, the PMOI published over 4,500 information packs on this issue or gave them to relevant officials. One of these packs included a list of the names of 32,000 people who were on the payroll of the IRGC in Iraq, an amazing and top-secret document. This list was obtained from within the IRGC in Tehran, and at least one of the sources was executed for leaking the information. An interesting point was that many senior officials in Nouri al-Maliki's government in Baghdad were on the list! Among other information, it included full names, bank account numbers, bank codes and amount of salary paid by the IRGC, for all of those listed.

Iran, moreover, had repeatedly thumbed its nose at the West's compromise offers, forcing Javier Solana, the EU's High Representative for Foreign Affairs, to concede in a speech in January 2005, 'There has been no progress. Iran continues to ignore us.' Even so, in the same debate, he and Benita Ferrero-Waldner, the Austrian Commissioner for External Affairs, again and again emphasised the need for ongoing discussion, debate and negotiation. 'People to people' contact is what is needed, Mrs Ferrero-Waldner assured the European Parliament, outlining the EU's strategy of opening our universities to Iranian students of nuclear physics and pouring Euros into a 'poverty alleviation fund'! In a speech before a plenary session of the European Parliament in Strasbourg and in front of Commissioner Ferrero-Waldner, I said: 'It almost beggars belief that EU taxpayers are helping to relieve poverty in one of the world's richest oil-exporting nations, whose leaders have corruptly embezzled billions and who choose to squander their cash on building weapons of mass destruction. Worse still, it is astounding that the European Commission boasts that we are training Iranian students in nuclear technology!'

In Washington, George W. Bush had placed the IRGC on the US list of terrorist organizations. This had, of course, infuriated Tehran and its apologists in the West, but it enabled the US to freeze the vast foreign financial assets of the IRGC and to target foreign companies doing business with them.

The IRGC have always comprised the backbone of the Iranian regime's system of oppression. In 2004 more than fifty former IRGC members sat in the 290-seat parliament, with others serving as mayors and provincial governors. Former IRGC commanders made up about two-thirds of the cabinet, including the president, Ahmadinejad, and the foreign minister, Monouchehr Mottaki, who was expelled as Ambassador to Turkey because of his involvement in assassination and torture. Former nuclear negotiator Ali Larijani and many other high-ranking officials were also ex-members of the IRGC.

The IRGC also supplied Tehran's key economic needs, enabling the fundamentalist regime to spread terrorism throughout the Middle East and even Europe. It controlled, and still controls, over 30 per cent of Iran's non-oil exports and more than 57 per cent of its imports. Its commercial annual revenue in 2004 was around \$4.8 billion.

The Qods (Jerusalem) Force, the main terrorist apparatus of the IRGC, has to this day more than 21,000 Iranian members and tens of thousands of non-Iranian mercenaries, including in Syria, Lebanon, Afghanistan, Iraq, Bahrain, Saudi Arabia, Jordan and many European countries. The Qods Force has dozens of garrisons across Iran in which it trains its non-Iranian operatives. In 2004 it boasted that at least 7,000 suicide bombers had enlisted for volunteer operations with the Qods Force; an IRGC general said they would be unleashed in waves across Israel and the Middle East if anyone attempted to attack Iran's nuclear installations.

When President George W. Bush unveiled his new strategy for dealing with the spiralling insurgency in Iraq following the 2003 invasion, he should have cast his eyes across the border to Iran. Repeated intelligence reports from the zone provided evidence of increasing Iranian subversion of Iraq. In fact, in 2004, the capture by the US military of Qods Force members of Iran's Islamic Revolutionary Guard Corps, who had infiltrated Iraq, further exposed the widespread, covert activities of the Qods Force in that beleaguered country. US and UK intelligence now had extensive details, provided by the Iranian opposition, of infiltration routes, Iranian proxy contacts and networks of operatives who moved arms, personnel and money from Iran to Iraq. The Qods Force secretly trained, financed and armed an extensive network in Iraq. It had embarked on creating a new terrorist infrastructure, calling it 'Hezbollah' to mimic Lebanon's Hezbollah. This Iraq network operated in Basra and Baghdad, and was in direct contact with the Qods Force and Hezbollah of Lebanon.

According to these intelligence reports provided by the Iranian opposition, agents of the Iranian regime were routinely transferring money from Iran to Iraq for terrorist operations. After a Qods Force envoy collected the money in Ahwaz in Iran, he was escorted by the Iranian regime's official security force to the Shalamche border crossing between Iran and Iraq, where he was handed over to Qods Force agents in Iraq. These agents would escort him to Najaf. In addition, the Qods Force used its affiliate currency exchange centres to send money to its front institutions and the new terror network directly from Qom in Iran to Najaf in Iraq. The Qods Force also set up a front organization called 'HQ for Reconstruction of Iraq's Holy

Sites', which had been smuggling arms and ammunition to Iraq disguised as containers intended to rebuild holy Shiite shrines.

Often these shipments would include sophisticated bombs used for attacking allied patrols. These so-called Improvised Explosive Devices or IEDs were not being manufactured in basements in Iraq, as was widely believed at the time, but in industrial complexes in the Lavizan neighbourhood of northern Tehran. Military sources confirmed that Iranian ordnance factories were producing an advanced form of IED, called Explosively Formed Projectiles (EFPs), which could penetrate thicker armour, were more difficult to detect, and as a result were far more lethal. There is little doubt that Iran had become the primary killer of US and UK forces in Iraq at that time, as the Iraqi insurgency spiralled. Just as President Bush prepared his plan to stabilize Iraq, Tehran continued to foment instability.

It was Leon Trotsky who said: 'It is not the people who vote that count, but the people who count the votes.' That was certainly true in the Iranian presidential elections of June 2009. No one could believe the election results or the figures the regime was claiming for voter turnout. The PMOI had undercover observers at 25,000 of the 40,000 polling stations throughout the country. They reported that turnout was extremely low. Their final estimate put overall turnout at around 15%. In other words, fewer than 8 million Iranians voted. The Mullahs, on the direct instructions of supreme leader Ali Khamenei, in a press release that was inadvertently leaked the day before the elections took place, announced that over 40 million people had cast their votes, with the incumbent Mahmoud Ahmadinejad winning by a landslide! Indeed such was the farcical nature of the Mullahs' efforts to rig the election, that Ahmadinejad won a huge majority even in the villages and districts of his main opponents.

This massive electoral fraud ignited a volcanic reaction across Iran. Hundreds of thousands of protestors took to the streets demanding an end to the Mullahs' theocratic dictatorship. Their courageous resistance against their fundamentalist rulers showed the free world that the regime did not speak for the Iranian population. The Mullahs ordered a brutal crackdown, with the expulsion of foreign journalists, the suspension of mobile phone and Internet networks, dawn raids on homes and universities and mass arrests.

The protestors, like the vast majority of Iranians, were opposed to the clerical regime in its entirety and their courageous demonstrations showed the will of Iranian society to uproot the religious dictatorship and establish freedom and democracy. Their slogans denounced the Khamenei dictatorship and supported democracy and freedom. The chants in the street were: 'Death to the dictator' and 'Iranians do not accept this disgrace'. The bulk of the protestors were young men and women, but they were not only students; they came from all walks of life.

The protests quickly grew, from objections to Ahmadinejad's rigged re-election, to wider protests about the oppression and corruption of the clerical regime. But as always the protestors paid a heavy price for their courage. Dozens were killed by the regime's storm-troopers, the Islamic Revolutionary Guard Corps and their handsomely rewarded Basij paramilitary thugs.

This was the moment the West could have intervened. The EU and US could have poured in support for the popular uprising, helping the ordinary citizens of Iran to overthrow their tyrannical rulers and restore democracy. Typically, the West did nothing. Iran rounded up thousands of suspected protestors in raids across the country and shipped them off to be tortured and executed, while the West watched in horror, like a rabbit caught in the headlights.

12

Interviews with Political Prisoners Tirana, Albania, May 2014

Abdal Nasser

'My name is Abdal Nasser. I was also in this prison in the cell right next to Hossein (Ebrahimi) [See chapter 10], although I didn't know it at the time. I hadn't seen daylight for months. I didn't see my mother and sister for three years. When I was teaching Hossein how to communicate through Morse I got angry and I would kick the wall. He was so difficult to teach. Once I was singing and asking what is your name? The guard came in and said, what are you doing, and I said, I am talking to God! And the prison guard told me he heard me say the name Hossein. I said that was Imam Hossein I was praying to! He said you have gone mad . . . and left me!

I was so alone and isolated that sometimes I preferred to be beaten up so I had some contact with another human being, even if it was only a sadistic guard. Finally one day Hossein managed to talk to me using Morse code and asked what is your name? I told him a nickname. We agreed to meet each other whenever it became possible. We fabricated a story in which I claimed I had stomach ache and he said he had a toothache, which got us out of our cells. We were forbidden from talking or making any physical contact with each other, of course, because they even thought we could communicate using Morse by tapping on each other's bodies.

One day it was very cold and I was hungry. I slept and dreamt that I had gone home and that my Mum was making my favourite kebabs. She shed tears of joy and I was eating all these kebabs and I was so happy that I had eaten my first full meal after three years. I woke up realising it was just a dream, so I tried to go back to sleep and continue with this sweet dream.

Soon I was separated from Hossein and we said goodbye to each other through Morse code. I was released from prison and escaped to

Iraq where I joined the resistance. Many years later, by sheer accident we came across each other again. I was not sure if it was really him, but then we used Morse to say hello and we found each other again!

I was in prison for a total of six years despite being sentenced to only 20 months initially. I was kept there for five extra years because they wanted to break me down.'

13

Amman

Following my election to the European Parliament in June 2009, I had been appointed as President of the European Parliament's Delegation for Relations with Iraq. This was a new delegation, and when the leader of the European Conservatives and Reformists Group approached me initially, he offered me the choice of chairing either the Iraq Delegation or the Canada Delegation. I told him that Canada was a lovely country that I had enjoyed visiting previously, but chairing such a delegation would be less challenging and less rewarding than taking on the more onerous task of Iraq. I duly found myself presiding over the first meeting of the new delegation, to which the Iraqi Ambassador to the EU had also been invited. Pleasantries were exchanged all round, and I pledged to do my best to improve relations between the EU and Iraq.

On Monday 26 October 2009 I set off to Jordan, where I had arranged a series of high-level meetings in Amman with the Foreign Minister, the Director for European Affairs in the Foreign Ministry, the Speaker of the House of Representatives and the Minister for Media and Communications. I had also arranged for key political leaders from Iraq to travel to Amman to brief me on the current escalating insurgency inside Iraq.

My first meeting in Amman was with a group of Iraqis representing the National Dialogue Front, a secular parliamentary group. There had been a horrific bomb outrage just on the edge of the Green Zone in Baghdad the previous day, killing 150 people and wounding over 500. They told me that this outrage was certainly politically motivated and a reaction to the formation of the new coalitions in readiness for the forthcoming general election in January 2010. Although it was quickly blamed on Sunni insurgents, such sophisticated explosive devices as were used in the attack could only have been smuggled into this high security zone with the knowledge and connivance of the Iranian Qods Force that roamed throughout Baghdad with impunity, as they told me. The massacre was almost certainly motivated by Iran and aimed at sending a warning to Prime Minister Nouri al-Maliki that he should re-join the pro-Iranian Shiite coalition with Hakim, Badr and Muqtada al-Sadr, in order to secure power again following the election.

They told me that current tactics used by the pro-Iranian factions were to threaten people not to vote in the elections and, through fear and intimidation, dramatically to reduce the number of people who would participate. This would then leave hundreds of thousands of blank ballot papers that could be falsified. All civil servants and police and military personnel were being ordered to vote for the governing Shiite parties, they informed me.

On the question of Iranian meddling in Iraq, they were adamant that Iranian infiltration to the very top of government had taken place to an unprecedented extent. Two of Prime Minister al-Maliki's senior staff were Iranian. His private jet and the entire crew were supplied by Iran. They also pointed out that many government ministers in Iraq had dual nationality with other countries, in order that if any were accused of corruption they could quickly escape arrest and flee from Iraq.

Later that morning I met with Dr Nabil al-Sharif, Minister of State for Media Affairs and Communications, and Ahmad S. al-Hassan, Director of European Affairs in the Ministry of Foreign Affairs. Dr Sharif said that Jordan had gone out of its way to support Iraq. King Abdullah was the only Arab leader so far to have visited Iraq since the war. As far as the forthcoming Iraqi elections were concerned, Dr Sharif said that it was essential that all of the political factions were included in the political process. No one must feel left out.

I raised the question of Camp Ashraf with the ministers and referred to the July 2009 massacre (see Chapter 15). I said that there was a new threat from Maliki to displace the 3,400 refugees to the desert in southern Iraq, and that this would create the conditions for another massacre. Mr Hassan suggested that perhaps I could resolve the situation by offering all 3,400 PMOI refugees visas to come to live in Scotland! I answered that I would if I could.

The Speaker of the House of Representatives, Abdel Hadi al-Majali, said a new, moderate, nationalist coalition in Iraq, following the general election, could outvote and isolate the extremist parties. But he said it was the US which supported the pro-Iranian parties in Iraq. He said that if the 'militia' won the forthcoming elections, it would point to a dangerous future. He felt that a Sunni could conceivably become the next Prime Minister of Iraq and that this would help to bring peace.

Later that evening, I had arranged to meet with Sattar Albayber, a member of the political bureau of the Iraqi National Accord movement and a candidate in the forthcoming elections. I had suggested meeting for coffee in the lounge of my hotel, the Intercontinental. As we began our discussion I noticed a man sitting opposite us, wearing jeans and a tee-shirt, who seemed intent on fiddling with his mobile phone. He momentarily met my gaze and quickly looked away. Seconds later I heard the characteristic click of his camera shutter and glanced up in time to see him quickly lower the phone to his lap, pretending to be reading a text message. I whispered to our Iraqi colleagues that I was sure we were being spied upon, and they laughed and confirmed that Jordan is awash with spies who photograph and report back to the Ministry of Intelligence on all meetings and goings-on within their territory. I later discovered that this information was also passed on to the Iraqi government, who had expressed an interest in keeping track of what I was up to in Jordan and who I was meeting.

I returned to Brussels and instructed my officials to issue invitations to the leaders of the main political parties in Iraq to come to the European Parliament to address the Delegation for Relations with Iraq, before the general election. I wanted to test the water for the likelihood of a non-sectarian, inclusive government being formed following the general election. A delegation of six members of the Iraqi Council of Representatives duly arrived in Brussels, led by Sadiq al-Rikabi, political advisor to Prime Minister Nouri al-Maliki. I met them at the VIP entrance, and as I shook hands warmly with al-Rikabi, he whispered loudly in my ear, 'We know whom you've been meeting in Jordan, Mr Stevenson, and we don't like it.'

As an opening remark, this was certainly blunt. OK, I figured, if the gloves are off it suits me. When we took our seats for the opening session of dialogue, I launched into a bitter condemnation of their treatment of the Ashraf residents, the massacre, the looting, the hostage-taking, the psychological torture and the siege of Ashraf. I said this was a breach of humanitarian law and a breach of trust, and it rendered my job as Delegation Chair almost impossible. I insisted on an end to the siege and the full cooperation of the Iraqi government in the re-settlement of the 3,400 Ashrafis to countries of safety. It became a sour and argumentative encounter, and afterwards my officials gently chided me about the need to maintain good diplomatic relations with the Iraqi parliamentarians. 'I am not going to take any lessons in diplomacy from these bastards,' I replied angrily.

14

Interviews with PMOI Refugees
Camp Liberty, August 2014
The Medical Siege of Camp Ashraf

Fatimah Alizadeh

'My name is Fatimah Alizadeh. In the second half of 2008, I was diagnosed with cancer. Prior to the US handing responsibility for the protection of Camp Ashraf to the Iraqis, I had three major surgeries performed on me. On 3 April 2009 I was getting ready for my fourth surgery when the Iraqi forces, under the direction of Movafagh Rubaiei, prevented the physician from entering Ashraf. On the same day three other female residents were also scheduled for surgery, but all the operations were delayed. After a week due to international pressure and a press conference about medical restrictions, the Iraqi Prime Minister – Nouri al-Maliki – was forced to allow the Iraqi doctors to perform the surgeries, and as a result, they started pressuring the residents.

For the fifth operation I was supposed to go to Madineh Al Taleb. Seven or eight fully armed soldiers accompanied me to the operating room. When I regained consciousness, all of the soldiers were around my bed. When I asked to see my doctor, the soldiers said, "You are a prisoner and you have to go to back to Ashraf." My doctor intervened, so I was allowed to rest for a couple of hours, after which the soldiers entered my room and said, "The ambulance is ready and we have to leave immediately." I was brought down several flights of stairs to the entrance of the hospital, but there was no ambulance waiting.

I waited nearly two hours in the sun for the ambulance to arrive. When the ambulance arrived there were eight people already in it. When we climbed on board there were a total of ten people inside the ambulance. One of the patients in the ambulance was Fathollah, who was suffering from stomach cancer and unable to sit down. Ten

65

critically-ill patients in one ambulance set out towards Ashraf. The driver was driving very fast, disregarding all the speed bumps on the road. Upon reaching Ashraf everyone was in a bad shape and in a serious condition.

At Ashraf, we were received by Dr Omar, who was actually an Iraqi officer who had been responsible for systematic mistreatment and torture of the patients, posing as a doctor. When we told him of our ordeal, he said, "At least you have it better than the Iraqi citizens!" We were then placed at the New Iraq Hospital where the Ministry of Information agents were using loudspeakers to yell profanities all night long, making rest and peace of mind for patients impossible. This was the psychological torture. Three months later, when I went to see my doctor for my next operation I found another person sitting next to the specialist. I asked him, "Who are you?" He responded: "I have orders from Dr Omar to supervise your visit so you don't talk about politics." Even the doctor didn't have the authority to make him leave the room.

Another time when I went for chemotherapy to Baghdad, my doctor gave me a series of medication for my chemo treatment so I could follow up my treatment in Ashraf. When we reached the checkpoint they confiscated my medication. It took a long time to be able to get my medication back. Another time, coming back from surgery in Baghdad, twelve people were placed in the same ambulance, one of whom was a patient with stomach cancer who had just undergone a gastroscopy procedure. He had a severe case of diarrhoea and was throwing up all the way to Ashraf. The atmosphere in the ambulance was unsanitary and intolerable. On that day Dr Omar was riding with us in the front of the ambulance, laughing all the way to Ashraf. We asked him to check the patient and he kept saying, "It is normal," and continued to laugh at the situation.

On several occasions when our brothers and sisters succeeded in getting an appointment through the New Iraq Hospital the guards at the checkpoint would not allow them to leave the camp to make their appointments. After months of pressure, they were allowed to leave for their appointments, but their actual departure from the camp was delayed in such a way that when they arrived in Baghdad after business hours, they had missed their appointments. I was supposed to visit my doctor every three months; I tried to see my doctor for two and a half years but I was not allowed to visit him even once. After two and a half years I was transferred to Camp Liberty and was able to finally see my doctor. My doctor, who was very concerned, informed me that the cancer had spread and my condition had now become critical.'

15

Camp Ashraf and the July 2009 Massacre

When the PMOI freedom fighters fled to Iraq during the Iran-Iraq war, Saddam Hussein gave them a large piece of desert in Diyala Province. Saddam was following the age-old tradition of 'My enemy's enemy is my friend,' rather than rewarding the PMOI for military services rendered, as has been alleged by the Mullahs. It was here, on this barren wasteland, that they built Camp Ashraf. Over the years it became a thriving small city, but when the US invaded Iraq in 2003, it was bombed and then surrounded by American forces. Indeed, in classified documents disclosed later at court hearings in the UK, it was shown that the Iranian Mullahs had demanded the bombing of Camp Ashraf, and other PMOI camps in Iraq, during Operation Iraqi Freedom in 2003. The British Government had subsequently assured Tehran it would oblige, and had urged the US military to carry out the bombing. The completely unjustified aerial bombardment of Camp Ashraf that then took place led to the loss of many innocent lives.

Despite this attack and despite the fact that the PMOI in Ashraf were heavily armed and well-trained, the residents bore no malice against the Americans and they agreed voluntarily to hand over their weapons in return for guaranteed protection. The American army and intelligence services carried out exhaustive interviews with every individual in Ashraf. Following 16 months of review and screening of each and every Ashraf resident, the US Government on 2 July 2004 recognised all of them as 'protected persons under the Fourth Geneva Convention' and 'Senior American officials said extensive interviews by officials of the State Department and the Federal Bureau of Investigation had not come up with any basis to bring charges against any members of the group' (*New York Times*, 27 July 2004). This meant that not a single person was engaged in any kind of terrorist or criminal activity, and that they posed no threat to the US military; each person in Ashraf was then issued with a photo-identity card on which the US Government guaranteed their personal safety.

Under this shield of American military security, Ashraf continued to thrive during the insurgency that raged elsewhere in Iraq. The residents of Ashraf were popular with their Iraqi neighbours in Diyala Province. They were industrious and produced numerous goods to sell locally, earning their keep and financing the gradual expansion of the camp's facilities. Foreign parliamentarians, lawyers and family members were allowed to visit Camp Ashraf, and glowing reports of the camp's well-ordered society were fed back to the West.

Of course the camp was regarded by the Iranian regime as a 'viper's nest' of PMOI opposition activity, and they made repeated demands on the Iraqi government to close the camp and deport all of the residents back to Iran, where they would face certain torture and execution. The Iraqi government, under the leadership of Prime Minister Nouri al-Maliki, a puppet of the Iranian Mullahs, was more than happy to comply with this request, but could not do so while the Americans provided protection to Ashraf. The Iranians, meanwhile, routinely arrested family members who were returning to Iran after visiting their sons and daughters in Ashraf. Many of these innocent mothers and fathers were subsequently executed simply for the crime of having visited Camp Ashraf. Indeed the Iranian Islamic Penal Code, articles 186-189, states that support for or membership of the PMOI amounts to the crime of 'mohareb' – waging war against God – the penalty for which is death.

The storm clouds over Ashraf were gathering. The seeds of tragedy were being sown. The US military had begun to make preparations to leave Iraq, and the 3,400 Iranian dissidents who now remained in Camp Ashraf were fearful of their fate once US military protection was withdrawn. In the EU, we were working feverishly to ensure their continued safety.

Now a senior White House official had confirmed that talks were under way between the US and Iraqi governments about the US withdrawing its protection and transferring control of Camp Ashraf to the Iraqi government. I was in no doubt that this action would constitute a grave betrayal by the US government. It was all horribly reminiscent of other great acts of betrayal in contemporary history, like the massacre of 2,700 Cossacks by the Soviets after they had been betrayed by the British military in Lienz, Austria, in 1945. Senior British military officials assured the Cossacks that they were being taken to a conference and would return to Lienz that same evening. Instead, they were driven under guard to a Soviet prison, where they were promptly accused of being Nazi collaborators and executed.

In the Balkans conflict, in July 1995, after the United Nations had declared Srebrenica a UN-protected 'safe area', 400 UN Dutch 'blue-helmet' peacekeepers stepped aside and allowed units of the Army of Republika Srpska, under the command of General Ratko Mladic, to massacre an estimated 8,000 Bosnian men and boys. In an urgent letter to US Secretary of State Hillary Clinton on 4 April 2009 I said: 'As you are aware, the situation of Iranian opposition exiles in Ashraf Camp in Iraq has become an international issue since the beginning of January this year, when US forces handed over the security of Ashraf to the Iraqi government. Since then we have witnessed several threatening comments by senior Iraqi officials against these Iranian refugees.'

I told the Secretary of State that the scene was being set for another epic betrayal and massacre in Ashraf, and asked the question, why do we treat our friends so badly and play into the hands of our enemies? PMOI supporters inside Iran have risked their lives repeatedly to provide the West with top-level secret intelligence about the activities of the Mullahs and the Islamic Revolutionary Guard Corps. It was the PMOI who first disclosed the existence of a nuclear weapons programme in Iran. But now we seemed set to abandon them to their fate. Handing over control of Camp Ashraf to the Iraqis would be like putting King Herod in charge of the nursery, but that was the scenario we were now facing.

The US forces who had been stationed at Ashraf since 2003, finally packed up and left on 1 January 2009, reneging on their safety guarantees to the 3,400 residents and abandoning them to their fate. Only a handful of USF-I (US Forces-Iraq) military observers were left behind to monitor the camp. The Mullahs in Tehran had been waiting for this opportunity. Now they could pounce. However a large group of US forces was based in the northern part of Ashraf, called

FOB Grizzly, monitoring the region. They knew what was going on around Ashraf but did nothing.

In late July 2009, the massacre that we had all predicted took place. The Iraqi military sent five Divisions of heavily armed troops with tanks and armoured vehicles to mow down unarmed men and women in a brutal assault that shocked the civilized world. On 28 July Colonel Saadi, the commanding officer of the Iraqi forces surrounding Ashraf, entered the camp to speak to the residents' leadership. He said that it was his intention to erect a police station in the camp near to the water-pumping station. The residents were wholly opposed to the plan, and around 2 pm, Colonel Saadi stormed off in anger. Two hours later, he returned leading hundreds of troops and police and stormed the camp, using Humvees and bulldozers to flatten perimeter fences and walls.

The Ashraf residents quickly formed a human chain to try to defend their territory, and they were mown down by troops opening fire with live ammunition and throwing stun grenades. Unarmed men and women were beaten with nail-spiked clubs and batons. The Iraqis claimed that they had come under attack from knives, stones and sharp tools wielded by the residents, which was completely untrue. The violent assault lasted for at least four hours until nightfall. The following morning, 29 July, the Iraqis returned to Ashraf around 10.15 am. This time there were an estimated 1,000 troops, police and members of the notorious 56th Brigade under the direct command of Prime Minister Nouri al-Maliki. They resumed the violence on the same scale as the evening before, firing live rounds at the fleeing men and women and hunting them down and crushing them under the wheels of speeding Humvees and armoured vehicles. Witnesses claimed that many of the attackers, although dressed in Iraqi uniforms, spoke perfect Farsi, indicating that they were Iranian or at least had been trained in Iran.

Video evidence filmed by some of the survivors showed how the Iraqi forces used extreme violence, including gunfire, water cannons and batons, killing eleven people and injuring 443, 42 of them seriously; two others died later due to their injuries and the denial of access to proper medical care by the Iraqis, who prevented doctors and ambulances from evacuating the wounded; UNAMI inspectors later found the Camp Ashraf ambulance riddled with bullets. It had been fired at repeatedly as doctors tried to ferry the wounded to safety. Following the attack, the Iraqi army and police went on a looting spree, stealing 49 vehicles and helping themselves to air-conditioning units, tables, chairs, generators and anything they could carry to furnish their own base on the camp's perimeter.

Ominously, 36 men had been seized during the attack and were subsequently and ludicrously charged with 'assaulting officials on duty'. They were detained in a local police station, many of them suffering broken limbs and head-wounds inflicted by the Iraqi forces during their arrests. On 24 August an investigating judge ordered their immediate release due to lack of evidence. The public prosecutor, undoubtedly acting on the orders of the Prime Minister, immediately revoked the release order and set a date for a judicial hearing of the case against the 36 in mid-September. He also lodged further indictments against each, accusing them of being illegal aliens who had entered Iraq without the correct papers. In protest, the 36 started a hunger strike from the day of their arrest.

Amnesty International, in its Iraq Report 2010 regarding the human rights situation in the country, wrote, 'Following months of rising tension, Iraqi security forces forcibly entered and took control of Camp Ashraf on 28 and 29 July. The camp houses some 3,400 members or supporters of the People's Mojahedin Organization of Iran (PMOI), an Iranian opposition group that had been under US military control since 2003. Video footage showed Iraqi security forces deliberately driving military vehicles into crowds of protesting camp residents. The security forces also used live ammunition, apparently killing at least nine camp residents, and detained 36 others who they tortured'.

Tahar Boumedra, Chief of the Human Rights Office of the United Nations Assistance Mission for Iraq (UNAMI), in his office in Baghdad, had begun to hear sketchy details of the massacre. He immediately applied to the Iraqi government for permission to take a fact-finding team to Ashraf. It took eleven days, despite his repeated protests, for permission to be granted. Pathetically, the Iraqi government argued that it required time for the residents of Ashraf to 'cool off' before it would be safe for the UNAMI team to visit the camp.

72

Tahar Boumedra and his team were finally permitted to visit Ashraf on 10 August. They took evidence from survivors, collected photos and video films of the attack, looked at medical reports and documented statements. They then confronted Colonel Saadi who had commanded the attack, and he admitted that he had been ordered to enter the camp by the office of Prime Minister Nouri al-Maliki. He claimed to have met fierce resistance from the residents, and said this was why he was forced to resort to using weapons. Mr Boumedra stated later that his team received no evidence that supported Colonel Saadi's version of events. Saadi became evasive, according to Boumedra, and admitted that 'mistakes had been made'. When questioned about the shooting, he said he had heard shots but had no idea where they had come from. He also claimed that he had seen PMOI residents throwing themselves under the wheels of the military vehicles!

Two days later, on 12 August, UNHCR met in Baghdad with Ali al-Yasseri, Director of Operations from the Prime Minister's office and head of the so-called 'Ashraf Committee'. He told the UN team that following the attack on Ashraf, the Iraqi authorities had discovered rockets and rocket launchers in the camp, proving the PMOI were intending to launch terrorist operations. The fact that the Iraqi Ministry of the Interior, the Governorate of Diyala Province and the US military and intelligence services had repeatedly searched the camp and discovered no weapons of any kind, exposed the absurdity of this claim. In April 2009, teams of the Iraqi Ministry of Interior with police dogs spent three days searching all parts of Ashraf and officially confirmed that they had found no weapons. Nevertheless, UNHCR decided to keep the ludicrous allegations about weapons being discovered in Ashraf secret and their apparent acceptance of al-Yasseri's absurd claims perhaps helped to explain their reluctance later to offer tangible help to the residents of Ashraf. Al-Yasseri later told Tahar Boumedra that the MEK had shot their own people during the attack of 28 and 29 July, to try to discredit the Iraqi forces.

Despite all the lies, excuses and propaganda, UNAMI found the Iraqi forces entirely responsible for the deaths, injuries and looting during the attack. Tahar Boumedra and his UNAMI team conducted interviews with some of the US military observers who had witnessed and filmed the entire massacre. Unable to intervene because of the US agreement with the government of Iraq over the withdrawal of American troops, they had to watch helplessly from the sidelines. They confirmed UNAMI's conclusion that the Iraqis were entirely responsible for the brutal assault and they even promised to provide a copy of their film if it wasn't classified. This film was, in fact, never handed over, presumably in case it upset the Iraqis; the Americans were still determined to back Maliki and to assure the world that, after all the horrendous costs of the Iraq campaign to the West in blood and treasure they had left behind a 'functioning democracy'.

It was shocking for me to watch a film by Fox News, showing a group of wounded Ashraf residents during the 28-29 July attack, asking American soldiers for help, but the soldiers, who had instructions from their high command, just ignoring them. This was a callous and scandalous attack made worse by the fact that we had predicted it was going to happen. We had urged the Americans to retain responsibility for the protection of the residents, warning that this duty must not to be handed over to the Iraqis.

I had written letters about this to the UN Secretary General Ban Ki-moon, to Barack Obama and to the then UK Prime Minister Gordon Brown. My pleas fell on deaf ears. No one was prepared to lift a finger. The PMOI were still on the US terrorist list, so there was a reluctance to do anything in Washington, and the FCO in Whitehall was still smarting from their humiliation at the hands of the courts, having been forced to remove the PMOI from the UK and EU terror lists. Ban Ki-moon was fully focused on the bloody insurgency in Iraq and refused to be diverted by what he surely regarded as a minor incident at Ashraf. The signals from the West were being received and understood in Baghdad and Tehran. The message from the West was clear: Do what you like to the PMOI – the West won't interfere.

UNAMI, the UN High Commissioner for Human Rights and Baroness Ashton, the EU's High Representative for Foreign Affairs, lodged strong objections with the Iraqi government and called for a full independent inquiry. Tahar Boumedra advised the Iraqi government that they should identify those responsible for the attack and hold them to account. Later he was shown a document drawn up by al-Yasseri from the Prime Minister's Office, which consisted of photos of a table on which were displayed hand grenades, pistols and knives, and an adjoining caption claiming that these were weapons discovered in Ashraf, proving that the PMOI was a terrorist organisation and had mounted a lethal assault on the Iraqi forces. Boumedra advised them not to circulate the document because it was so palpably amateurish and absurd as to be laughable. But as far as the UN and the West were concerned, the matter was now closed; it was already history and the calls for an independent investigation would not be repeated. The Iraqis literally had got away with murder!

PMOI supporters around the world now began hunger strikes in solidarity with the 36 residents detained following the massacre at Ashraf. 136 of the residents of Ashraf had also gone on hunger strike in sympathy. I addressed large protests outside the UN headquarters in Geneva and outside the European Parliament in Brussels. The judge in the Iraqi city of Khalis, where these 36 were detained, had issued three orders for their release, but the office of the Prime Minister blocked it and they were taken to different prisons in Baghdad, although they were each in a terrible physical condition. Finally, on 7 October 2009, the 36 hostages were released thanks to international pressure, but some of them were on their last legs.

Tahar Boumedra went to Ashraf to witness the return of the detainees. Two buses arrived at the gates of Ashraf surrounded by a heavy Iraqi military escort. The 36 had been dangerously weakened by 72 days of hunger strike, and none were able to stand up independently. Nevertheless, Colonel al-Saadi, who had masterminded the original massacre, was determined to prolong their agony. He insisted on the PMOI leadership in Ashraf signing a legal document stating effectively that the 36 were under a form of house arrest and would report instantly to the nearest police station whenever required to do so. This was completely outside the court's release orders and Tahar Boumedra and representatives from the International Committee for the Red Cross (ICRC) argued that it was illegal.

Meanwhile, with midday temperatures soaring, the 36 were made to suffer inside the buses, with no air conditioning and no water. Finally, in exasperation and to save their colleagues from further suffering, the PMOI leadership signed. But this did not satisfy al-Saadi, who demanded that Tahar Boumedra sign on behalf of UNAMI and that the Red Cross should also sign. Both argued that the document would have to be rewritten to indicate that they were only signing as 'observers' to the agreement and more time passed as al-Saadi sent the document away for revision. Finally, with all of the signatures appended, Boumedra was permitted to board the buses.

He said later that when the doors were opened the stench of putrefaction made him reel. Long-term hunger strikes cause the human body to start consuming itself and this quickly leads to organ failure. The 36 hostages were in a state of near-death. They had to be carried off the buses on stretchers and many had to be rehydrated with saline drips. The Office of the High Commissioner for Human Rights in Geneva quickly put out a press release *thanking* the Iraqi Government for the release of the 36 detainees and more or less congratulating itself on a successful outcome. There was no mention of the unlawful killings, the wounding of hundreds and the looting. This horror was quickly filed away, and together with the July massacre was never mentioned again in case it jeopardised relations with the government of Nouri al-Maliki. Indeed, the congratulatory tone of the UN press release almost amounted to a stamp of approval for Maliki's brutal assault. The craven cowardice of the West apparently knew no bounds.

16

Interviews with PMOI Refugees
Camp Liberty, August 2014
The Medical Siege of Camp Ashraf

Mahtab Madanchi

'My name is Mahtab Madanchi. In 2010 I was diagnosed with rheumatoid arthritis. This disease affected my hands, legs, neck and shoulders in such a way that within a time span of two months it left me completely paralysed, unable to accomplish the simplest tasks. I was bedridden for three months; meanwhile my legs and right arm became deformed leaving me unable to perform even the simplest chores.

Given that the outbreak of my disease coincided with the inhuman medical siege imposed on Camp Ashraf by the Maliki government, it took over a month to be able to see a physician, upon which I was told that the disease had reached an irreversible stage and the physicians could only put me on cortisone therapy.

I tried going to the Iraqi clinic with the hope of being sent to a specialist, but the officers from the Ministry of Information kept postponing my visits. When we were in Ashraf they used to send the patients to Baqubah hospital. They were unable to treat me in Baqubah and the only hospitals which carried the specific medication that I needed, Remicade, were in Baghdad. For over a year Maliki's agents stopped me from going to a hospital in Baghdad. Finally, after a year's delay and while I was suffering from excruciating daily pains, I was allowed to go to Baghdad. Needless to say, while I was in Baghdad the officers from the Ministry of Information, who accompanied us, intimidated and cajoled the physicians to make sure that we didn't receive the proper care we required.

After a month of delays I was sent to a Baghdad hospital to see my attending physician who had insisted I had to be administered Remicade without any delay. Upon arriving at the hospital the officers from the Ministry of Information forced us to return to Camp Liberty without even seeing the doctor.'

17

Ashraf Ultimatum

The UN Special Representative of the Secretary General in Iraq in 2009 was former Dutch Minister and Labour Party Leader Ad Melkert. He was sympathetic to the plight of the Ashraf refugees and conscious of the awkward position of UNAMI and UNHCR in being forced to cooperate with Nouri al-Maliki, despite the fact that he had repeatedly violated the core principles of international law and the UN Charter in his actions against the Ashraf residents. Melkert came to the European Parliament in Brussels in late 2009, and I co-chaired a hearing of the Foreign Affairs Committee with Elmar Brok MEP, where we asked him to outline his proposals for the future of Ashraf.

Melkert stated that we needed to identify a key person in the Iraqi government who could be trusted as a serious envoy. Up until now, people like al-Yasseri from the Prime Minister's office had proved to be unreliable, untrustworthy and unable to take decisions without reference to al-Maliki himself. 'Once we identify a trustworthy interlocutor,' Melkert suggested, 'we can assure the Iraqis that of course they have complete sovereignty over Camp Ashraf, but with that sovereignty comes responsibility for the wellbeing of the 3,400 residents, and that the UN will work hand in hand to ensure their safety in association with the Iraqi Government.' However, Melkert stated that this was only the essential first step and that he needed assurances from both the US and EU Member States that they would re-settle these refugees to get them out of Iraq as quickly as possible. Time was of the essence, he stressed, or further violence was likely.

Melkert returned to Baghdad and he and Boumedra met with Nouri al-Maliki's Chief of Staff, Dr Tarik Abdullah. Abdullah made it clear from the outset of the meeting that Maliki wanted no special treatment for the Ashraf residents, as he regarded them as having no legal status in Iraq. He emphasized that they were considered a foreign terrorist organisation, not only by Iraq, but also by the

US and many other countries, and their continued presence in Iraq created ongoing problems with neighbouring Iran. Notwithstanding all of these issues, Dr Abdullah said that he was prepared to allow a permanent UNAMI presence in Camp Ashraf so long as UNAMI remained neutral in that position. 'Those who are not with us are against us,' Abdullah said. He also agreed that the Iraqi government would cooperate with the re-settlement of the 3,400 residents to the US, EU and other countries, although he reserved the right to exercise Iraq's sovereignty over Ashraf and to temporarily relocate the 3,400 residents to another camp. This should be done before the elections scheduled for April 2010, a terrifyingly short timescale.

This news set the alarm bells ringing. I arranged an urgent meeting with Baroness Ashton, the EU's High Representative for Foreign Affairs, to urge her to encourage the 27 Member States to take their share of the Ashraf refugees. 'If they take 125 each, we will solve the problem overnight,' I said. In Baghdad, Ad Melkert called together ambassadors from six EU countries as well as the ambassadors from the US, Japan and Australia. He told them that this was a priority issue that required extreme urgency.

As expected, Nouri al-Maliki now issued an ultimatum. Camp Ashraf was to be closed by 31 December 2009. The timescale was impossible. A letter dated 15 November to the protocol section of the European Parliament underscored the decision: 'The Iraqi Government is left with no choice but to evacuate the camp based on principles of sovereignty, and transfer its residents to other camps in Iraq.' The letter went on to explain that the Iraqi government regarded the Ashraf men and women as terrorists and claimed that they had no status or protection under the Geneva Conventions or international humanitarian law.

This ultimatum from the Iraqis was tantamount to sending the residents to their deaths, and an obvious prelude to a massacre devised by the neighbouring Iranian regime. Camp Ashraf's residents were in fact all protected persons under the Geneva Convention. But since early 2009, when the US handed over the security of the Camp to the Iraqi government, Ashraf had been under a suffocating siege. Maliki had done everything possible to provoke a response from the West. Clearly he and his puppet-masters in Tehran were once again

80

testing the international water. If the West displayed its usual pusil-lanimous response to these provocations, then an all-out assault on Ashraf was inevitable.

On 19 October 2009 al-Yasseri brought a team to Camp Ashraf to meet the PMOI leadership and inform them of the Prime Minister's ultimatum that they had to get out of the camp. He said that buses would be brought to the camp on 15 December, and the 3,400 residents would be relocated to al-Muthanna province. The PMOI spokesmen, led by Mehdi Baraei, said that they were now regarded with outright hostility in both Iran and Iraq, and that therefore their only option for leaving Ashraf was for them to be relocated to countries of safety outside Iraq. He said that failing this solution, they would refuse to leave Ashraf.

As threatened by al-Yasseri, a convoy of buses duly arrived at Ashraf on 15 December, and the Iraqi army roared up and down the camp's streets in military vehicles using loudspeakers to blare out orders for the residents to board the buses. They had brought a large contingent of journalists to witness the entire evacuation of the camp. Of course not a single one of the residents agreed to leave. In fact many spoke to the journalists, telling them that they refused to move. Finally, after several fruitless hours, the buses left empty. This humiliating defeat by the Ashrafis caused a predictable reaction by Maliki. He now ordered punitive action against the camp's residents to soften them up and force them to leave.

Iraqi troops now guarded Ashraf and all visitors were immediately banned. Trucks filled with fuel, foodstuffs, chlorine for water purification and other basic necessities were routinely stopped at the gates and turned back. The Iraqi government had banned the Ashrafis from purchasing fuel in Iraq, so all fuel supplies had to come by road from Kuwait, at huge cost. On one occasion the drivers of two fuel trucks were arrested and held in a local jail for 20 days until released by a judge. Medical supplies were also turned away. The Ashraf workshops were no longer able to sell their goods to the local Arab population of Diyala Province, cutting off all sources of essential income. Lacking fuel to keep their generators working and rationing their dwindling food supplies, the 3,400 residents were now subjected to extreme psychological torture. Banks of giant loudspeakers began to be erected by Iraqi technicians around the perimeter fences of the camp. Over 300 of these speakers were used to roar endless threats and insults at ear-shattering decibel levels day and night, seven days a week, to torture the residents and destroy any chance of rest.

But the stress didn't stop there. Ominous and threatening news filtered out from the office of Prime Minister Nouri al-Maliki that senior Iraqi government officials had drawn up a list of 23 leading 'terrorists' from Camp Ashraf whom they intended to arrest, while the remainder would be deported to Iran. They also stated that any Iraqi citizen found to be providing aid to any of the 'terrorists' in Camp Ashraf would be prosecuted under Iraq's anti-terrorist legislation. Seriously ill patients from Ashraf who had previously been allowed to attend hospitals in Baqubah and Baghdad for surgery, to treat life-threatening cancer and heart disease, were now barred from leaving the camp. Ten died as a direct result.

The European Parliament adopted a strong resolution on Ashraf on 24 April 2009. We had to challenge many amendments from the regime's apologists in the parliament who tried to turn the text against the PMOI, as instructed by the Iranian embassy in Brussels. I was in charge of coordinating the meeting that prepared the final text for the resolution and we managed to defeat all those amendments in the voting session in plenary, and the resolution became quite an historic document, emphasising the rights of these Iranian dissidents as Protected Persons under the Fourth Geneva Convention and calling for their security and safety.

A year later in the European Parliament I started a written declaration (petition) calling for an end to the siege and the psychological torture of the Ashraf residents, and for their imminent evacuation to countries of safety. More than half of the 752 MEPs signed the petition, which became the official position of the parliament, (adopted on 25 November 2010). I drew attention to the provocative human rights breaches at the camp in repeated letters, articles, press releases and speeches, but to no avail. The EU, UN and US stayed silent and apparently indifferent.

Against this worsening background I remained deeply concerned that another bloody attack could take place at any time, leading to a Srebrenica-style annihilation of the unarmed refugees in the camp. It was clear that an urgent solution had to be found to the Ashraf crisis, but once again the international community seemed incapable of action. Ad Melkert and Tahar Boumedra called together a second meeting of the EU and US ambassadors in Baghdad, but were met with prejudicial statements and mutterings about terrorists and evil cults, based on propaganda circulated by the Iranian regime. The Mullahs were keen to propagate the rumour that many people were being held against their will in Camp Ashraf. They claimed that discipline was so rigorous that any dissenters were beaten and permission to leave the camp was routinely denied.

In fact, my close friends and MEP colleagues Alejo Vidal-Quadras and Paulo Casaca had both visited Ashraf (Paulo on several occasions), and had been deeply impressed by the residents. They were given complete freedom to interview anyone they wished, and prepared detailed reports on their visits when they returned to Brussels. Their reports rubbished the scare stories and smears being circulated by Tehran. Unfortunately, with the encouragement of the Iraqi authorities, these stories had gained some purchase amongst the diplomatic community in Baghdad and had even contaminated views amongst UNHCR and UNAMI staff.

18

Interviews with PMOI Refugees Camp Liberty, August 2014

The Medical Siege of Camp Ashraf

Hassan Habibi

'My name is Hassan Habibi. I am 48 years old and I am an electrical engineer. I came to Camp Ashraf in 1983. In 2003 after signing the agreement with the Americans, the protection of Ashraf became the responsibility of the US forces. Despite our objections, in 2009 the US transferred the protection of Ashraf to the Iraqis. It was obvious to us that the Iraqi forces were under the influence of the Iranian regime and were planning to close Ashraf and return the residents to Iran where they would face torture and execution. The Iraqi government besieged us and imposed a medical siege on the camp.

Subsequently the Iranian regime's agents, along with Iraqi forces, attacked the camp using armoured Humvees firing indiscriminately on the unarmed residents. On 28 July 2009, I was run over by one of these armoured Humvees, which left me severely wounded and unconscious. I suffered a broken pelvis fractured in four different places and a ruptured spleen. The ambulance that came for me was also riddled with bullets.

When I regained consciousness at Ashraf clinic I saw hundreds of wounded there. There was no room left and people were forced to lie on the floor. Even then the Iraqi forces would not allow anyone to leave the camp for treatment or allow Iraqi physicians to enter. After two days a group of American physicians who resided at the adjacent camp were allowed to visit us and they transferred eight of the critically wounded people, including myself, to Ballad hospital for treatment. Because of the delay in medical care, Alireza Ahmad Khah who was also wounded in his pelvis, passed away. He was lying beside me in a Humvee belonging to the American forces and he passed away as we were leaving Ashraf.

84

Another example was Siavoosh Nezamal Molki whose head was smashed by the Iraqis using a bat, causing a brain aneurism. He lost his life because of the delay in providing treatment. I was at the American forces' hospital for a month and a half, but they did not perform the internal surgeries I needed. They told me that I had to wait till January 2010 and they returned me to the camp. The National Council of Resistance issued a statement saying that they were willing to pay the expenses for the operations and would even send skilled physicians to Iraq to perform the surgeries or have me transferred out of Iraq for the operation, but none of these proposals were accepted.

Finally, in February 2011 when a mission from Geneva came to visit the camp and had asked to visit some of the wounded and injured, I was one of the people whom they met. After that I was able to leave the camp and go to Erbil in northern Iraq for my much-needed surgery. But the doctors in Erbil told me that because of the prolonged delay there was nothing they could do for me. I was returned to the camp with a Foley catheter stuck to my bladder. The medical siege has left me with a shortened leg and limited mobility. I am unable to lift anything. I have to live with a Foley catheter in my stomach for the rest of my life.

This situation is still going on in Camp Liberty and the residents have to go through the same ordeal trying to see a doctor or a specialist. They are not allowed to see a private doctor or go to a private clinic even considering the situation in Iraq; the public health facilities have a very low standard of care and hygiene due to a high number of patients. I had lost sight in one of my eyes and my other eye had the same symptoms. When I was finally allowed to go to the hospital to get my eye examined, a few armed guards constantly followed us, treating us like prisoners. They even entered the visiting room with the doctor. Due to the high number of patients the doctors would only spend a few minutes to listen to each patient before giving them a prescription. It is obvious that with such circumstances if a person has a complicated illness that needs closer attention, they would not be able to take care of it. I had requested many times to be sent to a private clinic but I was refused every time.'

19

Iraqi Elections

Until early January 2010, the international community was fairly confident that the main obstacles to holding a good, free and fair election on 7 March that year had been overcome and that the Iraqi government was showing great maturity and leadership in laying the foundations for a peaceful and fully accountable poll. However, the escalating extent of Iranian interference in Iraq was rapidly becoming a matter for grave concern. There had been an attempt to ban over 500 mainly Sunni politicians from the election process, including prominent parliamentarians and political leaders like Dr Saleh al-Mutlak. There was no doubt this was being done at the request of Tehran and by Shiite political factions that had allegiance to Iran rather than Iraq. It was having a major de-stabilising impact on the election process. The escalating political crisis led to a surprise visit to Baghdad by US Vice President Joe Biden, in an attempt to resolve the potentially explosive issue.

The previous December, Iranian military personnel had crossed the border into Iraq and seized control of the Fakeh oil field, hauling down the Iraqi flag and raising the Iranian one. This caused huge resentment inside Iraq, and it was no coincidence that a visit by Iran's Foreign Minister Manouchehr Mottaki to Baghdad shortly afterwards was aimed at settling the Fakeh oil field dispute based on an Iranian strategy for controlling the Iraqi election process. The Mullahs in Tehran were past masters at hostage-taking, and their seizure of the Fakeh oilfield provided them with a useful bargaining counter. Ahmadinejad's Foreign Minister Mottaki demanded the expulsion of the 500 anti-Iranian, secular politicians from the election process, and in particular Dr Saleh al-Mutlak, a senior parliamentarian who was a vociferous opponent of Iranian meddling in Iraq, in return for Iran's withdrawal from the Fakeh oil field. This was classic Mullah-style diplomacy. The Iraqi government complied, banning the politicians on trumped up de-Baathification charges, alleging that they were supporters of the former dictator Saddam Hussein.

In fact, the one common factor uniting the 500 expelled, secular politicians was that they opposed Iranian meddling in Iraqi affairs and some of them fiercely opposed the repressive measures against Ashraf. Indeed, Dr Saleh al-Mutlak, who led a sizeable parliamentary group, took part in a big gathering in Ashraf in June 2008. Then an amazing petition emerged, signed by three million Shiias in southern Iraq, in support of the Ashraf residents.

But the absence of key Sunnis from the electoral process was a calculated step aimed at handing victory once again to a Shiia-dominated, pro-Iranian government, paving the way for the constant acquiescence of Baghdad to the will of Tehran. But the Iranian regime didn't stop here. There was also the brutal assassination of key political figures, such as Dr Soha Abdallah in Mosul, the illegal arrest of Najem Harbi, head of the al-Iraqiya slate in Diyala province, together with an extensive campaign of arrests of al-Iraqiya supporters in Salaheddin and south Baghdad. Two brothers and a sister of Tariq al-Hashemi, Vice-President of Iraq at the time, who vociferously opposed the torture and repression of political prisoners, were assassinated.

Having excluded some of the key opposition figures from the election, al-Maliki then abused his position as Prime Minister and Commander in Chief of the Armed Forces, to prepare a comprehensive strategy for defrauding the Iraqi people out of their democratic choice. Evidence emerged of candidates being attacked and beaten by the Iraqi security forces in Karbala, and leaflets were distributed threatening violence and death to supporters of some of the nationalist and non-sectarian parties. Massive amounts of, allegedly, Iranian cash was distributed to buy votes, and in one case apparently pistols were purchased and handed out to villagers in return for their pledges of support.

I was so appalled at the endless flow of emails and reports of fraud and corruption that were streaming into my office on a daily basis that I applied to the European Parliament's secretariat to lead an election observer mission to Iraq. I was refused permission on security grounds. I therefore decided to set up an on-line election observation facility. I created a special website with a unique email address, and invited anyone with evidence of election fraud to send it to me, providing names of the guilty parties wherever possible. Through press conferences and press releases translated into Arabic, I spread the word throughout Iraq, and as the election drew closer I was inundated with emails. I received allegations from senior politicians, serving army officers, polling station officials, teachers, journalists and ordinary citizens, demonstrating that every aspect of the election was beset by squalid acts of fraud.

A senior member of al-Maliki's administration, a serving army general, even travelled to Brussels in the days immediately leading up to the election, to tell me that he had been ordered to drop hundreds of thousands of leaflets from helicopters over the predominantly Sunni suburbs of Baghdad, warning the population that if they voted for the secular Ayad Allawi they would be killed; he was disgusted by this and was prepared to risk his life to bring me the information. He told me that Iraqi troops were ordered to fire mortar rounds into the same Sunni areas to prevent the people from leaving their homes on polling day to vote. Many lost their lives as a result.

I discovered that tens of thousands of ex-pat Iraqis were refused permission to cast their votes in Europe, on spurious grounds relating to an alleged lack of proper identification. Inside Iraq, on the day set aside for military personnel and prisoners to vote, widespread cheating was reported. Entire regiments were denied the right to vote because they were considered hostile to al-Maliki. Over 1,500 youths were rounded up on the streets and imprisoned in Baghdad and other Iraqi cities, and told that they would only be released next day after they voted for al-Maliki.

Truckloads of boxes filled with voting papers pre-marked for al-Maliki were stopped at the Iranian border in failed attempts to smuggle them into Iraq. Polling station officials claimed they were ordered to stuff bundles of these pre-marked voting slips into their ballot boxes on polling day. At the end of polling, election observers were ordered to leave voting stations at gunpoint, the doors were locked and corrupt officials allegedly stuffed ballot boxes with pro-Maliki voting slips. They marked countless pro-Allawi voting slips with a second tick to render them invalid and altered figures on their final returns.

Having gathered extensive evidence of election fraud, I then sifted all of the emails to remove any trace of identities in order to protect the safety of the people who had risked their lives to contact me. Arabic emails were translated into English and as far as possible I tried to cite only evidence that had been corroborated by more than one independent source. But even with such rigorous editing, the volume of evidence still ran to 40 pages, which I published in book form and circulated widely throughout the European Parliament, the European Commission and to EU foreign ministers, diplomats and governments. The publication caused a volcanic eruption in Baghdad. Nouri al-Maliki himself called a press conference to denounce me as a liar and an enemy of Iraq. This drew even more attention to my document, which received widespread coverage across the Middle East, particularly in Iraq.

Despite all of these well-laid plans by al-Maliki and his Iranian allies, the repeated bomb blasts, death threats and intimidation failed to stop millions of courageous Iraqis from casting their votes for Ayad Allawi and his non-sectarian, nationalist party. I had met Dr Allawi in a long meeting in Brussels some months before. He initiated a very valuable alliance, the al-Iraqiya List, with the help of Dr Saleh al-Mutlak, Osama al-Nujaifi (the future Speaker of the Parliament) and Dr Tariq al-Hashemi (the future Vice President of Iraq), who were all totally opposed to the Iranian regime's meddling in Iraq.

Tired of the years of violence and corruption and the creeping, evil influence of Iran, brave Iraqis went to the polls in droves to cast their votes against al-Maliki and his henchmen. Press reports later said that if I had not exposed the fraud in the early part of the election, there is no doubt that Maliki would have won by a landslide. But my intervention led to increased media scrutiny and caused the later stages of the great fraudulent scheme to falter. In fact Ayad Allawi should have won a decisive victory, but the early attempts at rigging and manipulation left his party neck and neck with Maliki.

The final result showed that Allawi had won the election by two seats. This caused consternation in Tehran, and Maliki was ordered by the Iranian Mullahs to demand a complete recount of every single vote. This would have necessitated the re-deployment of over 400,000 counting agents and would clearly have provided Maliki with another great opportunity to cheat and emerge victorious. But Maliki was determined to cling to power at all costs. He even issued threatening remarks about a return to violence if the votes were not recounted. With three divisions of the Iraqi army owing their entire allegiance to him, these were not regarded as idle threats.

Meanwhile the EU, the US and the UN continued to play the role of the three wise monkeys! They saw no evil, heard no evil and spoke no evil. Alarmed that any allegations of a fraudulent election might sow the seeds of renewed violence that would thwart America's plans for imminent troop withdrawal, they instead insisted that the election was largely fair. Like Pontius Pilate, they were desperate to wash their hands of the whole Iraqi affair and move on. The mess and misery they left in their wake seemed of minor importance. They sowed the wind and four years later they were reaping the whirlwind.

In the meantime, on a visit to Semipalatinsk in East Kazakhstan on 6 April 2010, I had been invited, in my role as Roving Ambassador for the Organisation for Security and Cooperation in Europe (OSCE), to join the UN Secretary General Ban Ki-moon and Kazakh President Nursultan Nazarbayev, on a visit to 'Ground Zero' to mark the 20th anniversary of the closure of the former Soviet Union's biggest nuclear weapons testing site. We flew by helicopter from the airport at Semipalatinsk to Ground Zero where a tent had been erected and a press conference took place. Rather comically, in the middle of his address to the UN Secretary General, President Nazarbayev handed over a large, gnarled piece of melted glass, which, he explained, had once been solid rock but had been turned into glass by a nuclear explosion. Ban Ki-moon quickly handed the glass rock to one of his aides, who also quickly passed it to another aide and so it went on, like a game of 'pass the parcel'. No one was keen to hold on to this potentially lethally radioactive piece of history!

After the press conference we flew back to the airport at Semipalatinsk and I was invited to join the Secretary General and the President for a light lunch before we all departed for meetings in neighbouring Turkmenistan. A light lunch in Kazakhstan always includes a boiled sheep's head, and this was duly placed in front of Ban Ki-moon as the primary guest of honour. To my great surprise he knew exactly how to deal with the ceremonial slicing and serving of the grisly head, deftly cutting off an ear and offering it to President Nazarbayev with a graceful little speech hoping that it would help the President to hear the views of his people.

After several toasts with vodka, I took the opportunity to broach the subject of Camp Ashraf with the Secretary General. I told him that I was deeply concerned that there would be more bloodshed at the camp and that it was imperative that UN blue-helmets should be permanently stationed there after the withdrawal of US forces, to ensure the safety of the 3,400 residents. I also reminded him of the need to encourage the US and EU Member States to open their doors to these people once they had been registered as refugees by the UNHCR, in order that we could get them out of Iraq to countries of safety. President Nazarbayev and the Kazakh Foreign Minister looked rather nonplussed at this conversation and after the Secretary General had promised me that he would look into the matter when he returned to New York they quickly changed the subject. As we parted later towards our respective jets, Ban Ki-moon said to me, 'Anytime you are in New York, please come and see me in my office at the UN HQ.'

Back in Tehran, the Mullahs were rubbing their hands together in glee. Past-masters at manipulating elections in their own country, they were now looking forward to a new coalition government in Iraq which would include their Shiia acolyte Muqtada al-Sadr, the firebrand pro-Iranian cleric, whose Mahdi army killed scores of US and British troops and who now held the balance of power in the Iraqi parliament. The Sadrists had won 40 seats in the elections and were thus a powerful pro-Iranian bloc in bed with Ammar al-Hakim, head of the Islamic Supreme Council of Iraq (formerly the Supreme Council for the Islamic Revolution in Iraq). With their help, al-Maliki could yet re-emerge as the puppet Prime Minister of Iraq.

The coalition negotiations took eight months to conclude. Maliki had clung to power like a limpet, determined to use every means to stay in office. There were legal challenges against a number of Ayad Allawi's newly elected MPs, with attempts to have some disqualified on trumped-up charges alleging they were former supporters of Saddam Hussein's Ba'ath Party. Maliki had set up the so-called Accountability and Justice Commission under the illegitimate leadership of the notorious Ahmed Chalabi, widely seen as the man who persuaded America to invade Iraq, and his partner-in-crime Ali al-Lami, the virulently pro-Iranian witchfinder-general who saw a member of Saddam Hussein's Ba'ath Party in every corner. He once absurdly even accused US General David Petraeus of being a Baathist, and said that if he had been Iraqi he would have been arrested!

With these two thugs leading the charge, around 50 MPs who had won seats in the March elections were accused of being Baathists and denied the right to take up their seats in parliament. Most of these MPs were from the secularist, anti-Iranian ranks. But not content with the expulsion of its opponents, the pro-Iranian faction now exerted pressure on Iraq's judges to insist on a manual recount of the four million votes cast in Baghdad. The process started amid great acrimony on Monday 3 May, with many complaining that political pressure had been brought to bear on the judges in a direct breach of the Iraqi constitution, which guarantees non-interference in judicial affairs. The exhaustive recount changed nothing, ending with exactly the same result.

The newly elected Iraqi parliament met for the first time, under tight security, on 14 June. Under the Iraqi Constitution, a President must be elected within 30 days following the first sitting of the parliament. This deadline was due to expire on Tuesday 13 July, marking a crucial cut-off date for the Iraqi people. If the Constitution was breached, it meant all of the suffering, death, devastation and economic collapse resulting from the toppling of Saddam and the subsequent insurgency would have been in vain. Democracy was the only reason the beleaguered Iraqi people had endured all of this misery. If democracy was allowed to die with the breaching of the Constitution, then civil war and a return to violence and mayhem could be the only possible outcome. The international community had a duty to ensure that this was not allowed to happen. They had to defend the fragile constitution. If no President had been elected by 13 July then this should have automatically triggered the international community's invoking of Article VII of the UN Charter, whereby the UN and the international community would assume responsibility to prevent a return to violence and civil war. This was of crucial importance, as any vacuum created by a breach of the Constitution would quickly be filled by neighbouring Iran, already meddling extensively in Iraqi internal affairs and keen to extend its malign brand of fascist Islam across the whole of the region, so that it would become the dominant power.

Vice President Joe Biden visited Iraq on US Independence Day, the fourth of July, to re-affirm his commitment to a complete military withdrawal by the end of 2011, with 50,000 US military personnel leaving by August 2010. But during his visit, Biden didn't seem to be concerned about who formed the next government in Iraq. He seemed determined to shake the dust of Iraq from his shoes and to wash his hands of the whole mess the US was about to leave behind.

With escalating violence, almost daily suicide bombings and even the re-emergence of Muqtada al-Sadr's Mahdi Army on the streets of Baghdad, the signs were ominous. The sectarian divisions, which the election was supposed to have healed, had re-opened. The faith of the Iraqi people in the democratic process was being sorely tested. Iraq needed a stable, non-sectarian government of national unity. The task of setting up such a government should have fallen to the victor of the election, Ayad Allawi. But the meddling of the Iranian regime had rendered such a result unlikely. For Tehran, victory for the secular and anti-Iranian regime, Allawi was a red line. They had to have someone they could control, and that meant Maliki had to be somehow shoehorned back into the Prime Minister's office.

In an article by Ali Khedery which appeared in the *New York Times* in August 2014, the writer, who was the longest continuously serving American official in Iraq, acting as a special assistant to five US ambassadors and as a senior adviser to three heads of US Central Command, wrote that:

> After spending more than $1 trillion and losing some 4,500 soldiers' lives, American politicians cannot dare reveal a dirty little secret: Iraq has since 2003 devolved into a combination of Lebanon and Nigeria — a toxic brew of sectarian politics and oil-fuelled kleptocracy. The combination of religious rivalry and endemic corruption has hollowed out the Iraqi Government, as evidenced by the country's ongoing electricity crisis and the collapse of entire Iraqi Army divisions in the

face of an advance by the Islamic State in Iraq and Syria, or ISIS, into Iraq's second-largest city, Mosul, even though the Iraqi troops vastly outnumbered the militants.

Later in the article he said:

Increasing Iranian influence has only made matters worse. America sat back and watched in 2010 as Mr Maliki's cabinet was formed by Iranian generals in Tehran, thereby assuring its strategic defeat in Iraq. ISIS is a direct outgrowth of that defeat. Sensing an American vacuum, both Mr Maliki and his Iranian patrons sought to consolidate their gains by economically, politically and physically crushing their Sunni and Kurdish rivals. Consequently, today's 'Iraqi security forces' are almost exclusively Shiite, reinforced by militias financed, trained, armed and directed by Iran. Given Mr Maliki's blatant sectarianism and his complicity in Bashar al-Assad's campaign of genocide against Syria's Sunnis, Sunni radicalization and the spread of ISIS across the region were predictable.[1]

The same author in a long biographical article about Maliki in the *Washington Post* in July 2014 stated:

In short, Maliki's one-man, one-Dawa-party Iraq looks a lot like Hussein's one-man, one-Baath Party Iraq. But at least Hussein helped contain a strategic American enemy: Iran. And Washington didn't spend $1 trillion propping him up. There is not much 'democracy' left if one man and one party with close links to Iran control the judiciary, police, army, intelligence services, oil revenue, treasury and the central bank. Under these circumstances, renewed ethno-sectarian civil war in Iraq was not a possibility. It was a certainty. [2]

1. http://www.nytimes.com/2014/08/17/opinion/sunday/iraqs-last-chance.html
2. http://www.washingtonpost.com/opinions/why-we-stuck-with-maliki--and-lost-iraq/2014/07/03/0dd6a8a4-f7ec-11e3-a606-946fd632f9f1_story.html

Back in 2010, news soon emerged that the two major Shiite blocs – the State-of-Law coalition headed by Maliki and the Iraqi National Alliance (INA) backed by Iran – had done a deal which placed them only a few seats short of forming a new government. INA included Ahmed Chalabi and his Iraqi National Congress Party and the fiercely sectarian Shiite Ibrahim al-Jaafari. Now Tehran's attention turned to Ammar al-Hakim, a junior Shiia cleric who was the leader of one of Iraq's most influential Shiia groupings, the Islamic Supreme Council of Iraq (ISCI). The ISCI commanded the loyalty of the most powerful Shiia militia in Iraq – the Badr Organisation (formerly known as the Badr Brigade). Hakim was ordered by the Mullahs to throw his support behind Maliki.

Only the large Kurdish bloc remained to be persuaded to join Maliki's coalition, with tempting offers of being awarded the Presidency of Iraq as well as the role of Speaker in the Council of Representatives and ministerial office in the key role of Foreign Minister. The Kurds rapidly agreed. At last, months after the election, Maliki had his paper-thin majority, but it was enough for him to form a government. By 13 July, Jalal Talabani, the prominent Kurdish leader, was appointed as Iraq's President for a second term, meeting the constitutional deadline, but there was still no agreement on the distribution of key cabinet posts.

To break the deadlock, as there was still no cabinet in place eight months after the elections, the President of Kurdistan, Massoud Barzani, called for the creation of a national congress to resolve the differences and form a government. The national congress met in Erbil and was attended by the leaders of all the main political blocs including Ayad Allawi and Nouri al-Maliki. A nine article agreement was eventually adopted, which enabled Maliki to retain the post of Prime Minister, but promised the distribution of key cabinet posts covering defence, interior and security to Ayad Alawi's al-Iraqiya bloc and other political factions. Allawi was also supposed to chair the National Strategic Council to overview the decisions. The 'Erbil Agreement' was signed in the presence of US Ambassador Jim Jeffrey, although this binding agreement was then studiously ignored by Maliki, who retained a vice-like grip on all of the key defence, interior and security portfolios in his own Prime Minister's office, giving him almost dictatorial powers. Indeed, such was his abuse of the Erbil Agreement and his ruthless abuse of power that several prominent Iraqi politicians subsequently described him to me as being 'worse than Saddam'.

While this controversy raged in Iraq, with the Iranian Mullahs pulling the strings to secure a second term for their man Nouri al-Maliki, the controversial Iranian Foreign Minister Manouchehr Mottaki paid a visit to the European Parliament in Brussels on 1 June 2010. Mottaki had been expelled from Turkey when he had been Iran's Ambassador, following the discovery of a prisoner trussed and gagged in the trunk of an Iranian Embassy car trying to cross the border from Turkey into Iran. Alert Turkish border guards heard thumping in the car trunk and demanded it should be opened. When the prisoner was released, he said he was one of several PMOI dissidents who had been kidnapped off the streets of towns and cities in Turkey, then held in a dungeon beneath the Iranian Embassy in Ankara, where people were severely tortured before being sent back to Iran for execution.

I was outraged that this murderer had been invited to address a meeting of the Foreign Affairs Committee, so I organised a little welcoming party for him. When he arrived outside the committee room at 3 pm on 1 June, I was standing with a group of MEPs holding placards showing photos of Neda Agha Soltan, a student killed in 2009 during demonstrations against the Iranian President Mahmoud Ahmadinejad's fraudulent re-election. Mottaki had a large entourage of henchmen and bodyguards and was being pursued by a huge phalanx of camera crews and photographers. He momentarily paused when he saw our placards and I stepped forward and shouted in his face: 'You are a murderer and you are not welcome in the European Parliament.' Other MEPs joined in the shouts and catcalls, and his bodyguards immediately started to scuffle with us, trying to manhandle us out of the way, shouting 'Don't touch' to anyone who got too close to their boss. I yelled, 'Get your hands off me! Do not dare to lay your hands on an elected Member of this House. This is not Iran. We do not tolerate thugs here.' All of this was caught on film, much to the embarrassment of Mottaki.

As a postscript to this story, later that week, I got into one of the lifts in the European Parliament, heading to my office on the twelfth floor. The only other person in the lift was the First Secretary from the Iranian Embassy in Brussels. 'You were a bit hard on my Foreign Minister the other day,' he said.

'Why?' I asked.

'Calling him a murderer,' he replied.

'But he is a murderer,' I said, and we rode on up in stony silence!

20

Interviews with PMOI Refugees
Camp Liberty, August 2014

Akbar Saremi Speaks about His Father Ali Saremi

Akbar Saremi

'My name is Akbar Saremi. I am the son of one of the longest-serving political prisoners in Iran. My father was executed in January 2010 for being a supporter of the PMOI and for visiting me in Camp Ashraf. Thousands more like him have been and are arrested, tortured and executed in Iran for supporting the PMOI. My Dad spent a total of 24 years of his life in prison. He was imprisoned for a year under the Shah but was set free when protestors liberated them during the revolution. Under the Mullahs' regime he was imprisoned for a total of 23 years.

Under the Mullahs' regime he was arrested four different times. In 1981, he was arrested and imprisoned for six years for being a PMOI supporter and reading their newspaper. A year after my father's release from prison I decided to join the PMOI in their struggle against the regime. I had seen and felt the crimes of this regime, especially against my own family. When the regime realised I had gone to Ashraf and joined the resistance, they arrested and severely tortured my father in such a brutal way that he developed major back problems, forcing him to use a wheelchair to get around. My mother used to say that he was unable to stand on his feet or walk, and they would not allow him to leave prison for treatment. He spent years in prison in that condition before being released.

After the US invasion of Iraq, my parents came to see me in Ashraf. During the week that they stayed I gave them a tour of the camp and they met all my friends and took part in different events. Even before visiting Ashraf and while in prison, my father had remained a PMOI supporter. He was one of the prisoners who had resisted attempts by henchmen to break his morale. But even so, after seeing Ashraf and talking to many of the residents he had become a different person. He told me, "I am not the same person as I was before coming here; I will never forget Ashraf." He used to say, "I will do whatever I can to spread the message of Ashraf wherever I go." He added that the PMOI are unique in Iranian history and their sacrifice for the Iranian people is unmatched. My father was not an average man and never supported something unless he really believed in it. He was fluent in five languages – English, German, French, Arabic and Farsi. He was a writer and a poet who spent most of his life reading books and newspapers from all around the world. He was also the editor in chief of the Iranian newspaper *Arian Homeland*, which was banned after two years of publication for printing anti-regime articles.

When my father came to visit me in Ashraf he used to ask me, "Are you Akbar?" I asked him, "Why are you asking me that?" He said, "I kept hearing different stories about you while I was in prison." He went on to say that the first time he was in prison they had told him he had a visitor who had information about his son (me). When my father met with the visitor, he told my father that I had left the PMOI and was in a camp in Iraq and needed money. My father said "I was not sure if he was telling me the truth or not," but because he did not want to show any weakness in front of his jailers he told the visitor, "I don't care what he does, it does not concern me; he has chosen his own path." My father said the story occupied his mind for months and disturbed him, and he thought to himself, what if it was true.

The henchmen tried to break his resistance, using every dirty trick at their disposal. He said the second time he heard about me was after the US invasion of Iraq. He had been ordered to go to prison to report on my whereabouts, when they told him that I had been killed in the attacks by US forces. He said, "After hearing this news I decided to go to Ashraf and find out for myself. This is why I am in shock, when I find you alive in Ashraf."

Upon returning from Ashraf my father was arrested for addressing a gathering in Khavaran cemetery (the site of mass graves of political prisoners massacred in 1988). After his arrest, the regime realized that he had gone to Ashraf to visit me, and because of that they put more pressure on him to repent or he would be executed. He never gave in to their demands, and was executed just because he had gone to Ashraf to visit his son.

My father had been to Ashraf and had seen the high spirits of the resistance and he had taken that same spirit with him to prison and thus became a symbol of resistance in prison. He spread the same spirit to the rest of the prisoners. He kept sending messages and letters from prison exposing the regime's crimes at every occasion. During imprisonment he had written 25 different messages and letters to newspapers condemning the regime's crimes. His activities provoked more pressure and torture, which caused a heart attack, leaving him paralyzed down his left side and wheelchair-ridden. When they took him to the gallows, he was on a wheelchair. My mother told me that when my father was out of prison and working in our shoe store, he had printed pictures of Massoud and Maryam Rajavi and placed them under his counter. Whenever he sold a shoe he used to slide one of those pictures in the box for the customers, telling them he had put a present in the box for them. My Mum said, "I kept telling him this is dangerous but he never listened and kept saying, we have to put out the word for Ashraf and the PMOI."

After they executed my father they did not return his body to us and secretly buried him in one of the villages near his home town. My Dad was a well-known man, and when the villagers realized they were burying him they informed my family. The regime's Revolutionary Guards had told my family they were not allowed to hold a ceremony for him, but my family did not pay attention to the warning and held a large memorial service. The Guards attacked the memorial service and arrested my mother, and gave her a 10-year prison sentence. My mother was able to escape from Iran, leaving the regime empty-handed. She is now in Paris.

The memory of my father and all the other martyrs will live on forever and their struggle will continue.'

21

The Second Ashraf Massacre

On the morning of Thursday, 7 April 2011, I received a call in my office in Brussels from Tahar Boumedra. He had some deeply disturbing news. He told me that several battalions of the Iraqi army had taken up positions around Camp Ashraf, and that dozens of armoured personnel carriers, Humvees, bulldozers and other engineering vehicles had been strategically positioned around the camp's perimeter fence. Boumedra said that he was getting calls every half hour from the residents of Ashraf to update him on the escalating crisis. He said he was certain that another attack was imminent, and that he had spoken to a high-ranking army officer who of course had denied everything and assured him that nothing was going to happen.

At 4.45 a.m. the following morning, 8 April, the attack commenced. I began to receive a series of phone calls and emails as the attack progressed and the death toll of Ashrafis mounted. By 9 a.m. there were already 22 dead and hundreds seriously injured; three battalions of the Iraqi military had mounted the assault and they had now seized over one-third of the camp's territory. I was making frantic phone calls to Ban Ki-moon in New York, António Guterres at UNHCR in Geneva and Baroness Ashton in Brussels. I left messages informing them of this latest brutal assault on unarmed and defenceless 'people of concern' to the UN, urging them to contact Maliki immediately to demand a halt to the slaughter.

By the end of the day, the picture became clearer. Under the command of General Ali Gheidan,[1] commander of Iraqi ground forces, the three Iraqi battalions moved into Ashraf as dawn broke. They used tear-gas and smoke and stun grenades. The Ashrafis, who had been expecting an attack after witnessing the build-up of military

---

1. Gheidan was commander of the ground forces and was later responsible for crushing the Sunnis' peaceful rallies. During the ISIS attack on Mosul, he disgracefully ran away and was later dismissed for his cowardice.

forces over the past three days, immediately formed a human chain to try to prevent the army from moving further into the camp. The soldiers opened fire and snipers were deployed to shoot dead any residents who were trying to film the attack on their mobile phones. Humvees and armoured personnel vehicles were driven at high speed into crowds of Ashrafis, crushing them under the wheels. By evening, 28 Ashrafis were dead.

There had been a small US Force-Iraq (USF-I) observers' team stationed at Ashraf for weeks. This unit, under the command of Lt. Col. Robert Molinari, was based inside Ashraf and was fully aware of the Iraqi government's intentions to attack the camp. But despite pleas by the residents to stay, on 7 April, at 10 p.m., seven hours before the attack, his unit mysteriously disappeared. If they had stayed, the Iraqi forces would never have dared to attack. It emerged later, that in anticipation of a violent Iraqi assault on the camp, the USF-I soldiers had been told to leave the area so that they would not witness defenceless people being killed while they were under strict orders not to intervene. Nevertheless, the Americans reappeared on 10 April, following the massacre, and transferred ten of the residents who had the most life-threatening injuries to a nearby USF-I military hospital.

As the horrifying photos and videos of the massacre poured into my email account, I was stunned. We had warned repeatedly that another massacre was imminent and no one had listened. Now 34 unarmed civilians were dead, either gunned down or crushed by military vehicles. Eight of the dead were women, young teachers and artists with their lives ahead of them. Now I was staring at photos of their glazed eyes and blood-spattered heads and chests torn open by bullets, fired by soldiers from the 9th Infantry Division and 5th Armoured Division of the Iraqi military, sent to the camp under the direct orders of Prime Minister Nouri al-Maliki. For two years, I and other prominent politicians had warned that a massacre would take place. I had twice gone to Washington DC, most recently in March 2011, for meetings in the State Department, Congress and the Senate, to warn that unless Hillary Clinton made a public statement on the issue, blood would certainly be shed. I was ignored.

In repeated debates, conferences, hearings, letters and newspaper articles, I warned what was sure to happen. I wrote to the EU

High Representative for Foreign Affairs, Baroness Ashton, pleading with her to intervene. In a debate in Strasbourg I called upon her to warn the Iraqi government not to resort to violence over Ashraf. She replied that there were 'differences of opinion' over the issue. It took the death of another 34 unarmed civilians to force her to make a public statement condemning the attack. Too little, too late! Her complacency and that of other world leaders like Secretary of State Clinton had simply given the green light to Nouri al-Maliki to go ahead with his murderous attack.

The EU makes a great song and dance about its wonderful 'European values'. We pride ourselves on upholding human rights and standing up for the oppressed against bullies and aggressors. On 8 April, at 4.45 a.m. in Camp Ashraf, the hollowness of such claims was bloodily exposed. It seems that the EU had little more to contribute than hot air, and in the case of Ashraf, was not even prepared to offer that.

2,500 heavily armed troops and over 40 armoured vehicles, including tracked machines with mounted cannon like small tanks, invaded Ashraf and opened fire on the 3,400 refugees, gunning them down like rabbits in a field. Over 300 residents of the camp had been seriously injured, and the Iraqi authorities were preventing them from accessing proper medical treatment.

I watched horrifying films of the massacre posted on YouTube by residents of the camp. It was plain to see the refugees were fleeing for their lives as armoured cars accelerated across the camp, swerving left and right to mow them down, against a background of gunfire and explosions. This was a calculated and deliberate massacre and a gross violation of human rights. The reaction by the Iraqi government added insult to injury, and fuelled my anger at this crime against humanity. At first they claimed that no one in Ashraf had been killed and that their troops had been firing blanks. However, as pictures of the horror began to leak out across the internet, their story changed. Soon they claimed their 2,500 troops and 40 armoured vehicles had been violently attacked by a stone-throwing mob, and that they had been forced to repel this unprovoked assault. The odious Foreign Minister from neighbouring Iran even congratulated al-Maliki on a job well done, revealing clearly who was the real driving force behind the massacre.

The Iraqi Government denied Tahar Boumedra permission to go to Ashraf until 13 April, the normal weekly UNAMI visiting day; a UNAMI team and some senior officers accompanied him from USF-I. He went straight to the hospital in Ashraf, where the Iraqi doctor assured him that only three people had been killed. He noted that the hospital was empty, despite the fact that he had been told that over 300 people had been seriously injured during the massacre. The representatives of the camp's residents took Boumedra and his team to a makeshift clinic, where they found all of the casualties crammed into every available space, while one of the PMOI doctors tried to care for them. Many had shrapnel and bullet wounds. Others had suffered massive trauma from being crushed under vehicles.

Outside the clinic a crowd of Ashrafis had gathered, holding pictures of their murdered friends and relatives. A 14-year-old girl told Boumedra how her sister had been one of the victims. 'She was pleading for UNAMI's help and asking why no-one had come to their aid,' Boumedra said later. Boumedra's team was now split into two, with one half going to do the body count and take photos of the deceased, while Boumedra and two other UNAMI officials went to speak to the survivors. They were told that, just as in the first massacre at Ashraf, many of the military personnel involved could be heard to speak to each other and shout insults at the Ashrafis in Farsi. It was also clear that trained Iranian snipers had taken part in the assault, as single gunshot wounds to the head or heart had killed many of the dead.

It was evident that the lack of any meaningful criticism of Maliki following the first Ashraf massacre in July 2009 had emboldened him to strike again, underscoring his threat to use 'all possible means' to empty the camp by the end of 2011. Tahar Boumedra demanded an urgent meeting with Prime Minister Maliki's Chief of Staff, Dr Hamid K. Ahmed, and those in charge of the Ashraf file. They met the same day in Maliki's office. Dr Ahmed was accompanied by National Security Advisor Faleh al-Fayadh, Political Advisor to the PM, George Y. Bakoos and Security Officers Haqqi and Sadiq Mohammad Kazim. Despina Saraliotou from UNAMI and Ambassador Lawrence Butler, Foreign Policy Advisor to the Commander of USF-I, accompanied Boumedra.

Dr Ahmed chaired the meeting and opened by praising the ongoing cooperation between UNAMI and the Iraqi Government. Ludicrously, he emphasised the Iraqi government's commitment to upholding the highest standards of human rights in Camp Ashraf, while urging all possible haste to move the residents to a new location to enable the camp to be vacated by the end of the year. He made no mention whatsoever of the 8th of April massacre. No-one of the Iraqi side mentioned it.

Boumedra gave them a minute-by-minute account of his visit to the camp the previous day, enumerating the number of dead and injured they had found. He said the Iraqi side all stared at their notebooks, refusing to make eye contact and shuffling in obvious embarrassment. Incredibly, the National Security Advisor Faleh al-Fayadh then tried to deny that the attack had taken place at all, until Boumedra confronted them with pictures of the dead. Boumedra demanded an independent commission of inquiry to investigate the case and hold those responsible to account. Ambassador Butler supported him. Faleh al-Fayadh looked increasingly irritated, according to Boumedra, and angrily stated 'No-one will dictate to us how to do an inquiry.'

The international response to this premeditated extra-judicial killing was consistent with what had occurred following the first Ashraf massacre in 2009. Instead of issuing a withering condemnation and demanding an independent inquiry under UN supervision, UNAMI eventually issued a statement noting 'the initiative of the Government of Iraq to establish a commission of inquiry'. Riled by this limp-wristed response, Boumedra bypassed normal procedures and sent his damning report directly to the Office of the High Commissioner for Human Rights, Navi Pillay, in Geneva. Pillay did issue a strongly worded criticism of the Iraqi military's involvement in the massacre and called for a full, independent and transparent inquiry, with the prosecution of anyone found responsible for the use of excessive force. However, as usual, the UN failed to follow up on either the UNAMI or UNHCR statements, determined, as always, to follow their policy of appeasement rather than rock the Iraqi boat and sour relations with the murderous Maliki government. The then-US Senate Foreign Relations Committee chairman, John Kerry, described the raid as a 'massacre', calling for a thorough independent investigation, and emphasizing that the Iraqis must refrain from any further military actions against Camp Ashraf. Ironically, but perhaps unsurprisingly, when Kerry became US Secretary of State he completely forgot about his stern warning!

It is difficult not to condemn utterly America's betrayal of the Ashraf residents from start to finish. In fact it is interesting that the April 2011 and July 2009 attacks against Ashraf both occurred when the US Secretary of Defence, Robert Gates, was in Baghdad. In fact both attacks happened only hours after he met with Nouri al-Maliki, suggesting that the attacks could almost have had Washington's blessing!

22

Interviews with Political Prisoners in Tirana, Albania, August 2014

Fatimeh Nabavi Chashmi

'My name is Fatimeh Nabavi; I am 45 years old and a member of the PMOI. I was born into a religious family and my father is a cleric. During the 1980s, many of my friends and relatives were arrested and imprisoned for being supporters of the PMOI. Two of my relatives by the names of Hojat Emadi and Emad Nabavi were executed. When Hojat Emadi was executed they did not even inform his family of his execution. When Hojat's father was about to go to visit him in prison, the guards came to their home and brought Hojat's bloodstained shoes to his family and claimed that they had executed him and there was no longer any need for them to go to the prison to visit their son. Needless to say this was extremely shocking to Hojat's Mum and Dad, causing them to have nervous breakdowns.

In 1988, because of my support for the PMOI and opposition to Khomeini's regime, I was being pursued by the regime, so I was forced to leave my country and I later went to Ashraf. After the regime realised that I had fled the country, they put my family under immense pressure and surveillance. My family lived under constant fear of arrest and execution. My Mum had several nervous breakdowns. Having committed no crimes or broken any laws, in an attempt to exert pressure on my family, during the 1990s the regime forced two of my brothers out of the city and to exile. This was one of the tactics of the regime to try to make life miserable for PMOI families. My brothers spent many years away from their families.

Following the US invasion and the creation of a provisional government by the coalition forces in Iraq, the road to Iraq was opened. During that time many PMOI supporters travelled to Iraq to join the PMOI in Ashraf. In 2005 my brother went to Iraq and joined the PMOI. When he got to Camp Ashraf he told me that many young people would like to come to Ashraf. After a while my Mum and Dad along with my three brothers and sisters came to Ashraf to see me. They were amazed about the security of the camp. When my family was getting ready to go back to Iran, my brother Javad said that he would not return with the rest of the family and would instead stay in Ashraf to join the struggle against the regime. He is now in Camp Liberty.

At that time another relative of mine, by the name of Mojtaba Nabavi Chashmi, who had also come to visit Ashraf, decided that he did not want to go back to Iran and requested to join the PMOI in their struggle to bring freedom for the Iranian people. He is also now in Camp Liberty; Mojtaba was followed by Ammar and Marzieh and later by Assadollah, Saeed and Hadi, who were all part of my extended family. They all came to Ashraf and then requested to remain there. After a while Emmad, Vahideh, Maryam and Maryeh also came to Ashraf. This happened at a time when the regime wasn't paying much attention to people coming to Ashraf to join the Mojahedin. When they realised that the young people were coming and joining the PMOI in Ashraf, they started to put inhumane pressure on our families. They started with arresting my Mum, Dad, sisters and brothers. They took my 80-year-old father, who had not committed any crime, to prison and intimidated him in every possible way. They asked him why he had gone to Ashraf, and informed him that going to Ashraf to visit the Mojahedin was considered a crime. His interrogators told my father that he was not qualified to wear a clerical robe and from that point on he was not able to function as a cleric or go to the mosque and lead people in prayers. They also ordered him to stop supporting the PMOI. Their intention was to break my father but my father resisted their pressure. He said, 'I have no need for the clergy's robe,' and went back to Shahmirzad, the village where he had lived for years and was loved by all the inhabitants of the village. The people of Shahmirzad later asked him to become their prayer leader. The regime's agents kept on pressuring him to try to have him condemn the PMOI and stop his support, but my father never surrendered.

In prison his interrogator had told him, "You have become like a thorn in our side." After my father, they arrested and tortured my brothers. Two years ago I heard the news of my brother's arrest from Simaye Azadi television. Both my brothers were sent to prison in another province and not even allowed a visit by their wives and kids. My sister-in-law had just given birth, but they would not allow my brother to see his newborn baby. They kept on exerting this kind of pressure to break our family.

Maliki had promised Khamenei to increase the pressure on the PMOI. In keeping his promise he besieged Ashraf, and on 28 and 29 July 2009 launched a military attack on the camp. As it has been seen through the documented videos available, Maliki's forces attacked the Mojahedin using live bullets, axes, Humvees, high-pressure water cannons and bulldozers. The Mojahedin resisted empty-handed. My brother Mohammad Kazem, who was one of the singers in a traditional music group in Ashraf, had both his hands broken as a result of being hit with an axe. Both his hands were in plaster for three months and his comrades had to help him to accomplish his personal chores. He was not even able to lift a cup of water or brush his teeth.

In another attack, on 8 April 2011, my second brother Mohammad Javad was shot in the leg. On the same day my niece Maryam was also shot in the leg, and for months and because of the siege on Ashraf, the Iraqi government would not allow her to leave Ashraf to go to the hospital and to have the bullet removed. After several months the doctors in Ashraf managed to remove the bullet from her leg. She suffered severe pain for several months because of the inhumane medical siege imposed on Ashraf. The epic heroism displayed by the residents during the massacres of 28 and 29 July and 8 April did not cease on those days, but it has continued in the resistance of the survivors to this day, in the hope that one day we will get the answer to all our pain and suffering through the freedom of our people.

A few years ago I was diagnosed with Multiple Sclerosis. During the past few years of the medical siege on Ashraf and the inhumane psychological warfare waged on us, my illness has been getting worse on a daily basis. The medical siege added to the hardship we endured. My doctor used to tell me that, with your illness you have to sit in a place where there is a lot of shade and greenery, but I was instead forced into a place where there was no sign of any greenery or shade. I kept asking myself, what is our protected persons' status for? What happened when the Americans took our arms and promised us protection in return? Why did they lie to us?

Albania agreed to accept a number of the residents, and I was one of those people put on the list to go to Albania. In 2013, despite the fact I really wanted to stay with the rest of my friends, I was transferred to Albania. Through the insistence of my friends I was taken to hospital, where I started my treatment. My doctor informed me that I was suffering from epilepsy as well and my nervous system has been compromised. After a year of treatment and support from my friends, my condition has somewhat stabilised.

I also have a 26-year-old son who lives in the United States and who has got his Masters degree in Business Administration. Because of the siege placed on Ashraf and Liberty, he could not come and visit me when I was there. When I was transferred to Albania he came to see me. We were so happy to see each other after years of separation. My son told me that he was looking forward to seeing his father, but the inaction of international organisations with respect to Ashraf had led to a catastrophe, leaving him with the pain of not being able to see his father ever again, as he learned that he was one of the 52 killed during the 1 September 2013 massacre in Ashraf.'

23
Baghdad

In early 2011, I had demanded the right to take a small team of MEPs from my Delegation for Relations with Iraq to Baghdad. Our visas were issued in early April, just days before the massacre in Ashraf. This was fortuitous, as they almost certainly would have been withheld following the atrocities at the camp. So we were all set to go and we were given intensive security training and warned that there were considerable risks involved. We were told that travelling outside the so-called 'Green Zone' – the high security area in the centre of Baghdad – was lethally dangerous and should be avoided.

My team consisted of myself and three other MEPs, Mario Mauro (Italy), John Attar Montalto (Malta) and Jelko Kacin (Slovenia). We arrived at the International Airport in Baghdad on 25 April 2011. Baghdad was still a war-zone. The streets were entombed in heavy concrete. Tanks or armoured cars sat at every corner. Machine-guns poked out from behind heaps of sandbags. Concrete bunkers and watchtowers were everywhere. Politicians moved around the city in heavily armoured vehicles. For our high-speed journey from the airport to the Green Zone, we were made to wear full body armour and were taken in pairs inside armoured Lexus 4-WDs, with Iraqi drivers and European security guards, each brandishing sub-machine guns and pistols.

Our friendly British security guard was a former paratrooper called Mark, from Birmingham. He said he was married to a Scottish girl from Inverness, but only got home to see her every five or six weeks. As we drove out through the numerous security checks surrounding Baghdad's International Airport, he explained that we were about to drive along 'Irish Street, once the most dangerous street in the world.' Reassuringly he said that nowadays there are only occasional roadside bombs and isolated attacks on passing convoys like ours! I asked how well our Lexus would withstand an explosion from an improvised explosive device (IED), and he said that he recently saw a similar vehicle blown several metres into the air by one, then it landed on its roof and yet all of the passengers emerged unhurt!

With this information ringing in my ears, we raced on towards the city and the first major roadblocks, where queues of cars stood waiting to be searched and the occupants' identities checked. Mark pointed to two large craters in the road just outside the Green Zone, where suicide bombers had rammed cars into the waiting traffic only a week previously, killing 12 people and injuring more than 50. This was quite unusual, he said, as mostly now al-Qaeda were using a new tactic involving targeted assassinations of Iraqi military and police personnel, usually at roadblocks. 'They use handguns fitted with silencers and when the soldier or policeman taps on their window to ask for their ID, they open the window and shoot him in the face, before racing off to repeat the performance at the next checkpoint,' he explained cheerfully. 81 people had been killed in this way in the 16 days before we arrived.

High, thick concrete walls, topped with razor wire, surrounded our compound in the middle of the Green Zone. A Kalashnikov-toting guard stood at the main entrance gate. I was shown to my underground bunker-room where a notice pinned to the back of my door said: 'The signal for a missile/mortar attack will be a continuous warbling siren and flashing red lights.' A khaki-green helmet lay ominously on top of the bedroom drawers, next to a heavy set of body armour.

I soon discovered that missiles and mortars were a daily part of Baghdad life. Usually they were fired from the remote and desperately poor suburb called Sadr-city, named after Muqtada al-Sadr, the ferociously anti-American Islamic cleric who controls the black-clad Mahdi Army, and is now an elected member of the Iraqi Parliament. Muqtada al-Sadr takes his orders from Iran. He had openly threatened to reignite the insurgency if the Americans did not stick to their promise of complete withdrawal from Iraq by the end of the year. It was a serious threat.

On our way to visit the Polish Ambassador in the early evening we could suddenly hear sirens wailing. Mark got onto his walkie-talkie and announced that there was 'an incoming on the way.'

'An incoming what,' I nervously enquired.

'Oh it's probably just a rocket or a mortar,' said Mark. 'They're usually aimed at the American Embassy in the heart of the Green Zone, so we should be OK.'

Sure enough, a few seconds later the 'All Clear' signal sounded and Mark received a message on his radio confirming that the mortar had in fact landed in the River Tigris. As we were driving along the side of the River Tigris, this was not entirely reassuring.

At the Polish Ambassador's residence we met for dinner with a number of EU ambassadors. We were given an initial comprehensive briefing on the prevailing situation inside Iraq. We were told that Baghdad only had around six hours electricity per day, but they were hoping to reach up to 18 hours per day by the end of the summer, when temperatures can rise to over 50°C, and without air-conditioning, tempers can fray. Kurdistan in particular was thriving economically, with around 10% annual growth, against a background of relative safety and political stability. The general picture seemed to be that Iraq was gradually clawing its way out of the nightmare that it had suffered under Saddam Hussein's dictatorship, followed by the US/British invasion and the subsequent insurgency that left tens of thousands dead and the major cities devastated. There seemed to be a consensus among the EU ambassadors that Iraq was potentially open for business and we should do nothing to jeopardise the chance for lucrative business contracts. I can't say that I was convinced by their arguments!

I thanked the Polish Ambassador for his hospitality and said that we were here in Baghdad in the immediate wake of the horrific massacre at Camp Ashraf and it was my duty as Head of the Delegation to demand an independent inquiry into the 8 April atrocities, when 36 unarmed civilians from the PMOI were killed and many hundreds injured. I said that the EU must enter into urgent negotiations with the PMOI, the Iraqi government, the US and UNAMI to find a long-term solution to this crisis and to prevent further bloodshed. The re-settlement of the 3,400 residents of Ashraf to the US and to EU Member States was the only feasible option, and would have to be brokered before the end of 2011, the deadline set by the Iraqi government for the closure of Ashraf. However, negotiations could only begin if the

Iraqi government first withdrew its military forces from Ashraf, provided urgent medical attention for the critically injured, ended the siege of the camp and restored relative normality to the situation.

Each of the ambassadors spoke, condemning the attack of 8 April, but each qualifying their remarks with negative points about the PMOI. I said that it was pointless and deeply worrying to hear the usual Mullah-inspired propaganda criticising the 3,400 residents of Ashraf as being Marxist, a listed terrorist organisation and a cult. I said, "These people have been brutally attacked twice now. They are under siege in Ashraf and denied adequate supplies of food, fuel and water; 300 loudspeakers blaring insults day and night constantly harass them and you see fit to direct some criticism at them?" I was very angry, but I could see which way the wind was blowing.

The next morning, Tuesday 26 April, we met with Ad Melkert, Tahar Boumedra and the UNAMI team. I opened the meeting by raising the question of the lack of fulfilment of the Erbil Agreement and the failure by Maliki to fill the posts of Ministers of Interior, Defence and Security. I said that this was supposed to be a government of national unity, but was looking increasingly like a sectarian government. I said that the massacre at Ashraf had exposed the fault-line in Maliki's government, demonstrating clearly how he was prepared to abuse power and do the bidding of Iran. The massacre was a violation of everything the EU held dear, and was an appalling humanitarian tragedy for which a fully independent inquiry was needed to identify the perpetrators and bring them to justice. I reminded them that the European Parliament had twice sent strong resolutions to Iraq demanding an end to the intimidation and siege of Ashraf, with an appeal to the Iraqi authorities never to resort to violence.

The attack on 8 April showed contempt for the European Parliament and its Members, I said. I agreed that there had to be a long-term solution found for the residents of Ashraf, as the current situation was intolerable, and there was an increased risk of annihilation of the residents in a Srebrenica-style massacre. I asked Ad Melkert if UNAMI could not quickly embed a unit inside the camp to offer protection, or whether the US could offer military protection while a negotiated settlement was established. I asked whether the UN Security Council could raise this issue and demand protection for the residents of Ashraf. However, I said that there could be no negotiation with the Iraqi government over a long term solution to Ashraf while the residents remained under the threat of the Iraqi military that had now bulldozed a huge embankment from which they could threaten the remaining camp. The troops must be withdrawn, the siege ended, immediate medical assistance provided to the critically wounded and a state of peace and normality restored in the camp. Only then could any resolution be discussed between the EU and Iraq.

Ad Melkert said that the Iraqi government was determined to close the camp by the end of 2011. They had considerable interaction with Iran on this issue. He said the EU and US position was of vital importance in resolving this issue because UNAMI could only monitor the situation. They could not intervene. Nor would the UN Security Council discuss Ashraf. There was no question of that. UNAMI had demanded an international inquiry into the massacre. Iraq wanted a government inquiry with UN involvement. But if UNAMI was to get involved in any way, the army must withdraw first, he said.

'However,' Melkert continued, 'for the UN to be involved they must accept individual registration as refugees. For us, communication with the MEK is vital. We can talk readily enough to the camp leadership in Ashraf, but we need to communicate with the leadership in Paris. We need a channel for this, which you, Mr Stevenson, can provide.'

Our next meeting was with Osama al-Nujaifi, the Speaker of the Iraqi Council of Representatives. When I launched a tirade against the massacre, the Speaker said, 'As far as Ashraf is concerned a full investigation is underway into the events of 8th April. But you have to understand that the Iraqi Government has its own side to this story.' He was clearly not willing to engage any further on this issue.

We encountered the same reluctance to be drawn on Ashraf from our meeting with the chair of the Foreign Affairs Committee in the Council of Representatives, Humam Hammoudi, from the party of Hakim. His excuse was that this was a matter for the chair of the Human Rights Committee, rather than Foreign Affairs. It seemed as if everyone was astonished and embarrassed by the brutal attack ordered by Maliki. Mr Hammoudi did, however, emphasise the need for great friendship and cooperation between the EU and Iraq. I told him that premeditated, extra-judicial murders of unarmed civilians were not the best way of cementing good relations with the EU.

Continuing our series of meetings with the Council of Representatives, our next port of call was with the Chair of the Security and Defence Committee, Hassan al-Sunaid, a close ally of Maliki and several of his committee members. The Chairman said: 'Clearly the MEK is the main reason for your visit. We want Iran, Iraq and the MEK to sit together to settle this issue. We are not against the MEK and will always deal with them from a humanitarian position. But you should understand the camp is filled with weapons. I can take you there now and show you them. They attacked neighbouring areas near Ashraf. They attacked our forces. They constantly abuse our Prime Minister and government and call for their downfall. They have abused their position as guests in our country and are no longer welcome. But nevertheless our Committee on Defence and Security will investigate what happened on 8 April and punish those responsible.'

I thanked Mr al-Sunaid for his kind offer to take me right away to Ashraf to see all the weapons and evidence of terrorism for myself, and said that I readily accepted his suggestion. I asked when we could leave and he simply ignored my question!

We moved on to meet with Salim Abdullah al-Jabouri,[1] chair of the Human Rights Committee. He said that the members of his committee were deeply alarmed at what had happened on the 8th April, but they were aware of the Iraqi sovereignty situation and the situation regarding neighbours like Iran and the provocation to them from Ashraf. He suggested that the UN must take over and help to resolve the issue. But any resolution must respect Iraq's concerns over sovereignty and Iran.

We were met with a similar reaction from the Foreign Minister, Hoshyar Zebari, a prominent Kurd. He said: 'You must be clear that the Iraqi Government has no animosity towards the MEK. The US disarmed them and then the US and Bulgaria provided them with protection in Ashraf. I signed the handover agreement of Ashraf. The

1. Salim al-Jabouri became President (Speaker) of the Iraqi Parliament in September 2014.

residents agreed to follow Iraqi laws and we agreed that there would never be any forced extraditions to Iran. We agreed that we would respect their human rights. But now the MEK regard Ashraf as their liberated territory, as if they have conquered it in a war. They are our guests. They cannot seize part of Iraq and claim it as their own. Of course they are strong and effective lobbyists in the US and EU. But in 2009 we asked them to allow our police into the camp and it ended in a riot where 12 people were killed. This year, in April, there was an even worse attack. They have to realise that this is Iraqi land and they are Iranians. They even asked us if they could pay a rent for it! We supplied them with water, electricity and this is how they repay our friendship.'

Of course I knew that most of his allegations were baseless. The Iraqi government did not provide water and electricity to the Ashraf residents. In fact it was the residents themselves who pumped water from a nearby river, supplying more than 20,000 Iraqis in villages near the camp; US military officers officially confirmed this.

Zebari continued: 'Now Iraq and Iran are friends, so the situation has changed. We have tried hard to suggest voluntary repatriation to the Ashraf residents, but the trouble is that no country will agree to take them. This is unfortunate, because the government has taken a clear decision that there is no place for them in Iraq by the end of 2011. The government are prepared to work closely with UNAMI on a solution. Extensive talks have been held with Iran and the Iranians had agreed to voluntarily repatriate to Iran those who wished to return, with a cast-iron guarantee signed by both governments that they would not be arrested or prosecuted. They would even seek the International Commission of the Red Cross cooperation on this. Alternatively, Iran had even agreed to supply all 3,400 residents with Iranian passports so that they could go wherever they liked. So the last window of opportunity is now. We will try to help to re-settle them. As for the 8th April events, there is no clear answer on what happened, but we have launched our own investigation to uncover the truth.'

I said that there was a very clear answer to what happened on 8th April. It was a massacre by 2,500 heavily armed troops and armoured vehicles ordered by the Prime Minister. I asked if my delegation could go to Ashraf to see for themselves what had happened. Zebari said absolutely not. He could not permit us to visit Ashraf under any circumstances. It was out of the question. I then asked what would happen at the end of the year if all attempts to repatriate the residents of Ashraf had failed. In that case, Zebari said, they would be forcibly moved to an alternative camp.

Zebari then launched into an astonishing defence of Maliki's sectarian and divisive policies and added: 'Our democracy has acted as a spur for the Arab Spring in North Africa and the Middle East. Other countries want our freedom. That is why almost every suicide bomber in the Middle East was, for a time, sent to Iraq.'

I had been led to believe that Zebari's background and political inclinations differed greatly from those of Maliki, so I was dismayed to discover that he was now prepared to defend the Prime Minister's repressive sectarian policies, presumably in an effort to hold on to his own high-ranking post. It was disappointing to find an eminent Kurd like Zebari willing to distance himself from the honourable position of the Kurdish President Massoud Barzani. Zebari was even prepared to justify Maliki's attacks on PMOI members, claiming that they had been involved in assisting Saddam Hussein's repression of the Iraqi Kurds. This was an astonishing U-turn by Zebari, because I had seen his own testimony to a Dutch court on 14 July 1999 when he had written as the Head of KDP International Relations that: '[We] can confirm that the Mujahedeen [sic] were not involved in suppressing the Kurdish people neither during the uprising nor in its aftermath. We have not come across any evidence to suggest that the Mujahedeen have exercised any hostility towards the people of Iraqi Kurdistan.'[1]

Zebari's veiled threats and hostility to the Ashrafis were refreshingly countered by the Deputy Prime Minister, Dr Saleh al-Mutlak, who told us that he felt deeply saddened by the events at Ashraf. 'I said so to my colleagues in government. It hurts the reputation of Iraq after 5,000 years of civilization that we now resort to murdering unarmed

---

1. Colonel Wes Martin, a commander of US forces in Ashraf, testified under oath in a hearing in the Congress that when he was in Iraq, he showed this letter to Zebari and asked him to confirm it and Zabari said, 'Yes, I have written this letter'.

guests. These are unarmed civilians. We need to find a humanitarian solution that involves the EU, Iraq, Iran and UNAMI. But any solution must serve both the interests of the MEK and Iraq. I am happy to cooperate with you to find a solution.'

That evening, we were taken by our armed security guards to a meeting with the Iraqi President, Jalal Talabani, another senior Kurdish political leader. The Presidential Palace is outside the Green Zone, so we had been warned that we must spend no longer than 60 minutes in the meeting. 'Any longer,' Mark, our gun-toting guard said, 'will give terrorists time to target a mortar attack or an ambush, so you have to get out strictly after one hour.'

President Talabani began by apologising on behalf of Nouri al-Maliki. 'The Prime Minister is sorry that he cannot meet you, as he is currently in Korea.' In a rather too audible whisper, I commented, 'North Korea, I presume?' The President ignored this and continued by stating: 'I am personally against all forms of violence. Iran uses the MEK as an excuse to put pressure on us. I went to Tehran and asked them to stop sending arms to terror groups in Iraq. They responded by demanding we close Ashraf. In these circumstances what can we do? We cannot allow them to stay. Terrorists, supplied with weapons by Iran, are killing Christians and other minority communities almost daily.'

He repeated the allegations of Zebari about the role of the PMOI in repressing the Kurds and the Shiias and added: 'The MEK are hated by the Kurds and by the Shiites, although not by the Sunnis. Iran is threatening to launch rocket attacks on Ashraf if we don't do something. We need to act.'

This was quite a paradox, because I had seen Zebari's letter to the Dutch courts and I also knew that the PUK, the party of Talabani, after cementing strong links with the Mullahs in Tehran, had begun to repress the PMOI members in Iraq, even going as far as launching armed attacks against them. Dozens of PMOI members were killed in those unprovoked attacks. The PUK also boasted of handing over PMOI members to the Iranian regime, who were later executed (Agence France-Presse, 13 April 1991).

The next morning we emerged from our concrete bunkers to face another day in Baghdad. We were heading for the US Embassy, a vast complex covering hundreds of acres inside the Green Zone, and a routine target for terrorist mortar attacks. We had to go through tight security checks to get into the Embassy compound, and then we were led in to a large study and offered seats while tea and coffee were prepared. In due course US Ambassador Jim Jeffrey and a senior American diplomat stationed in Iraq, Ambassador Lawrence Butler, arrived.

I thanked the US ambassadors for their time and hospitality, and told them of my fears that Maliki was rapidly becoming a dictator, having breached the Erbil Agreement and seizing all of the key state powers for himself; I said he had clearly demonstrated his willingness to do the bidding of the Iranian Mullahs and to abuse his position as Prime Minister by ordering repeated violent military assaults on Ashraf and subjecting the residents to constant psychological torture.

Ambassador Jeffrey opened the proceedings by stating:

> The EU are our real partners. Iraq will be a major player in the new Middle East that emerges from the current upheavals. There is a fledgling democratic system here, rocky but beginning to come together. Security is improving. Attacks are down by 90% and US casualties are down. Electricity demand is rising faster than their system can cope with. Oil production is up from 2 million barrels a day to 2.1 million barrels per day and will reach 2.3 million barrels soon. In two to three years it will reach 3 million barrels per day. Iraq has around two thirds of the oil of Saudi Arabia, but there is a shortage of oil infrastructure because it currently has to be funded out of the capital budget. The US will certainly withdraw by the end of this year, although we will continue to train the police.
>
> I agree with Mr Stevenson on the need for the Erbil Agreement to be fulfilled. I participated in the drawing up and signing of that agreement and it is not acceptable that the three sensitive ministries have yet to be filled. Having said that, Maliki asked Ayad Allawi to draw up a list of five candidates and to choose one of them to be the Defence Minister. Allawi drew up the list, chose a candidate and submitted it to Maliki.

Maliki agreed and then Allawi changed his mind and said he no longer wanted this candidate. So Allawi is as much to blame for the hiatus as Maliki.

Iran is the most negative about it, as they don't want Allawi getting his hands on any power. Muqtada al-Sadr is an awful person and he leads an awful party who are in thrall to Tehran. He won 39 seats and does Iran's bidding.

It was quite astonishing that the American Ambassador was clearly trying to whitewash the role of Maliki in destroying the Erbil Agreement, while simultaneously trying to shift the blame onto Ayad Allawi. He said:

The MEK claim that they are protected persons under the Fourth Geneva Convention, but they know this to be untrue, as it was rescinded in writing together with all of their other rights of protection by the US military when our combat operations in Iraq ended. There will be no US forces left in Iraq by the end of this year, and the MEK cannot look to us for protection. They seem to think that the US Seventh Cavalry is going to come riding over the hill to protect them, but it is a dream. The Iraqis could cut off their electricity and water supplies during the summer when temperatures soar above 50 degrees centigrade and the camp will be finished. It doesn't only need military force to end Ashraf, and the MEK has to realise this.

When Ambassador Jeffrey was confronted with my protests at the irresponsible attitude of the US in this humanitarian issue, he changed his tone and said: 'Look, we are keen to help and we are keen to ensure that no-one will use military force to put pressure on Ashraf.'

I was dismayed, not only by the reluctance of the Americans to denounce Maliki as a criminal dictator, but also by their parroted criticism of the Ashrafis. They almost seemed keen to justify the massacre of the Ashraf residents three weeks earlier, and to whitewash the inaction of the US military in failing to fulfil its commitments.

It seemed as if they were also keen to renege on their guarantee of protection that the US military had pledged to every single Ashrafi. This was certainly a betrayal, and it depressed me to think that we were now being confronted by an ultimatum to close Ashraf by the year-end, and that the Americans were even backing this. However, the attitude of the Americans simply strengthened my resolve not to give up, but rather to campaign even harder to protect the residents of Ashraf and to find a peaceful solution to their plight.

24

Interviews with PMOI Refugees in Camp Liberty, August 2014

Hossein Farzanehsa

'My name is Hossein Farzanehsa. I was born in 1953 in an educated, prosperous family in Tehran. My father was one of the supporters of Prime Minister Dr Mohammad Mossadegh who was overthrown in an Anglo-American coup in 1953. My high school years coincided with the emergence of resistance organisations against the Shah. I entered university in 1972, which coincided with the celebrations of the coronation of the King. I was arrested and spent 15 days in jail. Two years later my brother Majid entered teacher-training college, and in 1976, due to his political activities, was arrested and sentenced to life in prison.

In prison he joined the PMOI. Once, when I had gone to visit my brother in jail, accidently I saw the leader of the PMOI, Massoud Rajavi, who was there with other prisoners to see their families. The families of the political prisoners played an important role in freeing their loved ones. Maryam Rajavi was responsible for coordinating the families of the political prisoners. Every Tuesday when we went to Qasr Prison, she used to give us specific guidelines to contact human rights organisations and journalists. My mother and I went to visit my brother Majid in prison every Tuesday.

After the revolution, the regime's attempts to monopolise power led to severe restrictions of civil liberties. On the other hand the Mojahedin National Movement in Tehran and other provinces started to form and grow. At this time all my family members were actively involved in the Mojahedin National Movement. My brother Majid was responsible for the student movement in Tehran, my sister Mahshid and I were active in the University of Tehran. My mother was active in the workers' movement and would accompany the Mojahedin to give speeches at different factories. Alireza and Fatimeh who were twins were active in the student movement as well.

Along with the growth of the Mojahedin National Movement the Khomeini regime kept on limiting people's freedoms on a daily basis; this went on until 20 June 1981. On this day in an unannounced demonstration, over 500,000 people in Tehran rallied, demanding their freedom. Khomeini ordered his guards to fire on the demonstrators, leaving many dead, and many more were arrested. My brother and sister Alireza and Fatimeh, who were only 15 at the time, along with my mother, were arrested. My mother managed to escape the guards after a few hours, but Alireza and Fatimeh were both put in prison for three years.

Following this event, the security forces would attack people's homes, and after arresting supporters or members of the PMOI, they would execute them. On 8 April 1981, my sister Mahshid and her husband Mohammad Moghadam, who were accompanying Massoud Rajavi's Deputy, Mousa Khiabani, and Massoud's wife, Ashraf Rajavi, were killed. After the martyrdom of my sister, the Revolutionary Guards attacked our home and arrested my father. They took my father and showed him my sister's body. They pressured him to cooperate with them but he resisted. At the age of 62 they put him in prison, where he suffered three heart attacks. They kept on taking him out of the prison and bringing him back time after time. He died of a heart attack in 1985.

The Revolutionary Guards killed my brother Majid on 9 June 1982 in Tehran. In August 1982 the house that I was living in was attacked, and five PMOI members were martyred as a result. I was able to escape the mayhem and go to another home. After a few months my friends helped me to go to Turkey, where I was able to reunite with the Mojahedin. In 1988, during the operation Eternal Light, my brother Alireza who was 23 years old at the time and was released from prison in 1985, was martyred. My wife Soraya Adibi was also martyred in that operation.

Years later, during the siege on Ashraf in 2008, I was diagnosed with prostate cancer. I had to wait for a month for an anaesthesiologist to come to Ashraf to have an operation. The lack of access to treatment in Ashraf and Liberty has caused serious problems for me. My cancer has spread, reaching a point of no return, and as a result I have to suffer on a daily basis.'

124

25
Erbil

We flew out of Baghdad on 28 April 2011 and headed to Erbil, capital of Kurdistan. The Kurdistan Regional Government (KRG) had maintained peace and stability for the past decade by sealing their border with the rest of Iraq, patrolling it with over 130,000 fierce Peshmerga militia. By stopping the incursion of terrorists and suicide bombers who were wreaking havoc on an almost daily basis throughout the rest of Iraq, the KRG had been able to develop healthy economic growth and relative prosperity. Kurdistan had also become a safe-haven for tens of thousands of refugees displaced by the Iraqi insurgency, and despite a lack of adequate housing, schools, hospitals and basic commodities, the Kurds were, nevertheless, willing to open their doors to Christians, Turkmen, Shabaks, Yazidis and other persecuted minorities who were fleeing for their lives.

Our first meeting was with Dr Barham Saleh, the KRG Prime Minister. He said: 'The quality of life here in Kurdistan is better than elsewhere in Iraq. We are moving towards 24 hours per day electricity supply from a position of only 12 hours last year. We should manage 18 hours per day this summer. But the PUK and KDP dominate Kurdish politics, and the "Facebook Generation" wants something different. The Opposition protesters demand an end to corruption and better services and jobs. We have had 60 days of riots in Iraq. Two clerics who were at the centre of calls for the overthrow of our government have been released from prison, actually against my better judgement, but this shows that the KRG cannot influence the independence of the courts here. There is not a single person in detention for political offences in Kurdistan.'

We went on to meet with the Speaker of the Kurdistan Parliament, Dr Kemal Kerkuki, before driving for some distance out of the bustling metropolis of Erbil to the Presidential Palace in Salahaddin, where we were met on the imposing steps of the huge building by

President Massoud Barzani. The President is an impressive person. He wears a traditional Peshmerga military commander's khaki uniform with a colourful turban on his head, making him seem taller than he actually is. President Barzani said: 'The uprisings in the Middle East mark a major turning point for the entire region. We have some major challenges in Iraq and I have only a two-term presidency. Terrorism is now our major problem, together with lack of services and corruption.'

I pressed the President on Ashraf. His response was very different to what I had heard from his party colleague Zebari in Baghdad and from the President of Iraq, Talabani, both of whom were Kurds. He said: 'This was a very sad and appalling affair. Thousands of people took refuge in Ashraf and it was shameful to do this to them. They must be protected. It is their right as long as they are our guests in Iraq and until there is regime change in Iran. I have told Maliki this, and expressed my deep concern.'

When we returned to Erbil, I was informed that Dr Ayad Allawi, the leader of al-Iraqiya and the actual winner of the last elections in Iraq, had travelled to Kurdistan to meet me. We met in a business room of our hotel, and Dr Allawi stated: 'The massacre at Ashraf was a black mark on Iraq's movement towards democracy. The human and moral side of this issue has been violated. These people should have been protected. It was done simply to please Iran.'

Dr Allawi told me that he had written to Maliki expressing four points:

1. The need for Iraq-Iran talks on Ashraf.
2. The need for talks between the Iraqi government and the MEK leadership in Ashraf.
3. The need for involvement of the UN in these talks.
4. The need for the involvement of the international community.

He continued:

We need an absolute assurance from Iran that they will stop meddling in our internal affairs. I would be happy to see the

126

3,400 Ashraf residents repatriated to the EU, but I fear that will take a long time. We need an interim solution, but not one that involves intimidation, killing and physical harm being used as a political tool. This does not represent a move towards democracy. This represents a move towards dictatorship!

Unfortunately it seems what Maliki is doing in Iraq is supported by the UN and the US. There were nine conditions agreed in the Erbil Agreement. None of them have been implemented. Instead, we have a series of oppressive institutions set up under the direct control of Maliki. He has two or three brigades and an intelligence outfit similar to the one Saddam used to have, as well as a so-called anti-terrorist group. All are answerable to Maliki and take their orders directly from him. When al-Iraqiya agreed to share power with him we did so in good faith, all to no avail.

There has been no division of labour. The economy is stagnant; the security situation is actually getting worse; 81 police and military personnel have been killed by pistols with silencers, at roadblocks and checkpoints, in the past 16 days.

I want to recreate the Erbil initiative again, but the international community fails to deal with this in a proper way. Meanwhile there are demonstrations across Iraq with many people killed and injured. Maliki responds by using sheer force against his own people. Many are arrested and held in secret prisons where they are tortured. We have a dictatorship in the making. I fought Saddam Hussein for 30 years and will never support a new dictatorship taking his place. We look to the EU for help.

Tehran had a red line on me becoming Prime Minister and that is why Maliki got the job. There is also huge corruption. This is a socialist economy. There is no free market.

We left Erbil from its spectacular new, marble , $500 million international airport, convinced that the autonomous region of Kurdistan has become a model of stability and economic progress for the rest of the Middle East to emulate. The Kurdish Regional Government has overseen massive inward investment, and the booming oil and gas industry has provided rapid economic growth. Erbil, the Kurdish capital, is now a mirror image of Western cities, with shopping malls, designer stores, luxury hotels and fine restaurants. Kurdistan stands as a shining example of what is possible in the rest of Iraq, if peace could be restored and a government of national salvation put in place. The Kurds also have a much more open society and a tolerance of alcohol which is missing in the rest of Iraq, so the cafes and bistros bustle with tourists and business people of every conceivable culture and religion. Terrifyingly, this haven of peace and prosperity has become a key target for the ISIS terrorists, and at the time of going to press, the Kurdish Peshmerga were fighting ferociously, assisted by US and coalition air strikes, to defend the borders of Kurdistan from an Islamic State incursion.

The oil sector in Kurdistan is, of course, a source of great wealth. Kurdish officials predict that Kurdistan could surpass Libya's output by 2019 by producing two million barrels per day, putting it on the list of oil-producing giants. But oil is a mixed blessing. It has strained relations with Iraq's central government in Baghdad, who regard many of the lucrative new Kurdish oil contracts as illegal. This has led to frequent violent clashes in the disputed border city of Kirkuk, which sits on top of one of the biggest oil fields in Iraq, ownership of which is claimed by both Baghdad and Erbil. As tensions mount, so pressure for Kurdish independence surges; it has long been a Kurdish dream to establish a 'Greater Kurdistan' connecting all of the Kurdish-inhabited areas of Iran, Iraq, Turkey and Syria. Indeed, the Kurdish diaspora is now reckoned to number over 40 million people worldwide, perhaps one of the greatest ethnic populations on earth with no actual homeland.

While Turkey and Iran remain opposed to the creation of an independent Kurdistan, the Turkish government has nevertheless pragmatically opened its borders with Iraqi Kurdistan and encouraged massive inward investment. It is largely Turkish businesses that have built the new infrastructure in Erbil and other Kurdish cities. Construction of a new oil pipeline linking Kurdistan and Turkey was completed in 2014.

All of this is a far cry from the horrific violence and oppression suffered by the Kurds under Saddam Hussein. Saddam's Ba'ath Party

Struan Stevenson meeting Prime Minister Nechirvan Barzani of Kurdistan, Erbil, November 2013.

Struan with PMOI protesters outside the UN headquarters in Geneva.

More than 100,000 people attending the PMOI rally at Villepinte, Paris, June 2013.

Struan with PMOI protesters outside the White House, Washington DC, July 2006.

Alejo Vidal-Quadras and Struan welcome Mrs Rajavi to the European Parliament, Brussels.

Struan hosts a press conference in Brussels for Iraqi Vice-President, Dr Tariq al-Hashemi, on 16 October 2013. On his left is Sid Ahmed Ghozali, former Prime Minister of Algeria.

Struan and Sheikh Dr Rafie al-Rafaee, the Grand Mufti of Iraq, at a conference in the European Parliament, Brussels, on 19 February 2014.

Struan with Patrick Kennedy at an NCRI rally at Villepinte, Paris.

Struan addressing the 'illegal' PMOI rally from a grassy knoll in Berlin, 10 February 2005.

(L-R) The late Lord Slynn of Hadley, Paulo Casaca MEP, Mrs Maryam Rajavi, Struan Stevenson MEP and Alejo Vidal-Quadras MEP, at a Friends of a Free Iran meeting in the European Parliament, Strasbourg.

Struan meeting President Massoud Barzani of Kurdistan in his palace in Salahaddin, Northern Iraq.

Struan with President Talabani of Iraq, Baghdad, April 2011.

Struan attending the PMOI's International Women's Day Rally in Berlin, March 2015.

The landscaped grounds and gardens of Camp Ashraf.

Mud and rock-strewn ground surround flimsy portacabins at Camp Liberty.

launched the infamous Anfal Campaign against the Kurds in 1986. This genocidal operation continued until 1989, and included the use of ground offensives, aerial bombing, systematic destruction of settlements, mass deportations, firing squads and chemical warfare. It is estimated that up to 100,000 non-combatant civilians, including women and children, were killed. The total death toll during Operation Anfal amounted to over 180,000. Around 4,500 Kurdish villages were razed to the ground. Schools, hospitals, mosques and churches were flattened.

But there are signs of a fresh start. A rash of new schools and universities are opening their doors across Kurdistan, offering hope of a better future to the next generation of Kurds. Meanwhile Kurdistan has become a magnet for refugees fleeing from the insurgency in the rest of Iraq, and from the civil war in neighbouring Syria. The West owes a debt of gratitude to President Massoud Barzani for the protection he has offered to these refugees. Kurdistan is a shining example of how peace and stability can in turn create economic growth and how economic growth has created jobs and prosperity for the Kurdish people and a sense of responsibility for persecuted minorities from neighbouring conflicts. It is of grave concern that the steady advance of the terrorist Islamic State (formerly ISIS) now threatens Kurdistan with a return to the days of genocidal war. Western intervention to back the Kurdish Peshmerga in their battle against the jihadists is essential, and is fair reward for Kurdistan's hospitality and protection for hundreds of thousands of refugees over the past decade.

26

Interviews with PMOI Refugees in Camp Liberty, September 2014

Mohammad Shafaei

'My name is Mohammad Shafaei. I was born in 1973 in Isfahan, Iran. I was studying medicine at the University of North Carolina at Greensboro, US. I was a sophomore student when I left the school to join the PMOI. All my family members were either PMOI members or supporters. In 1981, when I was 8 years old, the Mullahs' regime executed my father, Dr Morteza Shafaei, along with my mother, Efat Khalifeh Soltani, and my 16-year-old brother, Majid Shafaei. One year later, in 1982, my 27-year-old brother was tortured to death in the notorious Evin Prison. That same year, my 24-year-old sister, Maryam Shafaei and her husband, Hossein Jalil Parvane, were shot dead by the Revolutionary Guards (IRGC) in the streets of Tehran. My only surviving family member, my sister Zohreh Shafaei, was jailed in 1981 and released several years later.

With this background, I knew the PMOI from my childhood. I didn't know much about them at that time and I was not of an age to judge what is good and what is bad. I didn't know really why I'd lost all my family members. Why were they killed? I just loved my family and I knew that they were good people.

When I was 18 years old, I decided to leave Iran in order to escape the suppression of the Mullahs' dictatorship. When I went to the US, I had a better environment to investigate what is right and wrong. So, alongside my studies at the university, I researched about the PMOI; its goals, position, plans for Iran, its motivations and ideology and so on. I tried to get more engaged with the organization to identify it better. I started reading their publications, talking with their supporters, taking part in their gatherings and so on. I was very curious to find out if they were either on a right path or a wrong one. When I was in Iran, some people warned me not to engage in politics in order to enjoy life's beauties. Some supporters of the Mullahs, who knew my family background, warned me not to join the Mojahedin simply because my family members were PMOI supporters. They tried their hardest to demolish the reputation of the Mojahedin. So, with all these things happening, I wanted to decide my future with open eyes.

In 1981, Khomeini's regime closed down all the PMOI official headquarters in different cities and arrested members. So the PMOI had to hold its meetings in its supporters' houses. In the city of Isfahan, our home was the place for running such meetings and activities. On 2 May 1981 there was a meeting held in our home. At the end of the meeting, a crowd started demonstrating on nearby streets. The IRGC attacked the demonstrators and raided our home, which led to the arrest of my Mum and some others who were still inside the house. That was the first time that my Mum was arrested. They released her after a few days.

About two months later, when my Mum, Dad and I were at home, some Pasdars – agents of the IRGC – knocked on our door and asked for my Dad. They told us they had several questions, and they would bring him back within 30 minutes. He never came back and that was last time I ever saw my Dad. A few days later, the same thing happened to my Mum; Pasdars came and asked my Mum to accompany them. I began weeping. My Mum kissed me and told me: "I will never return. They didn't bring your Dad back and they won't bring me back." For a kid at the age of eight, there is nothing more precious than his Mum. So, I lost my control. I was hysterical. I attacked the IRGC agent by kicking and punching him. The Pasdar laughed at me and humiliated me. I could not see any mercy in his face but only hate and brutality.

Because there was no one left at our home to take care of me, my Mum asked our neighbour if she would look after me. The IRGC agents took my Mum and left me with a deep pain in my heart. A few days later, my uncle (my father's brother) who was living in the city of Shiraz, came and adopted me.

On one occasion I was taken to a prison to see my Mum. I passed through a huge gate. There was a jungle-like yard with large trees. I couldn't see any buildings there. They took me in and I was waiting beside a tree. They brought my Mum. She tightly embraced me.

I was kissing her. I was desperate for her love. I was so happy to see my Mum again, but my cheer turned to sorrow very soon. They told me in front of her that I wouldn't be allowed to see my Mum again. They obviously wanted to use me as a tool to pressure my Mum into denouncing the PMOI. They started to insult her. They were telling her to go back to her ordinary life and have a good life with her little boy. They told her if she didn't care about herself, she should care about her poor son. They continued by telling her that there was nobody to raise this kid. With no good guardian, he would become a criminal very soon . . . My Mum never paid any attention to them. She kissed me, and told me that she would never get back home and I would have to be strong. My Dad, Mum and Majid, my 16-year-old brother, were executed along with 50 other Mojahedin supporters in Isfahan on 27 September 1981.

While I was studying in the US, the more I researched about Mojahedin, the more I tried to engage in their activities. So I decided to move to Washington D.C. and enrol at George Mason University, to have the opportunity to get more involved in the PMOI movement which had a headquarters in Washington. In that period, I had the opportunity to meet some of the PMOI members. Most of them were former university students. One of them had quit school while he was working on his Ph.D. thesis. Another one was about to get his Master's degree, and so on. When I was looking at these people, I could see my dreams come to reality. These were clearly very good people with great morals and human values. Associating with them made me think about my own life more deeply. I could not continue my normal life any more. I could not think only about my own ambitions any longer. I was faced with a series of questions in my mind. These people I had met, like me, wanted to continue their studies. But if they didn't quit their schools, who would remain to fight in the front line against the Mullahs? Why should I remain idle and ask others to free my country?

On the other hand I was telling myself: "Why not finish your studies and become a good physician? In this case, you can benefit your people more. You have suffered too much already. It is enough. Why not enjoy your life? Get your Ph.D. in Harvard or Johns Hopkins University and become a well-respected person with a voice who can better represent your people and your country." This was a real dilemma. There was a growing fight inside me – many questions and answers. One night, that struggle reached its peak. It was the hardest moment in my life. I had reached the point where a decision had to be made. I could not escape from that decision, since I had enough knowledge of what was right and what was wrong. I didn't have any doubt about the rightness of the PMOI.

During my engagement with the organisation for more than a year, I realised that the PMOI had dedicated itself to the Iranian people and to free my beloved country. I made sure that the organisation was not fighting for its own benefit or simply for gaining power in Iran. I had reached a decision. I decided to become a Mojahed and devote my life to a free Iran. I decided to go to the front line and be a real freedom fighter. The National Liberation Army of Iran's base was in Iraq, so I decided to go to Iraq via Jordan. I quit my school. I packed up my belongings and left the US. I arrived in Baghdad on 7 April 1996.

In Ashraf I started to learn so many things, from how to drive and fire a Chieftain tank to computer science technology and the Arabic language. Now, I am a computer programmer. Before the Second Gulf War, I was a Chieftain tank gunner. I was also teaching computer science in Iran University at Ashraf. After the war, I mostly concentrated on developing required computer applications to computerise our workflows and systems in Ashraf.

I also learned many things from other Mojahedin in Ashraf. I learned how to sacrifice more and more for others. I learned how this sacrifice unites people and makes them love each other. I learned how to ignore others' faults and help them fill their gaps and fix their mistakes. In my whole life, I was dreaming of studying in top universities in the US. Finally, I ended up at Ashraf, which gave me more than a university education. It was a fabulous community of humanity, a utopia for any freedom fighter.

When I was in the US, I discovered that the Mojahedin never married. They dedicate all their energy to their cause. Men and women work closely together as brothers and sisters. I lived in Iran for some years. I could see how cruel the Mullahs are and how difficult it is to overthrow them. When I was in the process of making a decision to join the PMOI, I could guess that I would face many ups and downs, many pains and gains. I knew that it was not easy to be a warrior. I knew that I would have to sacrifice many things. I may get arrested like my family, or be executed like my Dad and Mum or be tortured like my brother. I was thinking about my Mum in that period. I may find myself in a situation where I have to make a tough decision, as my mother did. She had to choose between having a quiet life with her son having surrendered to the Mullahs, or to leave her son with no guardian and to stand firm on her position against the Mullahs.

Over many years, the Mullahs have plumbed the depths of atrocities and brutality. Some days I think about the street children in Iran; they are a Mullah-created phenomenon. I think about the innocent girls who are being trafficked under the Mullahs' misogynistic regime. They are my sisters and brothers. They are my sons and daughters. So although as a Mojahed I never married, I have a family. I am proud to have such a large family. I have all of them in my heart. I love them all. I dream of a day in a free Iran that every Iranian child can have a prosperous and safe future; so although I decided not to marry and shape my own family, my family now is the most populated family that anyone can imagine.

In Ashraf and Liberty, I was in a position to go to Iraqi hospitals as a companion and interpreter for our patients. I faced many attempts by mercenaries of the Iranian regime inside the Iraqi forces to sabotage those hospital visits and to interrupt the PMOI patients' therapy. I recall one badly wounded person who had been run over by an Iraqi armoured vehicle during Maliki's 2009 attack on Ashraf. He needed immediate surgery in one of Baghdad's private hospitals, but the Iraqi forces prevented him from going, using the lame excuse that he could be cured in a public hospital. Finally, I took him to that private hospital where he was operated on by a professional surgeon. He told me that the patient would never return to his normal life because of the long delay between the onset of his injury and the date of his operation.

Any time I accompanied a patient to a hospital we were watched by an agent from the Iraqi intelligence service, who stayed with us in the hospital 24 hours a day. His job was to intimidate doctors into denying treatment for the PMOI patient. He lay on a bed beside the PMOI patient all day and night. He did not allow me to communicate with the patient or the doctors. When I wanted to speak English to the doctors or nurses about my patient, he would yell at me, saying, "Speak Arabic." He told me, "You want to speak English with people to pass on propaganda about the Mojahedin instead of following the medical process."

One night, at 2 o'clock in the morning, one of my colleagues had a heart attack. I called the hospital in Camp Liberty. There was just one doctor on duty, and there was no oxygen available there to let my patient breathe. It took about two hours before the Iraqi police allowed us to go to Yarmuk Hospital in Baghdad, and my patient was having continuous heart attacks. On our way to the hospital, the police commander stopped us at a gas station. I told him that my patient was at the point of death and that we shouldn't stop on the way to the hospital. But he refused to listen. His orders were to cause us maximum pain. We finally reached the hospital with only minutes to spare and managed to save my friend. But we face such harassment on a daily basis.'

27

The Stevenson Plan

It was clear from all the discussions I'd had in Iraq that an urgent agreement, acceptable to the Iraqi government, the PMOI and the international community, had to be found to resolve the ongoing crisis in Camp Ashraf. Ad Melkert, the UN Secretary General's representative in Iraq, had specifically asked me to make contact with the leadership of the Ashraf refugees at their headquarters in Paris, to explore possible avenues for a long-term resolution. So, on my return to the EU from Iraq, I travelled immediately to Paris and engaged in intense discussions with Mrs Maryam Rajavi, Mohammad Mohaddessin, the foreign affairs spokesman for the PMOI, and other members of the leadership of the Iranian opposition movement. We made frequent conference calls to Ashraf to consult the PMOI leadership there. Together, we thrashed out a plan that provided the only viable alternative to violence and further bloodshed.

I realised that, without their agreement, there was little hope of a just, long-term solution. But there was considerable reluctance from the Ashrafis. They justifiably argued that Ashraf had been their home for almost three decades. Their friends and colleagues who had died were buried there. They had invested tens of millions of dollars on the development of the camp. They didn't want to move.

The proposal required the active involvement of the UN, the US and the EU. It recognised the Iraqi government's right of sovereignty over its own territory. But it also encompassed the rights of the 3,400 unarmed residents of Ashraf to protection under the Fourth Geneva Convention. The scheme laid the groundwork for negotiations involving the Iraqi government and set out a proposal to re-settle all of the refugees to countries of safety like the US, Canada, Australia, Norway, Switzerland and the 27 EU Member States, depending on . where they had previous associations, connections or family contacts.

The proposal, known as 'The Stevenson Plan' contained the following important pre-conditions:

Pre-conditions for any negotiation

In order to begin the negotiation for a long-term solution, the following conditions need to be met:

- Removal of Iraqi forces from the perimeter of Ashraf.

- An end to the siege of Ashraf (including lifting the ban on access to journalists, parliamentary groups, lawyers and family members of the residents).

- Immediate access of the residents, in particular those wounded, to medical services of public hospitals and private clinics in Iraq at their own expense.

- An independent Inquiry by a panel of jurists being launched into the incident of April 8, 2011 during which 35 residents were killed and hundreds wounded.

- Returning all the belongings confiscated on April 8 to Ashraf residents.

The plan envisaged groups of residents being moved from Ashraf to a new location, where they could be individually interviewed and registered as refugees by the UNHCR in a 'revolving door' system that would see them re-settled to countries of safety within weeks of being registered as refugees. I envisioned groups of up to 500 Ashrafis at a time being relocated to the new camp, interviewed and registered by UNHCR, then shipped out to countries of safety, almost before the next batch of 500 from Ashraf arrived. The plan also embraced the idea of UN 'blue-helmets' on permanent deployment at the camp to provide protection for the residents.

We all agreed that the security situation facing the refugees at Camp Ashraf had been in a perilous state for far too long. What was needed now was for all the main parties concerned to show the political will to resolve the situation once and for all and to ensure that justice prevailed over brutality. I tabled my plan at the next meeting of the Delegation for Relations with Iraq in the European Parliament and it was unanimously agreed. We also got the backing of the Foreign Affairs Committee of the Parliament. I then asked for the support of Baroness Ashton. Following the April massacre, Ashton, the EU's High Representative for Foreign Affairs, had called for a strong and united EU response and an immediate inquiry into the killings. She now agreed to support the 'Stevenson Plan'. Of equal importance was the fact that my plan also received active support from several political factions inside the Iraqi Parliament, including a letter signed by 74 Iraqi MPs.

So we had taken a decisive step towards solving the Ashraf crisis by convincing the residents to leave Iraq, while reaching a practical solution acceptable to the camp's residents, which would also serve the interests of the Iraqi government. This was a huge victory. But the reality was the Iranian regime had no intention of arriving at a peaceful resolution to the Ashraf crisis. The intentions of the Mullahs in Tehran were entirely destructive.

While we in the European Parliament, together with Mrs Rajavi, the PMOI, NCRI and other friends of the Iranian resistance, had started a campaign to sort out the transfer of the residents to third countries, suddenly we heard that the American diplomat, Larry Butler, had shown up in Ashraf, urging and threatening the residents to accept his plan to move to another camp inside Iraq. In fact the US government began to put pressure on Ashraf in line with the policies of the Iranian regime and Maliki, against the interests of the residents.

His concept, again aimed at clearing Ashraf of all of its residents within the timescale set by Maliki and before the departure of the last of the US troops from Iraq, involved re-locating groups of Ashrafis to a series of different former US bases spread across Iraq. The Ashrafis, who said that this played directly into the Iranian Mullahs' 'divide and rule strategy', understandably vetoed this idea. They feared that once they were split up into smaller groups they could be annihilated at will, away from public view. They said they would rather stay within the fragile confines of Ashraf, where at least the world was watching and where it was more difficult for Maliki and his Iranian puppeteers to mount another massacre. But in any case, Larry Butler put a lot of US diplomatic effort into promoting his plan and it diverted much of our focus for at least three months, while we tried to convince people that it was a bad idea and that the Stevenson Plan was the only viable alternative. Butler had arrogantly even threatened the people in Ashraf with the prospect that if they did not move, then 'Soon we will have to mourn at your funeral!'

Both the residents and Tahar Boumedra, who used to go with Larry Butler to Ashraf every week at that time, gave me regular reports on the situation. It was very clear to us that the idea of relocation within Iraq was in direct contradiction to our plan for evacuating all of the residents out of Iraq. At that time Ad Melkert was the UN Secretary General's special envoy to Iraq and he refused to collaborate with the US plan for relocation within Iraq because he was fully aware that such a plan would be harmful to the residents.

Butler visited Ashraf seven or eight times between May and July and deployed all sorts of pressure to try to force the residents to leave Ashraf for another camp. The residents categorically rejected his demands. They said only if the US would accept full responsibility for the protection of any new camp would they even consider such a transfer. The Ashrafis offered several different plans of their own by way of a compromise. One of their suggestions was that all of the residents would be transferred to the US and held temporarily under surveillance, while other candidate countries were found for their permanent residence. Another was that the US would ask a friendly neighbour like Turkey, Jordan, Kuwait or Saudi Arabia to allocate a piece of arid land so the residents could build it up themselves as a temporary safe haven while permanent homes in third countries were found. But the US rejected all of these ideas. It seemed they were keen to avoid anything that might upset the Mullahs.

Butler's last trip to Ashraf was combined with a deeply immoral act for an official envoy. He had brought with him a *New York Times* journalist whom he falsely introduced as an American diplomat. The subsequent article written by this journalist was published on 23 July in the *New York Times*. Two weeks later this dishonest action was criticised by the *New York Times'* own editor in an article entitled: 'A reporter shields his identity and an Iranian exile group's viewpoint goes missing.'

I and other MEPs repeatedly insisted that all our energy and efforts must be focused on transferring the residents directly from Ashraf to third countries; finally Butler's plan was ditched and he had to leave Iraq with his tail between his legs. Ambassador David E. Lindwall, who in his first trip to Ashraf on September 2011 stressed that the idea of relocation to camps within Iraq belonged to the past, replaced him.

When we got rid of Butler in July, everything began to get back on track. But now we had to resolve another problem involving the UN High Commissioner for Refugees (UNHCR). The residents rightly stressed that the PMOI had been recognised as political refugees in Iraq since 1986, and that as such the UNHCR should recognise them collectively as political refugees and start looking for third countries to which they could be safely relocated *en masse*.

The UNHCR did not accept this argument, and said that first of all each person would have to resign from the PMOI and then ask for political asylum as individuals. The NCRI and many world-class jurists published legal opinions strongly rejecting the UNHCR claims. I, along with Alejo Vidal-Quadras and some influential American friends of the Iranian resistance, also expressed our opposition and the UNHCR finally accepted that membership of the PMOI was not related to becoming a political refugee.

So, on 24 August 2011, I travelled to the UN headquarters in Geneva to get the approval of the UN High Commissioner for Refugees, António Guterres, to the Stevenson Plan. I described my April visit to Iraq only days after the massacre at Camp Ashraf had taken place, and I explained that none of the key points of the Erbil Agreement had been implemented; that Prime Minister Nouri al-Maliki was therefore in full control of both the military and security forces, which ultimately gave him the power of a dictator and the ability to carry out attacks on Ashraf. I outlined the key conditions of the Stevenson Plan and asked for his support.

António Guterres expressed equal concern over the massacre and stated that the UNHCR had been working toward and had achieved a better relationship with the Iraqi Ministry of Migration and Displacement (MoMD). Nevertheless, he stated that it had always been a challenge to engage with Prime Minister al-Maliki. He further explained that he had sent al-Maliki a letter the previous week concerning the very serious human rights and humanitarian problems in Camp Ashraf and had requested an extension of six months to the closing date of the camp, which had been set for the end of 2011. He said his letter also described what the UNHCR was willing to do to resolve the situation, given the fact that Iraq was not a signatory of the 1951 Human Rights Convention.

He explained that the biggest problem the residents of Camp Ashraf faced was the refusal by potential receiving countries to take any of them. To explain this, he mentioned that a first group of 200 people had applied for refugee status with the UNHCR in Baghdad, yet until now not one of them had been resettled. He stated that a more open attitude towards resettlement was crucial to unblock this situation, implying that the Ashrafis themselves were resisting leaving the camp. I told Guterres that the Italian embassy was leading the way in their new attitude towards resettlement, having already issued seven visas for people with serious illnesses and injuries due to the attack in April, and had begun the process of issuing another seven.

With regard to *prima facie* refugee status for the residents of Camp Ashraf, Guterres stated that the UNHCR was unable to grant refugee status for a 'blanket group' in this case, since the residents of Camp Ashraf had different backgrounds.

I mentioned that one of the roadblocks to resettlement in the US was that the PMOI remained on the US State Department list of Foreign Terrorist Organisations (FTO). Nevertheless, I explained, the federal courts in Washington D.C. had ruled that there was absolutely no reason for the PMOI to remain on this list and it was expected that a reviewed list was to be issued, hopefully within the next few days. Andrew Harper, Head of the UNHCR's Iraq Support Unit, added that the PMOI were also on FTO lists in Australia and Canada, which are the other two major receiving countries with regard to refugees. However, if they were to be removed from the US foreign terrorist organisation list, Australia and Canada would most likely follow suit.

I ended the meeting by stating that the US and Canadian embassies had been to Ashraf to study the situation, and I enquired whether anyone from the UNHCR had visited Camp Ashraf. Guterres replied that they had requested a joint mission with UNAMI, which would take place within the next few days. I thanked Guterres for his efforts and said that I would immediately convey to the residents of Ashraf the urgent need for each to write a letter to the UN seeking refugee status. I passed this news to lawyers representing Camp Ashraf. Within four days, 3,400 letters were duly delivered to Guterres in Geneva.

In September 2011, we had a feeling of triumph, believing that we had made a big step forward. We were looking for a suitable place for UNHCR to hold their interviews. UNHCR officials had checked various locations and chosen some sections of Ashraf as suitable for interviews and had even started preparations. The interviews were scheduled to begin in October. But again the Iranian regime, Maliki and the USA, this time through UNAMI and the UN envoy in Iraq, raised obstacles by again insisting on the relocation of all 3,400 residents within Iraq.

Maliki disliked Ad Melkert, and in a blatant act of political capitulation Ban Ki-moon decided not to renew his term in Iraq; at the end of August 2011, Melkert left the country for good. The farewell meeting between Melkert and Maliki turned into a diplomatic incident because of Ashraf. The *Washington Post* headline of 29 August 2011 was: 'On last day in Baghdad, UN envoy denies embracing Iraqi PM's plan to deport Camp Ashraf exiles'. The article added:

> The departing head of the U.N. mission in Iraq on Monday bluntly disputed Prime Minister Nouri al-Maliki's account of their farewell meeting, saying he did not embrace the government's efforts to deport a group of Iranian exiles by the end of the year. The public disavowal was rare for the U.N. office in Baghdad, which goes to great lengths to avoid engaging in political disputes. A deadly April raid on the camp by Iraqi forces drew international criticism of Baghdad's treatment of the group, and al-Maliki responded by pledging to deport the Ashraf residents by the end of the year. In a statement after they met to say goodbye Sunday, al-Maliki said U.N. envoy Ad Melkert affirmed U.N. support on a bevy of matters, 'including the issue of Camp Ashraf and the

necessity of implementing the Cabinet's decree to deport its residents outside Iraq by the end of this year.' In one of his last acts after two years as envoy to Iraq, the mild-mannered Melkert flatly said that was not true.

'The U.N. continues to advocate that Camp Ashraf residents be protected from forcible deportation, expulsion or repatriation,' Melkert's office said in a statement Monday. It said Melkert reiterated the position during his meeting Sunday with the prime minister.

28

Interviews with PMOI Refugees in Camp Liberty, September 2014

Amir Ali Seyed Ahmadi

'My name is Amir Ali Seyed Ahmadi and I was born in 1980 in Tehran. I continued my education to the second year of tech school. For some time in Tehran I was employed in various workshops carrying out the repair and maintenance of vehicles. I was born into a religious family, and by the time I was 6 months old, due to the fact that our house was raided by the armed forces of the regime for the "crime" of supporting the PMOI, all of my family members, including my mother and uncle, were killed. Due to the hatred the regime had for my mother, father and the PMOI, they held me inside Evin Prison for four years. There I was under the care of PMOI supporters. This was how I came to know the PMOI and how I began my political life. Two of my uncles were executed during the 1988 massacre of political prisoners and I went with my grandmother to receive their belongings. From then on I have always tried to get revenge for the blood of these martyrs and all the other martyrs who lost their lives in the pursuit of freedom and their quest to establish a popular, just and free state in Iran.

Following the July 1999 uprising staged by college students against the regime throughout the country, I began my activities as a supporter of the PMOI. A few months later I came to Ashraf and joined the National Liberation Army of Iran, because I saw them as the only solution to overthrowing this dictatorial regime. Following the 1988 massacre of political prisoners I will never forget my grandmother's resistance and dignity in the face of vicious Revolutionary Guards members when they gave her the belongings of her executed loved ones. They never even informed her about the location where her sons were buried. My aunt also suffered psychological problems resulting from the execution of her brothers and when I called her recently she was still suffering from these illnesses.

I came to Ashraf with the help of friends, and after three days of hiking I crossed the border into Iraq. Before the 2003 war I was a member of the NLA and I received the necessary training in order to carry out my duties in the war against the Mullahs' regime. After April 2003 and the US-led war against Iraq, we voluntarily handed over our weapons to US forces. After that, in Ashraf, I started working in trailer workshops, but Maliki's government – at the behest of the Iranian regime – prevented us from continuing these income-generating activities. This is a long story, but one cannot fight and lead an ordinary life at the same time. As a result, I decided to give my all so that my people could have everything.

During the July 2009 attack by Iraqi forces against Ashraf, one of my very good friends by the name of Sha'ban Souri received many blows to the head and face. He was suffering from extreme pain for many days afterwards. However, he didn't say anything and didn't allow anyone to realise the excruciating pain he was going through. As a result, 20 days later he suffered a stroke due to DVT, and he died in a helicopter while being transferred to a US hospital in Balad. I will never forget Sha'ban. Also my father was killed in the September 2013 massacre in Ashraf. When I see these scenes I become more determined than ever regarding the path I have chosen to overthrow this regime, and I pledge yet again to continue his path.

On 8 April 2011, I was hit in the leg with a metal rod wielded by the Iraqi forces attacking Ashraf. They attacked us just to prevent us from using one of the camp's roads. On that day I saw many scenes of sacrifice by my friends. We were all backing each other up. Thirteen of my close friends were injured and wounded in that attack, and two of them are still suffering from the blows they received to their heads.'

29

Martin Kobler

Martin Kobler, who came to Iraq at the end of October, replaced Melkert. He took up the Ashraf file in an unconventional manner. It seemed that everything had been decided before he arrived in Iraq. Clearly he had already reached agreements with Iran, Maliki and the US, who were determined to use him as a tool for promoting their plan for the total closure of Ashraf and the internal relocation of the 3,400 residents. They had settled on a new location called Camp Liberty, a former US military base near Baghdad airport. Maliki, with the backing of Kobler, prevented the UNHCR interviews from going ahead in Ashraf and stated that interviews would only be possible in Camp Liberty.

Here, it was proposed, the residents could be individually interviewed by UNHCR, registered as refugees and quickly flown out to countries of safety. The 'revolving door' strategy that I had lobbied hard for now seemed a reality. But first we had to assess the suitability of Camp Liberty and we had to convince the Ashraf residents to move there.

I had received news of Kobler's appointment in August 2011. I was informed that Kobler, a German diplomat and former advisor to the Green Party's former Foreign Minister, Joschka Fischer, had replaced Ad Melkert as the UN Secretary General's Special Representative. The news did not fill me with confidence. The Green Group in the European Parliament, dominated by the German Greens, were almost universally the biggest apologists for the Iranian Mullahs and, consequently, had a gut hatred of the PMOI instilled in them by the endless propaganda dished out by their friends in Tehran. I was constantly battling against outright prejudice from the Greens, and I was now alarmed that a Green had taken on the key role of Special Representative of the UN Secretary General in Iraq. My fears turned out to be well-founded. Ad Melkert had become increasingly critical

146

of Maliki and the UN was nervous that good relations with the Iraqi Prime Minister and his government were being jeopardised. They decided he had to be replaced by someone more compliant.

Kobler asked to meet me in Brussels in October 2011, before he went to Iraq to take up his post. He told me that he was coming to the European Parliament and said that he had arranged a special meeting room in which we could talk. I found this rather strange, as in my role as President of the Delegation for Relations with Iraq I had a large meeting room of my own attached to my office. I soon discovered why Kobler had arranged the meeting in this way. It was the first indication of his true agenda. I was not the only person he had invited to the meeting. He had summonsed his Green Party colleagues, all known enemies of the PMOI, including the senior Green Group foreign affairs advisor Sabine Meyer, also a German, with close links to the Iranian Embassy in Brussels. Meyer and I had crossed swords on many occasions. Her prejudice against the PMOI was visceral, and I suspected that she was being manipulated by the Iranian regime. I was disturbed that Kobler had chosen to invite unelected officials from the Greens to a meeting between him as an ambassador and me as a parliamentarian.

Kobler opened the meeting by stating that in his opinion I was the only person who could persuade Mrs Rajavi in Paris to order the 3,400 Ashraf residents to agree to relocation to a new camp inside Iraq. Kobler said that unless they re-located they would almost certainly be subjected to a violent assault, and he wanted to do everything in his power to avoid further bloodshed. I countered by stating that we should not tolerate threats of violence by Maliki, and that in any case, the leadership actually in Camp Ashraf would take the final decision on whether or not they would relocate. At this point Sabine Meyer interrupted me to say that I was talking rubbish and that the PMOI were an evil sect who took all of their orders from Maryam Rajavi. I was furious. 'How dare you interrupt,' I said. 'I am elected to serve as a Deputy in this House and I have been privileged to chair the Delegation for Relations with Iraq. I am not going to be interrupted and contradicted by a mere parliamentary official from the Green Group or indeed any other group.' Sabine's eyes flashed in anger. She tossed her long, blond hair aside and began scribbling furiously in her notebook. However, she took no further part in the meeting. For once I had silenced her!

I told Kobler that I had visited Iraq immediately following the massacre at Ashraf in April and had been denied permission to visit the camp by the Iraqi Foreign Minister himself. I bitterly condemned Maliki's government for the murderous attacks they had carried out, and I said it was appalling that we were now being threatened with more bloodshed unless we managed to vacate the camp by the end of the year. I explained to Kobler that if the real intention of the Iraqi government was to move all the Ashraf residents out of Iraq, then the best way surely was to transfer them from Ashraf to third countries; things would be much simpler and smoother, and I explained we had already spoken with UNHCR about it and they agreed with this idea. But, I argued, moving them to another place in Iraq would make things much more complicated, would delay the process and might endanger the residents more than before. I told Kobler that I agreed with the residents for not accepting a move to another camp inside Iraq. Of course, I accepted the reality of the situation and told Kobler that I would do what I could to help avoid any further bloodshed. I explained my initiative, which I had floated with Mrs Rajavi on my return from Iraq in the spring; Kobler said he liked the sound of the Stevenson Plan and he'd look into it, although what he was advocating was in clear contrast to my plan.

According to Tahar Boumedra, when Kobler finally arrived in Baghdad in October, he took everyone at UNAMI by surprise. From the outset, he stated that it was his single priority to get the 3,400 residents of Ashraf moved to another location in total submission to Maliki's orders. He then began a series of bizarre manoeuvres to achieve this goal, alienating his senior staff, four of whom subsequently resigned, including Tahar Boumedra. Soon we heard that Kobler's wife had been appointed as German ambassador to Iraq, and she also had taken up residence in Baghdad. It seemed as if the Koblers were creating a cosy little sinecure, which required total commitment to and support for Maliki.

Meanwhile, Catherine Ashton, the EU foreign policy chief, in seeking to promote a peaceful resolution to the Ashraf crisis, had appointed in September 2011 a special envoy for Ashraf, Jean de Ruyt, a Belgian senior diplomat and former ambassador to Poland and the UN in New York. At around the same time, the UN High Commission for Refugees (UNHCR) declared that the Ashraf residents were to be considered formally as asylum-seekers, and urged Iraq to postpone any closure of the camp. Amnesty International reiterated this call on 1 November. It seemed that we were beginning to make real progress.

In Iraq, Kobler was hard at work. Such was his dedication to the Ashraf task that towards the end of 2011 and the beginning of 2012, he met five times with the Iranian ambassador to Iraq, Hassan Danaifar, a well-known Qods Force commander, to discuss Ashraf. Following these meetings, Kobler drew up plans for the eviction of the 3,400 residents from Ashraf.

In various meetings with me and other MEP colleagues, Kobler claimed that at least half of the residents would willingly return to Iran after their transfer to Liberty, if they were given the chance to do so. He had said the same thing to the Iranian ambassador.[1] He argued that Ashraf was under the total control of the PMOI, and so the residents did not have freedom of movement and were unable to leave the organisation. His assumption was that if they were relocated to Camp Liberty, many of them would take the opportunity voluntarily to return to Iran.

He was also keen to advocate the removal of sick people from Ashraf and their relocation to the Hotel Mohajer and the Hotel Yamamah in Baghdad, where, he argued, they could be better cared for. Dan Fried, Special Advisor on Camp Ashraf to the US Secretary of State, also strongly recommended that even disabled residents should move from Camp Liberty to one of these hotels.

It is certain that following his many meetings with the Iranian ambassador to Iraq, Kobler knew the Hotel Mohajer and the Hotel Yamamah had been taken over by the sinister Iranian Ministry of Intelligence (MOIS) and were effectively the equivalent of their 'Gestapo headquarters' in Baghdad. Moving any PMOI patients or disabled people to these hotels would be tantamount to signing their death warrants, and yet this was the proposition being actively pursued by Kobler and Fried.

1. Fars News Agency, 22 and 24 January 2012.

Kobler had decided that the key to moving everyone out of Ashraf was to draw up a Memorandum of Understanding (MOU) between UNAMI, the Iraqi government and the PMOI. By November 2011 he had been working on the draft text for more than a month, but each time he submitted something to the Iraqi authorities they rejected it, complaining that the Ashraf residents had no legal status in Iraq and should therefore not be recognised as such in the MOU. Iraq was not a signatory to the Geneva Convention on Refugees and refused to recognise the status of the Ashrafis as refugees or asylum seekers. The Iraqis insisted that this ruled out moving the Ashrafis to a refugee camp, where they would have had freedom of movement. Instead, they insisted that Camp Liberty should be designated as a temporary transit location or TTL, where the 3,400 residents would be temporarily accommodated pending their removal to third countries. The Iraqis made it clear that Camp Liberty was to be a detention centre.

Instead of fiercely resisting this tragic breach of human rights, Kobler bent over backwards to reach a compromise with the Iraqi government. 'Time is of the essence. Human rights are not important. We have to save lives,' was his mantra to the UNAMI staff in Baghdad, according to Tahar Boumedra. By the end of November, over 20 versions of the MOU had been drawn up and rejected by one side or the other. Finally, in frustration at the delays, Kobler decided that he would unilaterally sign an MOU agreed only between him and the Iraqi government, even although it had been rejected by the PMOI. Kobler spoke in the UN Security Council session in New York about Iraq on 6 December 2011. On his return, representatives of the PMOI met him in the European Commission in Brussels with Jean De Ruyt on 7 December and told him that the residents were not prepared to move to another location inside Iraq unless the UN was prepared to deploy Blue Helmets to guarantee their safety.

To aid this process, I had proposed a plan on 5 December and sent a copy to Kobler and Mohammad Mohaddessin. My intention was to submit this plan before their meeting and to get the agreement of the PMOI and the Ashraf residents for it.

In the plan I wrote:

This agreement and each of its items should be taken in its totality as a package signed and guaranteed by the UN, US, EU, GOI and the Ashraf representatives concerning the closure of Camp Ashraf and the relocation of all its residents, with no exception, to Camp Liberty, as the temporary resettlement camp, under the guaranteed protection of the UN and with the UN flag flying over the camp, until such time as the last person leaves Camp Liberty and Iraq for re-settlement in a third country or any other place he/she wishes to go.

Protection of the camp will be provided by UN Blue Helmets or a combination of Blue Helmets and American private security companies. The protection will be guaranteed by the UN, US, and EU, and will be monitored by UNAMI permanently. The Ashraf residents are prepared to pay the expenses for employing private security companies.

By mentioning the use of private security companies, I was trying to minimise the Blue Helmets issue, which I knew was opposed by Kobler. The PMOI agreed to my plan and tabled it at their meeting with Kobler on 7 December. But Kobler refused to talk about anything other than the unconditional evacuation of Ashraf. He seemed to have a single objective, the closure of Ashraf. But nevertheless, he promised the PMOI representatives that he would not sign any agreement with the Iraqi government without their consent.

Several days later, Kobler, who had returned to Baghdad, called Mohaddessin and requested a meeting with Mrs Rajavi. He travelled from Iraq to Paris in mid-December and spent ten hours in discussions with her, during which he made many false promises in a bid to convince her to agree to the move to Camp Liberty.

In Paris Kobler promised Mrs Rajavi once again that he would not sign the Memorandum of Understanding with the Iraqi government without the agreement of the PMOI. But on the evening of 25 December 2011, he signed the MOU with Faleh al-Fayadh and then called Mohaddessin on the phone at midnight, claiming he had been forced to sign it! The news agencies in Iraq had already reported it. Kobler said that he would leave Baghdad early the next morning to fly to Paris to meet Mrs Rajavi on the afternoon of 26 December. When Mohaddessin asked for the text of the MOU to be emailed to him, Kobler said that this was not possible because New York had to see it first!

The MOU signed by Kobler amounted to an agreement forcibly to evict the residents of Ashraf and to imprison them in the Camp Liberty detention centre. It was an abject betrayal of the 3,400 Ashrafis. In complete breach of all international conventions, the MOU specifically denied access to Camp Liberty for NGOs, parliamentarians and diplomats, and clearly determined the status of the refugees from Camp Ashraf as detainees, despite the fact that none had ever been charged, far less tried, for any offence. The 3,400 defenceless men and women were about to be forcibly evicted from their 36 kilometre-square home of almost three decades and sent to a prison compound measuring only half a kilometre square. Kobler argued that having the residents incarcerated in a detention centre was better than seeing them all killed, effectively denying the Ashrafis their basic fundamental rights at a stroke and even denying them the right to life, as the choice they were now being confronted with was to move to Camp Liberty or die.

When news of the MOU was delivered to the residents of Camp Ashraf, they were outraged, accusing Kobler of acting on behalf of Maliki rather than on behalf of the UN. 'How can the UN justify entrusting the victims to their murderers?' they asked. When Kobler signed the MOU on 25 December, he had falsely said that Camp Liberty was in a state of readiness. The Ashraf representatives had asked him many times if they could accompany him to check the camp. They had even proposed to send a group of 100 people first to prepare the place for the rest. But Kobler rejected such demands and insisted on the residents' immediate transfer to Liberty.

When Kobler came to my office in the European Parliament he was accompanied by Clare Bourgeois from UNHCR and Hillary Clinton's special envoy on Ashraf, Dan Fried, a gnarled little man with a disconcerting twitch and a foul temper, who until now had been working on resettling prisoners from Guantánamo Bay. I had asked Alejo Vidal-Quadras, Vice President of the European Parliament, to join our meeting. Kobler insisted that his mission in seeking to relocate the Ashraf residents to Camp Liberty was entirely humanitarian and designed to save lives.

He had brought with him a large volume of photographs of Camp Liberty which he proceeded to use to explain how the facility, although small, was well-equipped with good quality trailers for sleeping accommodation, as well as communal dining halls, kitchens, showers and toilets. He said the camp only required some minor repairs, which the Iraqi government had promised to carry out. Dan Fried and Clare Bourgeois urged us to intercede with Mrs Rajavi and plead with her to persuade the Ashrafis to move to Camp Liberty to prevent further bloodshed. The large-scale photos that Kobler displayed were certainly impressive. Alejo said the camp looked better than anything he had experienced as a young conscript in the Spanish army. I said the accommodation looked better than the boarding school I had been sent to in Scotland as a boy. We both agreed that we would pass on our views to Mrs Rajavi in Paris and urge her to persuade the residents of Ashraf to move to Camp Liberty. Little did we know how comprehensively Kobler had fooled us; only later, after Tahar Boumedra had resigned from UNAMI in anger and frustration at Kobler's naked betrayal of the core values of the UN, did we learn the truth.

Boumedra recounted how Kobler had ordered a large team of UNAMI staff in Baghdad to take the best photos possible of the facilities at Camp Liberty, avoiding anything dirty or dilapidated. He then ordered the whole UNAMI team to Photoshop the pictures repeatedly until he was satisfied that they provided a well-doctored and positive impression. All signs of swampy ground, broken sewerage pipes, cracked panes of glass and rusting metals, were carefully painted out. The final volume of photos was a masterwork of dishonesty, designed to fool elected parliamentarians and win approval for the MOU. It was a disgraceful deception.

The aim of Kobler's trip to Brussels was to deceive friends of Ashraf in the European Parliament and to convince EU officials who, under our pressure, were following the issue of Ashraf. Kobler and Dan Fried wanted to show that Liberty had acceptable living conditions. An internal report prepared by one of Kobler's officials who had attended his Brussels meeting revealed how he wanted to damage the PMOI and Liberty residents and to force the European Parliament to exert pressure on them. A part of this report, which was sent to me in error, regarding a meeting on 2 February 2012 with Elmar Brok, Chair of the Foreign Affairs Committee stated:

> The US representative reported the 2 messages that he had carried from Clinton:
>
> It is important that Rajavi starts to hear other voices from parliamentarians than only those ones who support her and Ashraf. Hearing only from one side (parliament & senior officials) gives her some hope to rally more voices with the objective that Kobler and US will move away therefore Ashraf can stay forever.
>
> Importance that those individuals granted refugees status by UNHCR are moved out of TTL ASAP. While US have not taken any decision, discussions are on-going to consider those who have been recognised as refugees, together with those with family links or those who had former residence in the US.
>
> Elmar Brok agreed at the end of the meeting to issue a press release the same day and invite SRSG (Kobler) to the next Committee meeting (later in Feb or March).

Although Kobler was telling us on 2 February how good Liberty was, the UNHCR shelter expert Martin Zirn had written on 19 January that Liberty was far from meeting humanitarian and human rights standards and its infrastructures were so deficient that they could not be quickly completed and repaired. Kobler, however, had not shown us this official report, and when the PMOI revealed it a year later, he failed to explain why he had insisted that everything in Camp Liberty had been OK.

The reality was that Camp Liberty was in a dreadful condition, as Kobler well knew; it was entirely unfit for human habitation even for a small number of people. For 3,400 people it would be little less than a concentration camp. By consigning the Ashraf residents to detention with no interaction with the outside world, no visits from family, lawyers, parliamentarians or diplomats, Kobler had effectively betrayed the core principles of international humanitarian law. He had designated the Ashrafis as prisoners, despite the fact they had never been convicted of anything. This was a scandal on an international scale. At meetings involving large groups of PMOI supporters around the world, the chant of 'Shame on you Kobler,' could be regularly heard.

Despite the PMOI's feeling of abject betrayal by Kobler over the final signing of the MOU on Christmas Day 2011, Paris now reluctantly agreed to persuade the 3,400 residents of Ashraf to prepare to move to Camp Liberty. They were encouraged in this by Kobler's promise that they would be under 24/7 guaranteed protection by UNAMI, which was another lie. Kobler now informed the Iraqi government that he had reached agreement with all parties for the evacuation of Ashraf to begin, but it was quickly realised that the facilities at Camp Liberty were in such a poor condition that the first transport of residents had to be postponed until emergency repairs could be carried out.

As a goodwill gesture and to demonstrate the flexibility of the Ashraf residents in the face of extreme provocation, it was agreed that the first 400 Ashraf residents would move to Camp Liberty on 17 February 2012. They had not been permitted to visit the place they were about to move to, to assess what they would need to make it habitable; they were not allowed to take most of their personal belongings with them; and they were only allowed to take along 10 vehicles out of some 150 they owned. They were to have no freedom of movement and the surface area provided inside the camp was less than 1.5% of Ashraf's total surface area, with a police station and a large number of police present inside this restricted zone. There were no tarred pathways and ramps for wheelchair users or the elderly, only rough gravel walkways. The old, rusting electricity generators were obsolete and half of them didn't work.

When Kobler refused to allow a small group of the residents to go to Liberty to check and prepare the place in advance, I wrote a letter to him to make arrangements for me and some of my colleagues in the European Parliament, together with lawyers representing the Ashrafis, to travel to Baghdad and visit Liberty and then go to Ashraf to reassure the residents. But, as usual, Kobler did not reply.

I wrote a letter on 1 January 2012 to Jean de Ruyt, Martin Kobler and Dan Fried:

Now that they have accepted the condition of displacement inside Iraq and an initial 400 residents are ready to go to Camp Liberty with their belongings and vehicles, it is absolutely perverse for the Iraqi authorities to deny them the right to take these possessions with them or indeed to send an advance party of engineers to inspect Camp Liberty and ascertain their key requirements prior to moving there. Denial of these basic requests simply convinces the people of Ashraf that they are being humiliated and imprisoned, rather than moved to a temporary staging-post *en route* to re-settlement outside Iraq.

This letter, like so many others, was not answered, and so the first group of 400 Ashraf residents were taken to Camp Liberty on 17 February. On the day of the transfer, the sadistic Iraqi Colonel Sadiq ensured the 400 refugees were subjected to every conceivable humiliation. They were held up for hours and exposed to repeated searches and ID checks. Many of their personal belongings were confiscated and looted by Sadiq and his men. The whole process was designed by Sadiq to be a sort of torture. In any case, clearly this transfer was unnecessary when the residents had already accepted the European Parliament's plan for relocation to third countries. They had each individually applied for asylum to the UN's High Commissioner for Refugees in August 2011, and had the Iraqi government allowed the UNHCR refugee status interview procedure to begin at that time in Camp Ashraf, a significant number of them would by now have been relocated out of Iraq.

But when the first 400 Ashrafis finally arrived at Camp Liberty in February 2012 they were deeply shocked by what they found. Instead of the first-class facilities in this former US military base they had been shown in Kobler's doctored photos, they found themselves in a shabby slum, with flimsy, dilapidated containers for living accommodation, broken-down sewage pipes, intermittent electricity and no running water. These 400 people, around half of them women, were now completely at the mercy of the Iraqi military, commanded by the notorious Colonel Sadiq, one of the alleged ringleaders of the two previous violent massacres. The refugees were humiliated and abused. Requests for vital medicines and basic mobility equipment for the disabled were refused. Attempts to have a main water supply connected at the refugees' own expense were repeatedly blocked. Even basic sun-shelters to protect the residents from the blistering 55°C summer sun were rejected. 18,000 concrete T-walls that had protected the trailers in the US military base from mortar or rocket attack had been removed and the camp was now a sitting duck for such attacks. Requests for body armour and hard hats, which were stored at Ashraf and had been purchased in 2006 following an agreement between the residents and US forces as civilian defence equipment, were summarily refused.

Army and police patrols surrounded and constantly patrolled the half-kilometre square prison camp. In total breach of the UN's own rules on refugee camps, the people were imprisoned, unable to leave the camp's perimeter fence; no-one was allowed in or out without the guards' permission. In a cruel display of sadism, Sadiq ordered lorries laden with tons of basic food supplies to be unloaded for inspection, leaving the food to rot in the sun for hours, before it was examined by Sadiq's guards.

And yet all of this inhuman treatment was allowed to continue right under the noses of a large contingent of UN monitors, directly supervised by Martin Kobler. But the UN had already shown that it was unwilling to intervene again. Kobler had even praised al-Maliki's 'patience' and amazingly claimed that Camp Liberty was totally fit to house the remaining 3,000-plus residents.

In response to the first swathe of complaints I received from the group who moved to Liberty on 17 February, I wrote to Kobler insisting that the police station should be moved promptly out of the camp. I argued that while Liberty was a small area of only half a kilometre square with all the entries and movements controlled by the police, and while Moslem women lived in the camp, far from being proof of Iraqi sovereignty, the police presence would only contribute to tension and possible confrontation. I said that this was the most important issue to be resolved, without which the relocation project would certainly end in total failure.

Happily, I was not a lone voice. Some US lawmakers still believed their country had a moral duty to intervene. Seventy-nine congressmen wrote a letter to Secretary of State Hillary Clinton demanding that Washington keep its word.

On 15 January 2012, I wrote to de Ruyt:

> On various occasions I have tried to convince the MEK leadership to forgo their rights and I have been mostly successful. However, until I can conscientiously assure myself that Liberty is not a prison, I cannot advise them further to sacrifice their rights. I, you, Martin Kobler, and a couple of MEK lawyers could go to Liberty and see the place up close for a few hours and then go to Ashraf and explain what we have seen to the residents. I am sure this would be helpful to all parties. I can promise you that in such a case, the residents, the camp's leadership and the leadership in Paris would trust and listen to me. Then the GoI would also be forced expeditiously to work out the minimum requirements in Liberty.'

De Ruyt did nothing, and indeed resigned from his post in March 2012, having made no impact whatsoever.

So, over the course of the next twelve weeks, a further 1,200 Ashrafis were forced to go through the humiliating process of endless searches and security checks before being transferred to Camp Liberty. The stress was so great that on one occasion one of the residents died of heart failure. He was a young engineer, Bardia Mostofian, who died just one hour after arriving in Liberty. Iraqi doctors said that his death was due to stress and exhaustion. This tragedy happened on 21 March 2012, the first day of the Iranian New Year celebrations, which was turned into a day of mourning. He was amongst the third group of 400 transferred to Liberty. The residents had asked Kobler several times to postpone this transfer for a few days until after the new year, so they would be able to celebrate in Ashraf, but Kobler refused and said that this was out of the question; he forced them to go on 20 March, putting tremendous pressure on the residents.

There were now 1,600 refugees crammed into a half-kilometre square corner of the camp, forced to live in squalid containers under the constant surveillance of the Iraqi police and military. But despite these shortcomings the Iraqi authorities refused to help. They even refused to allow the residents to help themselves. They prevented them from building ramps and pathways over the rough, gravel surfaces for the elderly and disabled. They prevented the movement of special toilets and ambulances for the sick and disabled from Ashraf to Liberty. They prevented the building of shelters to hide from the blistering sun. Worse still, during the transfer of the fifth group to Liberty, when half-way there, six of the special septic-tank emptying vehicles for pumping out black water, which were being taken to Liberty as part of an agreement with the Iraqi government, were stopped and then sent back to Ashraf. This blatant breach of the agreement, coupled with the fact that it would become impossible to clean out the septic tanks at Camp Liberty, disgusted the rest of the people and they refused to move to Liberty. Up to this point around 2,000 had already been transferred to Liberty, and over 1,200 were still in Ashraf. The process of transfer was halted.

Kobler had said in February 2012 in Brussels that the Iranian Ambassador in Iraq would not give him a visa for a trip to Iran until the transfer of the residents from Ashraf to Liberty had been substantially completed. Now, after the transfer of the fifth group, he was given a visa and he immediately went to Tehran.

On 24 April, Maliki's security adviser, Faleh al-Fayadh al-Ameri, said on Iraqi state television that it was natural 'to discuss the issue of the Mojahedin terrorist organisation with the Iranians'. The security advisor added, 'Mr Martin Kobler has talked in detail with Iraqi and Iranian parties in order to provide the requirements for implementation of the understanding which has been agreed on between him and Iraq to close Camp Ashraf and put an end to the presence of this organisation on Iraqi territory.'

This was a shocking violation of the law of asylum, to allow a repressive regime like Iran to interfere in the treatment of its opponents.

The International Committee In Search of Justice (ISJ) representing 4,000 parliamentarians across the Western world, declared in a statement on 9 May, 'Mr Kobler's visit to Tehran exactly on the day after the relocation of the fifth group of the residents raises, more than ever, a series of questions and concerns, especially since during his trip to Europe in February, Mr Kobler told the European side that the Iranian Ambassador in Iraq had set the PMOI's transfer from Ashraf as the precondition for his visit to Iran.'

In May 2012, the UN Committee on Arbitrary Detention published a highly critical report in which they said the status of the people incarcerated in Camp Liberty amounted to arbitrary detention. They ordered the Iraqi government to lift all of the restrictions on the residents. As usual, they were completely ignored.

Worse still, during the transfer of residents from Ashraf to Liberty, it was noted that four representatives of the Iranian Embassy had been invited to observe what was taking place; in addition, agents of the Iranian Ministry of Intelligence had been allowed to set up a base right next to Camp Liberty. These were dangerous and provocative actions sanctioned by the Iraqi government, and certainly constituted a breach of human rights for the unarmed, civilian refugees concerned.

When the transfer of residents from Ashraf to Liberty was stopped, Kobler began a big campaign through the US government, other UN bodies and even friends of Ashraf across the world, to force them to surrender. Frankly, it was a new experience for us to see a special envoy of the UN Secretary General working so hard seemingly at the behest of the Iranian regime.

The representatives of the Ashraf residents, in numerous letters to the UN Secretary General and US officials, had put forward the demands from the residents that should be met to enable the relocation process to recommence. Mrs Rajavi and representatives of the residents also stated that, because of Kobler's close links with the Iranian regime, they would no longer be prepared to meet him. But after the intervention by some senior American supporters of Ashraf, Mrs Rajavi relented and agreed to meet him in the presence of a group of American and European friends.

So on 1 January 2012, a meeting took place in the NCRI headquarters in Paris which included three sides: Kobler with his staff, Mrs Rajavi with NCRI officials and a delegation of seven European and American dignitaries, including Alejo Vidal-Quadras, Vice-President of the European Parliament, Paulo Casaca, founder of Friends of a Free Iran in the European Parliament, Rudy Giuliani, former mayor of New York, Michael Mukasey, former US Attorney General, Ed Rendell, former chair of the Democratic Party and former Governor of Pennsylvania, Louis Freeh, Former Director of the FBI and Senator Robert Torricelli. In this high-level meeting it was agreed that the relocation of the next convoy would only resume after some steps, which were part of the residents' requirements, had been implemented. But despite all the promises made by Kobler, most of the points were neglected. Fraught negotiations continued for months until on 26 July, Mrs Maryam Rajavi met Kobler again in Paris and she made it clear that the sixth convoy would move from Ashraf to Liberty immediately after the eight outstanding basic humanitarian requirements had been fulfilled. This plan was sent to Ambassador Dan Fried on 30 July. Despite this, Faleh al-Fayadh, Prime Minister al-Maliki's national security advisor, told a press conference in Baghdad on 31 July that the involuntary relocation of the Ashraf residents was inevitable and that the Iraq government intended to force them out of Ashraf. This was the clearest threat of violence yet and was obviously the outcome desired by the Mullahs in Tehran, who were putting constant pressure on Maliki to murder the remaining residents.

The Ashrafis' demands were straightforward and readily achievable if the Iraqi government wished to cooperate. They wanted fresh water piped from the main Baghdad water supply. They wanted six specially adapted containers to be transferred from Ashraf to Liberty in which their disabled residents could live in comfort. They wanted their own generators transferred from Ashraf to Liberty so that they could be sure of a reliable supply of electricity. They wanted to sell their former homes and properties in Ashraf and not have them looted and plundered by the Iraqi regime. They wanted the appropriate materials to build paths over the rough gravel in Liberty so that lame and disabled people could move around and they wanted canopies to help them shelter from the blistering sun. They wanted some minibuses, forklift trucks and water, sewage and fuel tankers either purchased new or transferred from Ashraf to Liberty.

What was so difficult about fulfilling these basic requirements? The answer was crystal-clear. The Iraqis had a different agenda, dictated by Tehran. It was an agenda that included the intimidation, coercion, bullying and terrorising of the PMOI residents in Liberty and Ashraf. That is why they had surrounded Ashraf with blaring loudspeakers for years, subjecting the residents to constant psychological torture; that was why they mounted two vicious assaults on the camp killing many innocent people; that was why Colonel Sadiq even insisted on the daily food trucks going into Liberty being laboriously unloaded by hand so that his guards could inspect the loads, which meant that many tonnes of perishable foods were then left sitting in sweltering heat for hours, so that the food rotted and was wasted. This was also the reason why they had at that time withheld permission for more than 50 days for the burial of two residents of Ashraf who had died in recent weeks from the long-term effects of injuries they received in the July 2009 attack. They had also refused to release the body of Bardia Mostofian who suffered a fatal heart attack due to stress and fatigue on the very day he arrived in Camp Liberty from Ashraf, more than five months ago. This was callous and anti-Islamic behaviour, and was cruel not only to the residents of Ashraf and Liberty but to Mr Mostofian's friends and family. But once again it served to underline the ruthlessness and needless brutality of the Iraqis.

I recognised this cruelty and condemned such tactics, demanding that we were joined in this condemnation by the UN, the US and the EU. Mealy-mouthed appeasement of bullies and murderers was not acceptable. The world was watching Liberty and Ashraf, and the UN, the Americans and the EU would be judged on the results.

However on 16 August, a four-sided agreement was signed by the residents, the US government, Iraq and the UN, on which basis the residents agreed to move to Camp Liberty based on assurances by the US. The document stated:

The US commits to working towards resolution of the remaining humanitarian issues at Camp Liberty that materially affect the daily lives of the residents including sustainable mechanisms to provide water and electricity,

and

Commits to support safety and security of the residents until the last of the residents leaves Iraq.

On this basis the residents again began the move to Liberty. During August, September and October, over 1,100 were transferred to Liberty, and around 100 stayed in Ashraf to look after the final disposal of their movable and immovable belongings.

Rather than intervene to help the residents, Kobler now instituted a policy that actually allowed some of his UNAMI staff to harass them even more. UNAMI monitors, who were originally supposed to protect the rights of the residents from the violent and aggressive activities of the Iraqi forces, were now employed as collaborators or prison wardens, psychologically pressurizing the residents. One of the worst was an Afghan called Massoud Dorrani who had accompanied Kobler to Iraq from his previous posting in Afghanistan.[1]

Neither Dorrani's administrative rank nor his background qualified him to occupy this position. But acting as Kobler's special agents, Dorrani and his colleagues relayed messages from Iran's intelligence agents to the residents, mostly consisting of foul abuse and insults, causing extensive protests and complaints. They made repeated and unwarranted entries into the sleeping quarters of women and men during the night and into the bedrooms of the disabled, causing outrage and disturbance. The main aim of Dorrani and his colleagues was to encourage the residents to give up their opposition to the Iranian regime, leave the ranks of the PMOI and return to Iran or to go to hotels in Baghdad which were under the control of the Iranian regime's intelligence ministry. As part of this process, Dorrani took photos and films of the private quarters and lives of the residents without their consent, and then he drew up dossiers, which contained false accusations against the residents.

Kobler eagerly exploited these dossiers, writing letters on a weekly basis to Mrs Rajavi, Mohammad Mohaddessin, myself and Alejo Vidal-Quadras, with copies going to numerous US, European and UN personalities, claiming that his monitors were not allowed to visit everywhere in the camp or to talk privately with people, and that they were routinely being humiliated and boycotted by the residents. In his letters he claimed that the camp's PMOI leadership was clearly violating the residents' rights! I knew from my personal

1. Before going to Iraq, Kobler had been the Deputy Special Representative of the UN Secretary-General in Afghanistan.

acquaintance with Liberty's residents and many telephone conversations with them, together with regular examination of Camp Liberty Daily Reports and my familiarity with the repeated bad behaviour of Mr Kobler, that he was in fact not implementing the goals of the UN but rather playing into the hands of Iraqi officials and the Iranian regime, who had every intention of liquidating the inhabitants.

After several tortuous transportations, usually numbering 400 to 500 Ashrafis at a time, all except for a small number of the former residents of Camp Ashraf had been moved to the tiny prison compound of Camp Liberty. By agreement with UNAMI, UNHCR, the US, the EU and the Iraqi government, 101 residents had been left behind in Camp Ashraf to look after the property and prevent looting. In Camp Liberty the siege by the Iraqi authorities continued apace, with ongoing restrictions on access to fuel, food, medicines and other essentials, and a reluctance to allow necessary repairs to be carried out to the broken-down sewerage, water and energy infrastructure. Meanwhile the UNHCR interviews were conducted at a snail's pace, with only two or three residents a day being taken for interview to see if they could be approved for full refugee status.

On 9 February 2013, the inevitable happened. A rocket and mortar attack left eight dead and nearly 100 wounded. Having been denied hard hats, protective vests, concrete T-walls and even shovels with which to dig protective shelters, the 3,300 residents crammed into half a kilometre square of flimsy portacabins were sitting ducks. When 45 Katyusha rockets and mortars rained down into their tightly-packed, prison-like compound at 5.45 am, they were blown apart and incinerated while they slept.

There was no doubt that this rocket attack had been well planned and professionally targeted; it could only have been carried out by the Iraqi military, obviously with Qods Force help from Iran. Indeed the launch pad from which the rockets had been fired was discovered shortly afterwards. It was well within the tight security zone that surrounded Baghdad Airport and Camp Liberty. A brick wall had been specially constructed around the launch pad. It would have been impossible to approach this area with a truckload of Katyusha rockets and mortars without passing through five separate security roadblocks. Only the Iraqi military could carry out such an attack and they were only able to do so on the direct orders of Nouri al-Maliki. I raised an outcry in the European Parliament and fired off angry letters to Ashton, Ban Ki-moon and President Obama, saying that our repeated negligence had cost lives once again.

On 27 February 2013, I wrote a letter to Kobler's deputy, Gyorgy Busztin:

> On many occasions Kobler assured us that Liberty complied with humanitarian standards. Now it has been revealed that a UNHCR expert had said the opposite. I am appalled that I was deliberately deceived in this way. We truly did not think that a Western diplomat and a senior UN official would part so far from professional integrity.

Despite our vociferous protests and demands for UN and international help, the West sat on its hands. Maliki was delighted and ordered another rocket attack on 29 April 2013, when 20 explosions rocked Camp Liberty, luckily largely missing their target, as this time no one was injured.

Again our cries of protest were ignored. Our repeated request for the return of the concrete T-Walls, helmets and protective vests fell on deaf ears, despite the fact that these were the minimum protective requirements that could help to reduce future casualties from further rocket attacks. On 15 June 2013, Liberty was attacked once again by rockets, a day after the fraudulent presidential elections in Iran. It came as no surprise to us that Khamenei was keen to divert international attention from these elections. In this attack, two people were killed and many wounded. This time the residents were better prepared and sought cover after the first missiles exploded, so the number of casualties was not as high as the Iraqis and their Iranian puppet-masters had no doubt hoped.

But a further deadly rocket attack occurred on 26 December 2013, killing four of the residents and wounding about seventy. After each attack, of course, the Iraqi authorities repeatedly denied any involvement and said that they would hunt down the perpetrators.

However, in a rare claim of responsibility for attacks on the PMOI, Wathiq al-Batat, the commander of the al-Mukhtar Army militia, admitted his group had fired the rockets at the camp. This relatively new Shiite militia was supported and funded by Iran and tolerated, if not actively encouraged, by the Iraqi authorities, particularly when its objective was to kill members of the PMOI. The UNHCR called on the government of Iraq urgently to scale up security measures in the camp to ensure the safety and security of its residents. Maliki probably chuckled with delight every time he received such a plea. He knew that Kobler and UNAMI would do his bidding and he knew that he could murder the PMOI residents with impunity, as the West would do nothing.

I now felt a deep sense of guilt over the fact that, having crammed over 3,000 people into this death camp, the US and EU promptly washed their hands of the whole affair and abandoned these innocent men and women to their fate at the hands of the Iraqis. The great liar and sociopath Maliki, having signed an MOU accepting responsibility for the safety and protection of the refugees in Camp Liberty, was now happily engaged in their serial murder with the full encouragement and assistance of his backers in Tehran. Kobler, in a breathtaking and shameless show of concern, even publicly thanked the Iraqi Government for their pledge to investigate the murders! He was joined in this charade by his wife, Britta Wagner, the German Ambassador to Iraq, who not only publicly thanked the Iraqi government for their pledge to uncover the perpetrators of the bloody attacks on Camp Liberty, but even congratulated her husband and UNAMI for their sterling efforts to resolve the Ashraf crisis by transferring everyone to the new camp!

For the residents of Liberty, enough was enough. They now began a protest of deliberate non-cooperation, refusing to be interviewed by the UNHCR and refusing to speak to UNAMI and Kobler.

Behind the scenes, Mrs Rajavi had been negotiating at the highest level through European friends with the Albanian government in Tirana, from early 2012, to see if they would accept a significant number of refugees from Camp Liberty. They had arrived at a breakthrough agreement, with the Albanians willing to accept all or most of the residents as refugees. Their humanitarian initiative was supported by UNHCR and the US. In November 2012, Ambassador Dan Fried, the special Ashraf Envoy appointed by Hillary Clinton, after returning from Tirana, wrote to Mohammad Mohaddessin:

> As you may have heard, the Government of Albania has confirmed privately that it is prepared to accept for resettlement up to 210 former Ashraf residents. I urge you and the MEK not to make this offer public, but to work quietly with UNHCR to help your people leave Iraq in safety for a better future.

The PMOI were meanwhile negotiating with Albania to accept a much larger number of refugees. In January 2013, a senior delegation from the PMOI had gone to Tirana and met the Prime Minister Sali Berisha, who was sympathetic to the idea of increasing the number of PMOI members taking refuge in his country, but he insisted that the issue must not be made public. The Albanian government was particularly keen to do everything quietly, beneath the radar, so as not to stir up international controversy and cause a diplomatic split with the Iranians.

When news of this highly sensitive and confidential negotiation reached Kobler, oblivious to such niceties, he promptly issued a press release on 15 March 2013, taking full credit for the breakthrough, announcing that he had negotiated this amazing deal with Albania; he then turned his fire on the PMOI, arguing that the non-cooperation protest by the refugees was putting the whole operation in jeopardy. This in fact spooked the Albanians, who became much more cautious about accepting additional refugees.

On a subsequent visit to Camp Liberty, Kobler was surrounded by a group of angry PMOI women shouting that he had betrayed them. Displaying all of the typical traits of a bully confronted by his crimes, he came near to nervous collapse, rendered speechless and terrified by a handful of unarmed women. He retreated quickly from the camp to jeers of derision.

In an attempt to defend his controversial record, on 29 May 2013 Kobler came to the European Parliament to address a meeting of the Foreign Affairs Committee. He got a hostile reception, although some German MEPs felt it was their duty to defend him.

But many MEPs accused the UN Special Representative in Iraq of deceit and demanded his resignation or dismissal, protesting that he had attempted to deceive parliament in the past, had presided over a disastrous decline in the domestic situation in Iraq while doing little to criticise the Iraqi government and had brought progress on the re-settlement of 3,400 refugees in Camps Ashraf and Liberty to a virtual standstill through his incompetence.

During the meeting Kobler reiterated his usual litany of misinformation, complaining that UN monitors had difficulty in accessing residents of Camp Liberty and that there was a general lack of cooperation from the Camp management and the PMOI leadership in Paris. At the same time he tried to ignore the most pressing and immediate issue, namely the safety and security of the residents facing rocket and missile attacks in that tiny, prison-like compound. He was challenged three times by MEPs to explain why hard hats and protective vests that were left behind in Camp Ashraf had not been returned to the residents of Liberty to provide them with even rudimentary protection. His feeble reply was that this was a matter for the Iraqis. Kobler's remarks were so contradictory that even the chairman of the committee, Elmar Brok MEP, stated: 'I find what you have said today almost unbelievable. Accurate information should be provided to us through impartial channels.'

I pointed out the lack of any proper response by Kobler to the massive increase in executions and human rights abuses in Iraq and the lack of proper attention by Kobler regarding the ongoing popular uprisings in cities across Iraq. I also reminded Kobler that he had signed the Memorandum of Understanding regarding the transfer of the residents of Camp Ashraf to the prison of Camp Liberty with the government of Iraq without the consent of the residents of Camp Ashraf. I accused Kobler of deceiving members of parliament on the conditions in Camp Liberty by showing us doctored photographs. I said that he had guaranteed that the 3,400 residents would enjoy safety and security at Camp Liberty and they would be rapidly transferred to third countries, both of which were lies. I pointed out that Tahar Boumedra had resigned from UN-AMI in protest at the behaviour of Kobler and had testified to the US Congress under oath that Kobler had doctored photographs of

Camp Liberty with the sole intention of deceiving MEPs and other decision-makers.

Jim Higgins, MEP from Ireland, said to Kobler, 'You say the government of Iraq considers the Ashraf and Liberty residents as terrorists. But they have been removed from the US and EU terror lists and you, representing the UN, should state that they are not terrorists. Why do you not take a correct position on this? What you are doing is very hypocritical. Can you tell us what you have achieved in view of all the money that you receive? You should be fired. The UN Security Council should fire you'.

Vytautas Landsbergis, a former President of Lithuania, pointed out: 'Scores of Iraqi politicians condemn you. Why do you involve Iran, a foreign country, into this issue in Iraq? Why do you bring Iran into the issue of the status of Camp Liberty and refugees that the Iranian regime hates so much? Eighteen political dignitaries [who had visited Ashraf before] have issued a statement and have called on your conduct to be examined in a court. They have stated their readiness to testify before this court and have called for an investigation into your conduct.'

Tunne Kelam, MEP from Estonia, said: 'Mr Kobler, you have become a controversial figure in Iraq. It is said that you are too close to the government of Iraq. You provide no reasonable explanation regarding the safety of the Liberty residents. You signed the MOU with the government of Iraq but there is no guarantee for the safety and security of the residents. You put 80 percent of the blame on the inhabitants of Camp Liberty. This is very hypocritical and unacceptable.'

Ryszard Czarnecki, a Polish MEP, said: 'You showed us pictures that you claimed demonstrated that Camp Liberty would be an excellent place. But none of these promises were true. The residents do not trust you. You are part of the problem, not part of the solution. Don't you think it is about time that you should resign and leave?'

Kobler, becoming increasingly agitated in the face of such relentless disapproval, turned his fire on the PMOI. He said, 'As Europeans, MEPs should look at the internal structure of the PMOI. You should not support structures that do not provide individual freedoms.'

Following the meeting of the Foreign Affairs Committee of the European Parliament, I told the media, 'This once again underscores the need for Kobler's immediate dismissal by the UN Secretary General.'

We did not have to wait long for the UN Secretary General's response. In July 2013, only eight weeks after his final shambolic appearance before the European Parliament's Foreign Affairs Committee, Kobler was dismissed from his post in Iraq and sent to the Congo. His cosy sinecure with his wife, the German ambassador to Iraq, had been ended. Such was the public outrage at Kobler's appalling record in Iraq that Ban Ki-moon had no choice but to remove him! In his place, on 2 August 2013, the UN Secretary General appointed Nikolay Mladenov as his Special Representative in Iraq. Mladenov was a former Bulgarian Foreign Minister, and until 2009 had been a member of the European Parliament. I knew him from his time as a member of the EPP-ED majority group, when I had been Vice President. He was also a close friend of the Czech diplomat and former MEP Jana Hybášková, who was known for her hostility towards the Iranian PMOI and who was now the EU's Ambassador to Iraq.

30

Interviews with PMOI Refugees in Camp Liberty, September 2014

Mahmoud Royai

'My name is Mahmoud Royai. I was born in Tehran in 1963 and I have a diploma. In 1979, after the anti-monarchy revolution, I became disillusioned with the new government due to the discriminatory and deceptive atmosphere and the reactionary and intolerant ideals of Khomeini. I was, by contrast, inspired by the honesty and righteousness of the People's Mojahedin Organization of Iran. I trusted their programme and became a supporter.

I was part of a middle-class family and all the educational and recreational opportunities at hand left me with no shortage in this regard. Yet while continuing my studies, I continued my support of the PMOI and assisted in selling their books and newspapers and participated in their meetings and gatherings.

On 30 August 1981, when I was 18 years old, I was arrested on charges of supporting the PMOI and sentenced to ten years in prison for selling PMOI newspapers, taking part in meetings and completely legal demonstrations staged by the PMOI. From that time forward, either in the harsh times of interrogation when I wished I would die just to get relief from the pain of torture, or when I entered Ghezel Hesar Prison and before I entered the ward when they shaved my head and eyebrows and forced me to eat them, I didn't think I could survive one year of all these hideous conditions in the notorious prisons of Evin and Ghezel Hesar. Despite all that, thanks to the unprecedented resistance shown by PMOI inmates and our presence as a group, we shared each other's pain and fate, which kept me alert and alive for 10 years in Evin, Ghezel Hesar and Gohardasht prisons under various physical and psychological pressures, while up close I witnessed torture, group executions and the 1988 massacre of political prisoners.

171

Despite the fact that according to the regime's own laws I had not committed any crime and my activities were completely public and legal, in September of 1981 I was on death row and if it wasn't for my father's efforts and those of my friends and relatives, one of those very nights when PMOI supporters were being executed in groups every few minutes, I too would have been gunned down and executed. During those nights we could hear the sounds of the final bullets being fired into the heads of those being executed, and often we counted more than 300 shots in a single night. In the ten years that I was in Evin Prison my father had used nearly all of his assets and belongings to secure my release, and my family was constantly under pressure, facing threats and humiliation by the IRGC.

In 1991, I was released from prison on the condition of a guarantee provided by an official government employee, virtually a signed blank cheque, providing official property papers worth around $80,000 to the prosecutor's office. My mother and father also had to give their pledges and guarantees to this kind of bail bond. The goal of these guarantees was to prevent me from getting anywhere close to the resistance or opposing the bloodthirsty monsters of the Mullahs' regime. As an IRGC member said very clearly to my parents, 'If he does anything, rest assured that he will be executed. Of course first his home will be confiscated, then his guarantors will be arrested and the blank cheque will be used.'

After being released from prison I was faced with a huge paradox. On one hand I couldn't deny all the crimes, torture and executions and keep my pride and conscience silent and yet on the other hand there were my mother and father who had lost their health while I was held in Evin and Gohardasht Prison and they couldn't tolerate me not being close to them any more. I was their only hope and they didn't want me to leave. They had literally used up all their assets to have me freed, and all they had in life was their home and family. If I continued the struggle they would lose everything. It was a very difficult decision. Once I tried to discuss it very vaguely with my father so that maybe my conscience would be a little bit relaxed, so that after I left Iran they wouldn't be caught off guard. I said I should continue my education abroad and not be forced to see the IRGC members that had killed my friends for no reason at all, which makes me very upset.

My father said: "I have lived a long and proud life, but in the past ten years because of my love for you, I tolerated all kinds of humiliation, hardship and difficulties and I stayed alive with this only hope. If you go I won't survive another month." I didn't say anything any more, but I had made my decision and I knew that, despite all the threats to the path ahead that I had chosen, I saw that joining the ranks of the PMOI was the only way to repay my people and continue the path of the martyrs. In 1995, after months of effort, I was able to reach Dubai through a passport that I had obtained, and four days later, with the help of my friends, I arrived in Baghdad. I learned later on that my father passed away exactly one month after I left the country and my mother remains ill.'

31

The Final Ashraf Atrocity

Under the agreement of the UN and US, 101 residents had remained behind in Camp Ashraf to negotiate the safe disposal of their movable and fixed properties, valued at many millions of dollars. Lawyers employed by the Ashraf residents to negotiate the sale of their properties were threatened by the Iraqi regime and scared off, while Prime Minister al-Maliki, acting on the instructions of his sponsors in Tehran, cut off supplies of water, food and electricity to the camp in late August in an attempt to oust the remaining residents and loot their belongings.

Around midnight on Saturday 31 August 2013, several battalions of the Iraqi military and special SWAT forces, acting on orders directly from Prime Minister Nouri al-Maliki, stormed the camp under cover of darkness. The attack began at 6am on 1 September. Anti-tank rocket-propelled grenades and mortars were fired into the sleeping quarters of the refugee camp, and the fleeing residents were then machine-gunned. 52 deaths and dozens of severe injuries resulted. Many of the residents were handcuffed and then summarily executed by being shot in the back of the head. Nine seriously injured residents were carried to the camp clinic by their colleagues, but were then executed by Iraqi military personnel on their hospital beds. Seven injured residents, six women and one man, were kidnapped.

Their mission was clearly to take a few hostages and kill all of the rest. The 42 survivors were the ones who the killers could not find, which explains why General Jamil Shemeri, commander of Diyala police, who had personally taken part in this operation, hearing that there were some survivors, demanded to know how the hell they were still alive?

The systematic massacre continued into Sunday 1 September for some hours, and despite repeated pleas for the UN or US to intervene, there was complete silence and inactivity from both. While under attack, the Ashraf residents directly telephoned UNAMI, the

174

American Embassy and the NCRI headquarters in Paris. Indeed some of the bodies found later were still clutching phones. The Second Secretary in the US Embassy in Baghdad, who was informed 30 minutes after the start of the massacre, replied that he would urgently follow this case. But it was only after 12 hours that a local UN official finally went to the scene, by which time the massacre was over. By then the Iraqi government was already denying that any of their military had entered the camp. The international media, focused on the unfolding civil war in Syria, studiously ignored this new atrocity at Ashraf and there was little or no coverage. I watched horrifying films of the atrocity taken by some of the Ashrafis. In one film, Iraqi soldiers can be seen shooting dead unarmed civilians and then, spotting the cameraman, running towards him firing their weapons. The soldiers can be seen bursting through a door where the cameraman had taken refuge and the final footage shows them raising their Kalashnikovs and firing a burst directly at the camera, which then tumbles to the ground. This brave Ashrafi died filming his own murderers.

This final massacre at Ashraf was as avoidable as it was predictable; myself and many members of parliament, congressmen, senators and leading judicial and military figures in Europe and America had warned for months that a massacre was imminent. In late August, intelligence reports from inside Iran made clear that the Mullahs saw the Syrian crisis and the West's ineffectiveness as ideal cover for a brutal strike. Despite warnings to US Secretary of State John Kerry and others of the inevitability of an attack, no action was taken to protect the unarmed men and women in Ashraf, who subsequently forfeited their lives.

Having achieved their objectives in Ashraf while the West continued to bicker and dither over the crisis in Syria, I warned that we could now expect similar pre-emptive action against the 3,000 residents in Camp Liberty. Despite being under the supposed protection of the UN, these refugees had suffered several vicious mortar attacks leading to 10 deaths. All evidence pointed to the involvement of the Iraqi regime and their Iranian allies in these attacks.

I warned that as Ban Ki-moon, Ashton and Obama wrung their hands in feeble impotence, the killing of the innocent would continue apace. Tehran and Baghdad, both supporters of the brutal Assad regime in Syria, were rubbing their hands together in glee that the West could simply ignore the gassing with chemical weapons of over 1,400 people in Damascus and the scorching of school children with napalm in Aleppo. What perfect cover for their own vicious assault on Ashraf! I said that to ignore this criminal and barbaric attack on Ashraf would be to give the green light for a full-scale massacre at Camp Liberty. The Ashraf agony could have been avoided if the West had heeded the warnings. The liquidation of Liberty would inevitably follow unless al-Maliki and his Iranian sponsors were held to account now. 'Maliki and his Nazi thugs must be indicted for war crimes,' I said. 'The West must sever all further aid to Iraq until Maliki has been arrested.'

The case of the seven hostages has not yet been solved. Their fate remains a mystery. Despite clear evidence that showed they were being held in Baghdad by the Iraqi government immediately following the massacre, the Americans did nothing to seek their release. In fact the Americans first said privately, and then publicly, that the hostages had been taken to Iran on the first day of their captivity, despite the fact that the PMOI, UNHCR, the EU envoy in Baghdad and Baroness Ashton had all confirmed that to their certain knowledge the hostages were still in Baghdad.

Encouraging news arrived in late 2013 that the Spanish courts had indicted Faleh al-Fayadh, Iraqi Prime Minister Nouri al-Maliki's top Security Advisor, for war crimes. This move clearly confirmed Maliki's role in these crimes against humanity. The Spanish courts accused Faleh al-Fayadh as the 'person responsible for grave breaches of the Fourth Geneva Convention (GCIV) and First Additional Protocol committed as from May 2010 in the latter's capacity as Chairman of the "Ashraf Committee" attached to the office of Prime Minister al-Maliki, and in particular for his alleged involvement in the massacres of 8 April 2011 and 1 September 2013 of "protected persons" under the Fourth Geneva Convention residing in the city of Ashraf (Iraq), in conjunction with the reported offences of 35 murders and 337 cases of wilful injury on 8 April 2011 and 52 murders and 7 abductions on 1 September 2013, along with torture and bodily harm to Ashraf residents.'

The Order also stated that 'Killings, injuries, noise bombardment, denial of food and healthcare – nothing can happen at Ashraf without the knowledge of the Committee members and in particular of Faleh al-Fayadh. In the civil and military hierarchy he was the person in charge of the operation on 8 April 2011 under the orders of the Prime Minister, who is Commander-in-Chief of the Iraqi armed forces. In security matters throughout the country, including Ashraf, Faleh al-Fayadh is the person in charge.'

According to the court decision, 'On 1 September 2013 the Iraqi military forces surrounding and occupying Ashraf permitted the cold-blooded massacre of 52 residents – of the roughly 100 residents who had not been forced to move to "Camp Liberty", all with protected person status under the Fourth Geneva Convention. A further seven "protected persons" were abducted during this assault and have yet to be released, and neither have the Iraqi authorities said where they are. Property belonging to the residents was looted, several buildings were destroyed with explosives and one was burned down.'

This breakthrough indictment came as a blow to Maliki, who continued to lie and deny involvement in the series of massacres and abductions that had targeted the unarmed and defenceless refugees in Camps Ashraf and Liberty. The charges were also an acute embarrassment to the State Department officials in Washington who, instead of holding the Iraqi Prime Minister to account, had accepted Maliki's lies and lamely tried to provide cover for his crimes. Maliki had, contrary to the Erbil Agreement signed shortly after the last Iraqi elections, retained control of all of the key Iraqi ministries of Defence, Interior, Intelligence Services and Police. He therefore could not deny responsibility for atrocities carried out, almost on a daily basis, by his military and intelligence networks, including the series of attacks on Ashraf and Liberty and the abduction on 1 September of the seven hostages. Sadly, many EU governments and even the EU's High Representative for Foreign Affairs, Baroness Ashton – had taken their lead from the US State Department and made pathetic comments about a lack of evidence to prove Maliki's guilt. The Spanish court's decision blew such comments out of the water.

The charges by the Spanish courts opened a new chapter, which may hopefully, one day, lead directly to an indictment of Maliki himself. As such, I applauded the initiative of Maryam Rajavi, President-elect of the National Council of Resistance of Iran, who called on the hundreds of PMOI hunger strikers worldwide, many of whom had been on hunger strike since the massacre of Ashraf residents on 1 September, to call off their protest. I applauded the hunger strikers for their courage and fortitude in bringing global attention to the horrific crimes against defenceless Iranian dissidents who were supposed to have been under the protection of the Iraqi government.

With 8,000 Iraqis killed in 2013 in almost constant terrorist outrages, Maliki's answer was a system of secret prisons, mass executions, torture and repression. His sectarian dictatorship was driving Iraq relentlessly towards civil war. And yet Maliki had been the preferred choice of the US State Department. The PMOI and NCRI began a big campaign in the US to condemn Maliki's policies and to convince Washington to distance itself from him. In September and October 2013, before Maliki's trip to Washington, the Congress, Senate and many distinguished Americans condemned this visit and urged Obama to put pressure on Maliki to release the seven hostages.

The Iranian community turned up in their thousands outside the White House during Maliki's meeting with Obama, capturing many headlines in the media. These protests soured Maliki's visit to Washington, and as a result he cancelled several meetings and returned to Baghdad a day earlier than scheduled.

Now others were beginning to realise that the favouring of Maliki had been a grave mistake. Maliki's frosty welcome in Washington in November 2013 was a clear manifestation of this changing view. His reception can be compared to the warm welcome given to Massoud Barzani, President of Iraqi Kurdistan, in Turkey in November that year. Barzani was now increasingly viewed as the most important political figure in Iraq, and one who could play a key future role in ending the deadly spiral towards civil war.

The upshot of the final atrocity at Ashraf was predictable. The 42 survivors and witnesses of the 1 September massacre were quickly moved to Camp Liberty and the Iraqi authorities finally achieved their objective of seizing the property of the camp's residents, worth millions of dollars. Buildings, vehicles, electrical goods and generators were looted. The final act of a criminal conspiracy was laid bare for all to see. Homicide, slaughter, abuse, kidnapping and robbery of defenceless men and women, listed as asylum seekers and refugees, had all been tolerated and condoned by the UN, US and EU; this was a shameful chapter in human history and the situation was far from being resolved.

32

Interviews with PMOI Refugees in Camp Liberty, September 2014

Reza Haft Baradaran

'My name is Reza Haft Baradaran and I was born on 24 May 1952. I graduated studying cinema from the School of Television and Cinema. I was studying French literature in 1981 when Khomeini carried out a "cultural revolution" and closed all the universities in Iran. On 22 February 1982, when I was in my office, the Revolutionary Guards and Ministry of Intelligence forces suddenly arrested me; this is despite the fact that I had ten years of experience in Iran's state-run television. But I was also making a film with a couple of my friends that during Khomeini's rule would never have been approved or allowed to be broadcast. We had made three long movies and a number of long documentaries, showing them in private gatherings. These films revealed how freedom lovers were tortured and murdered, and how the country's wealth was plundered. The films also invited and encouraged people to join in protests and uprisings.

Following the 1979 revolution I came to know the PMOI very closely indeed. At the same time I also came to know Khomeini's men who had gained control over state-run TV. The opposing behaviour of these two groups quickly made me realise that Iran's society was heading towards a huge battle and I had to choose sides. On the one hand I saw Khomeini and his forces that had just gained power and were busy "recruiting" to consolidate their rule. They suggested I take the post of production manager of programmes aired by Channel Two (which was a very profitable post); just on one "simple" condition that involved my cooperation in identifying and annihilating dissident forces, especially PMOI supporters.

On the other hand I also had relations with the PMOI and their leader, Massoud Rajavi, who described freedom as the crown jewel and the main objective of the revolution; he sought freedom for everyone, all groups, short of taking up arms. I chose the PMOI, despite the bloody path laid out before me. One day I witnessed the execution of pregnant women and the rape of schoolgirls on the night of their execution. The justification for this barbarity from the jailers was that these girls should not go to heaven without first having experienced the pleasures of marriage.

My choice was the PMOI because I was witnessing the Mullahs' theocracy and intolerance and I knew it wouldn't take long for the Iranian people to be plunged into fundamentalism. Another issue helped me make this decision even faster. From the very first days of the 1979 revolution I was approached to go as a filmmaker to Afghanistan along with a delegation of individuals hand-picked by the president and Khomeini's office. Our secret mission was to recruit Afghan forces that would then spread Iranian influence inside Afghanistan. The Mullahs' regime said that they would prepare non-Iranian independent reporter's documents for me and if I was arrested I should deny everything. They proposed to give me a huge amount of money for this mission. I didn't accept their offer, but I quickly realised that this fundamentalist entity had not only targeted the freedoms of the Iranian people, but they were also seeking to spread their malign influence to other countries. Very soon an organisation was formally established by Khomeini's regime and given the name of "Supporting Liberation Movements". Witnessing such things convinced me that the only solution was the PMOI.

As I have said, in February 1982 I was working at the Network 2 TV station when IRGC and plainclothes agents of the Ministry of Intelligence suddenly raided my office, arresting me in front of my colleagues, yelling that my crime was buying and selling narcotics. I was immediately blindfolded and taken to the torture chambers of Ward 209 in Evin Prison, where I was placed on a torture bed, which I had read and heard a lot about but I had no experience of. Therefore I could see with every single cell of my body how inhumane this fundamentalist ideology was.

At first they began hitting my bare feet and other parts of my body with hoses so my skin would become swollen, and then they used electric cables which had open wires so that my swollen skin would rupture and my muscles would literally spill out and my bones would be exposed. When they brought my pregnant wife and one

181

and a half-year-old daughter to the torture room to put more pressure on me, I came fully to understand the line of separation that had been traced between the PMOI and Khomeini's evil ideology. With my swollen feet so badly bruised that it was almost impossible to walk, nevertheless they made me carry my baby daughter and forced me to walk around the torture room, hoping that I would stumble in pain and fall. Under such torture it wasn't important for them what I had done or had not done. However, their hysterical hatred against the PMOI and Massoud Rajavi himself was astonishing for me to see.

I was transferred from solitary confinement to the general ward (each room was 6 x 6 metres with 130 inmates in Ward 2 of Evin Prison, 2nd floor, room 5). Seeing the diverse social background of those arrested made me realise why the IRGC was so hysterical in their hatred. From university professors, freedom-loving military personnel, administrative employees, engineers, workers, small business traders and a widespread spectrum of college and high school students, they all represented the broader social hatred toward Khomeini's regime. Khomeini came to realise that the only way to remain in power was to fill this social void with brutality and repression.

I was sentenced to five years in jail. However, I was released three years later as a result of a huge bail paid by my family through an intermediary. Following my release from prison, having two small daughters, housing and financial problems kept me busy for some time. They had denied me the right to work and no private firm would dare to hire me. Finally, with the help of my friends, I was able to afford the cost of leaving the country through the mountains, going first to Turkey and then to the bases of the National Liberation Army of Iran inside Iraq. In the course of this escape I was ambushed no fewer than nine times by the Mullahs' regime forces, but each time I miraculously survived.

I later sent my two little girls, 11 and 9 years old, abroad so that their lives would not be compromised because of me and so they would find their own paths. This was probably one of the hardest decisions of my life. Two children whom I had so many big dreams for, I was now leaving in the hands of fate. On 22 October 1992, I saw that my little girl, Saba, had followed her older sister's path just a few months later and joined the PMOI and come to Ashraf. It was like someone had given me the world.

I truly loved Saba. She had been brought to prison 40 days after she was born and remained in prison until she was about two years old. The day I saw her in Ashraf was amazingly refreshing, but little did I know that a very hard test was on the horizon. On 8 April 2011, I had plans to see my older daughter and say happy birthday to her. However, from the very early hours of that day Maliki's forces began to attack Ashraf under orders from the Iranian regime and made my wishes vanish into thin air. I was informed that my little girl, Saba, had been shot in the leg and that I must accompany her to a hospital in Baghdad. When I saw her I realised how dangerously injured she was. She was losing a lot of blood. They could have taken her to a hospital much sooner and with simple surgery they could have saved her life. But they didn't, and they made me and her choose between Saba's death and succumbing to the Iranian regime's demands of leaving the PMOI.

There was a surprising level of coordination between the Iraqi doctor at the Ashraf hospital and the Iraqi security forces. The Iraqi officer, by the name of Major Yaser, turned a simple 90-minute trip to Baghdad into a 14-hour wait. He and another intermediary came to me to say that if I chose to separate myself and my daughter from supporting "Rajavi" they would let my daughter undergo surgery at the best hospital in Baghdad and then we would be sent to any country we wanted, the US, France or any other European country. Just separate yourself from "Rajavi", they said. Their message was very clear and so was the decision made by Saba and I; I told the Iraqi officer that we are guests in your country and we don't want anything special, just take us to the hospital soon, please. Saba summoned all of her remaining energy before she died and said, "Dad, why didn't you punch him in the face so that he wouldn't dare to repeat what he said?"'

33

Paris

The first big PMOI Rally I attended was in June 2007. It was held in a huge aircraft hangar near Paris. The PMOI stage a mass annual rally every June, and the momentum gradually built up over the years so that now they attract over 100,000 ex-pat Iranians from around the world. The list of speakers is formidable, with former Prime Ministers, ex-Presidents, parliamentarians, senators, congressmen and women, former US State Governors, former FBI and CIA Chiefs, military generals and renowned international celebrities. Addressing an audience of this size can be a daunting and exhilarating experience.

Alejo Vidal-Quadras, Vice President of the European Parliament, accompanied me to my first PMOI Rally in 2007. At this time there were around 50,000 supporters in attendance, and as we approached the venue in Villepinte, north of Paris, we could see row after row of buses filling all of the surrounding car parks and even spilling out onto the hard shoulder of the nearby Autoroute. Inside, the vast hall had been decked out with banners, flags, balloons and streamers and giant screens and loudspeakers conveyed the speeches to the excited audience. Alejo and I watched bemused as film footage was screened of heavily armed and uniformed PMOI soldiers marching and riding on tanks dating back to the 1990s when they had a conventional army in Iraq. There were resounding cheers from the audience at the warlike messages that accompanied these films.

Alejo and I were surprised. We were fighting on several continents to have the PMOI removed from terrorist lists, arguing that this was a legitimate, peaceful opposition movement, and here they were publicly celebrating their military past, which could have been misused to keep the PMOI on the blacklists. We raised this with the NCRI and argued that it was counterproductive. The 2008 rally and all subsequent rallies to date have been entirely free of all military overtones. Our advice was being taken on board.

Alejo and I have been regular attendees at these gigantic rallies ever since. It is deeply frustrating when we encounter politicians and civil servants who tell us that the PMOI is irrelevant as an opposition movement and has no support within Iran. We point to the 100,000 Iranians who come to Paris every year and remind them that all of these people have extended families back in Iran that could number over one million. We also have to challenge such ignorance by reminding them that support for the PMOI carries the mandatory death penalty in Iran, and it is therefore hardly surprising that there are no mass opposition rallies in Tehran and other Iranian cities. A look at the demography of Iran and the composition of the exiled Iranians who take part in the PMOI rallies, shows that this movement has a good base of support amongst the middle classes and the people living in cities and urban areas of Iran.

These annual rallies in Paris are incredibly well-organised. The countless speeches by renowned political leaders are beamed into Iranian homes from the PMOI's own satellite TV network, itself strictly illegal under the Mullahs' repressive regime. Many people have been executed simply for donating money to keep this TV station going. Unquestionably, Mrs Rajavi leads a most formidable, well-organised and well-funded opposition movement, with a manifesto that I would be happy to stand for election under. Over the years, Mrs Rajavi and foreign affairs spokesman Mohammad Mohaddessin have both become fluent English-speakers. Recalling their limited ability to speak English when we first met, this has been a truly remarkable achievement and a sign of their relentless quest for excellence.

On Saturday 23 June, 2012, the PMOI held its largest ever gathering outside Iran in the enormous Parc des Expositions halls at Villepinte, north of Paris. Around 100,000 participated in the rally. I took part in similar events in the same place in 2013 and 2014. Typically, at these annual events, more than 500 prominent political personalities, parliamentarians and jurists from 40 countries and five continents are present. More than 1,300 coaches are chartered to bring participants from throughout Europe to the venue. Speakers from the US usually include people like former Democratic Party Chairmen, Governor Howard Dean and Governor Ed Rendell, former US Ambassador to the UN, Governor Bill Richardson, Congressman (1995-2011) Patrick

Kennedy, former New York Mayor, Rudy Giuliani, former Chairman of the Joint Chiefs of Staff, General Hugh Shelton, Senator Joe Lieberman, Former FBI Director Louis Freeh, former Attorney General Michael Mukasey and President Obama's first Assistant Secretary of State for Public Affairs, Philip J. Crowley. Also the rally is usually attended by a large group of American officers who were based in Ashraf after the US invasion of Iraq, including Colonel Wes Martin.

Other speakers from Europe generally include European Parliament Vice President Alejo Vidal-Quadras, Vice President of the Italian Senate, Emma Bonino, EU Commissioner (1999-2010), Günter Verheugen, Former Irish Prime Minister, John Bruton, French Foreign Minister (2005-2007) and UN Under-Secretary-General, Philippe Douste-Blazy, former Director of the French Anti-Espionage Agency, Yves Bonnet and German Bundestag Speaker (1988-1998), Rita Süssmuth, plus a long list of parliamentarians from other European States. Members of parliaments from Afghanistan, Jordan, Palestine and other Middle Eastern countries also address the gathering.

The keynote speaker at these events is of course always the Iranian opposition leader Maryam Rajavi, who is elected by the National Council of Resistance of Iran (NCRI), the Iranian parliament-in-exile, as 'president for a six-month transitional period after the fall of the Mullahs.'

In my speech to the June 2012 rally I reported on an incident that had happened during the previous week in the European Parliament. A group of Iraqi government officials had come to Brussels for meetings. 'They wanted to attend the routine monthly meeting of my Delegation for Relations with Iraq. I made a background check and realised that the delegation included the notorious Colonel Sadiq, who had been indicted by the judges in Spain for his complicity in the alleged murder of 47 people in the two massacres in Camp Ashraf and his involvement in torture and oppression,' I said. 'The Parliament's security officials stripped Sadiq of his security pass and did not allow him into the building. We do not welcome alleged murderers in the European Parliament. Now we have sent a lesson back to Iraq.'

I continued: 'But you know the appalling thing about this whole episode was that on Monday there was a press conference in Washington at the State Department and an anonymous official told the press that the United States was proud to support this Iraqi delegation coming from Baghdad to Brussels. Indeed Ambassador Dan Fried, the US special envoy for Ashraf, had even flown across the Atlantic to meet the group and attend their meetings in Brussels.'

I was supported by Alejo Vidal-Quadras who said: 'We were very shocked when we knew that Colonel Sadiq, who conducted attacks against Ashraf, shooting dead dozens of unarmed civilians, was part of this Iraqi delegation to the European Parliament. We did not allow him into the Parliament, mostly for environmental reasons, because in the European Parliament we like to breathe clean air.'

Alejo Vidal-Quadras also addressed Maliki, rebuking him for sending 'criminals' to the European Parliament. 'Our difference is that you put criminals in command of top jobs while we put them in prison!'

In fact the encounter with the Iraqis had been a tense and fraught affair. Led by the Deputy Foreign Minister Abbawi Aziz, the delegation from Baghdad had included, apart from the notorious murderer Colonel Sadiq, George Bakoos, Maliki's personal advisor responsible for dealing with Ashraf. There were also officials from the Ministry of Justice, Iraqi intelligence, the Secretariat of the Prime Minister's Cabinet, the Human Rights Ministry and even two generals. The intention, fully endorsed by US Ambassador Dan Fried, was to convince my Delegation for Relations with Iraq that the Iraqi authorities were looking after the 3,400 residents of Ashraf and Liberty in an exemplary fashion, and that they were certainly not responsible for any of the attacks or massacres that had occurred.

On learning that Colonel Sadiq was part of the visiting delegation, I phoned Security and told them to stop him at the outside entrance and strip him of his pass. I said on no account was he to be allowed into the building. The group was supposed to arrive at my meeting at 15.00 hrs. Finally, at 15.25 hrs. they appeared, looking very red-faced and angry. They told us that they were horrified that Colonel Sadiq had been stopped at the entrance and prohibited from coming to our meeting. I exploded and said, 'Colonel Sadiq was directly involved in commanding the massacres of innocent men and women at Camp Ashraf. He's been indicted by the Spanish courts on a charge of murder and we do not welcome murderers in this House.'

George Bakoos was almost choking with rage. 'This is a grave injustice and an acute embarrassment to the people of Iraq,' he screeched. 'You would rather support terrorists like the PMOI than listen to the true facts from us!' At this, Alejo Vidal-Quadras let fly, 'Do not try to lecture us on freedom and democracy in the European Parliament,' he yelled. 'We will not take lessons from murderers and torturers.' The meeting broke up in disarray, with each side shouting abuse at the other. I was overjoyed when I heard that Sadiq was arrested in Paris two days later and held for 24 hours in prison. He was released pending further enquiries, but he immediately fled back to Iraq and resumed his role at Camp Liberty even more aggressively. But the apparent collusion of the US State Department and Ambassador Dan Fried, in his attempt to facilitate the attendance of a murderer at a meeting of my delegation, had deeply angered me and soured relations between us.

Fried compounded my anger by stating that decisions on removing the PMOI/NCRI from the US State Department Terror List, for which the US Federal Courts had set a deadline of the end of September or the courts themselves would remove them from the List, could be influenced by whether or not the remaining 1,200 residents got out of Ashraf quickly. In other words, if 1,200 unarmed asylum-seekers refused to move quickly from Ashraf to Liberty it meant the PMOI were terrorists! I had always understood the Americans believed in freedom and justice, but this really plumbed the depths. Kobler and Fried repeatedly warned me that their number one priority was the safety of the people in Ashraf and Liberty. Why in that case did they not object to the appointment of Colonel Sadiq as Camp Commandant at Liberty? Why had they not insisted on the Iraqi government upholding the terms of the MOU they signed with Kobler on behalf of the UN?

Notwithstanding these frustrating setbacks, there was a glimmer of light at the end of the tunnel. The Albanian government had generously agreed to accept 240 of the sickest and most elderly residents from Camp Liberty and had provided them with a multi-storey building, where most of them were residing. In May 2014, Alejo and I went to Tirana in Albania. We were given a guided tour of the building, looking at the sleeping quarters, offices, dining-room and kitchens. The residents were full of praise for the Albanians who had given them access to first-class hospital care and were now cooperating with them on a daily basis. All of this was being paid for by the PMOI.

Alejo and I had set up meetings with Edi Rama, the Prime Minister of Albania, Saimir Tahiri, the Minister of the Interior, and with President Bujar Nishani. We also had arranged to meet the Speaker of the Albanian parliament and the leader of the main opposition party. Our meetings were highly productive. For the most part, the Albanian leaders were young, deeply committed politicians, keen to see their country become a full member of the European Union. They were also delighted to have been able to assist with the re-settlement of 240 of the Camp Liberty refugees, although they were bemused as to why Albania, a tiny country on the periphery of Europe, could provide such humanitarian shelter, while the 28 EU Member States seemed incapable of doing anything.

Our main objective in coming to Tirana was to ask the Albanian government to take even more of the PMOI refugees. We explained the mounting crisis in Iraq and the fact they faced imminent annihilation if no one had the courage to step in and help with re-settlement in the way that Albania had. We pointed out that no matter how many PMOI refugees came to Tirana they would be self-financing, productive and would benefit the Albanian economy.

Albania certainly was an eye-opener for Alejo and me. Back in Brussels I told friends that we had witnessed a miracle. It was something that even Mother Teresa, the iconic Albanian saint, would have been proud of. I said that only a year ago the 240 PMOI refugees had been prisoners in Liberty Concentration Camp. They were wounded, exhausted, sick and facing daily psychological torture by Nouri al-Maliki's Iraqi thugs. They lived in constant fear of rocket attacks and assassination, which had claimed the lives of over 100 of their companions. They were denied access to proper medical care and surgery, and had watched helplessly as some of their closest friends had died.

Then, I said, the miracle happened. The great humanitarian Albanian government stepped in and agreed to re-settle these ill and exhausted refugees. They were flown to Tirana and teams of skilled doctors and surgeons began work on their long progress back to recovery. I recounted how when Alejo and I had visited the large social centre in Tirana that is home to these survivors of the horrors of Iraq, we found a bustling community. We joined these wonderful people in songs and celebrations. It was a joy to see people who had been on the edge of death smiling and laughing and living once again a life of peace, fully integrated into Albanian society and ready once more to continue the fight against the Iranian oppressors. Their courage, their sacrifice and their refusal to give in were inspirational.

I wrote to the Albanian President and Prime Minister thanking them and thanking the fantastic team of young Albanian doctors and surgeons and the many other key lawyers, teachers and professionals who had become the close friends of the PMOI in Tirana.

Alejo and I found Albania to be a country of charming, warm and friendly people. This was not the country of pickpockets, criminals and thugs portrayed by the Western media. Indeed, this is a country that suffered from years of totalitarian rule. The President of Albania, several senior government ministers and many ordinary Albanian citizens explained to us that this is why they value and cherish political opposition movements like the PMOI. This is why they value freedom and democracy and share our quest for justice and human rights in Iran.

Many of these talented young people from Albania travelled to Paris for the annual PMOI Rally on Friday 27 June 2014. This was the biggest gathering yet, with an estimated 110,000 supporters attending from 69 different countries and over 600 parliamentarians and prominent political figures from five continents. Two former prime ministers of Albania, Sali Berisha and Pandeli Majko were present, and gave passionate speeches in defence of the PMOI and Liberty residents, and warmly welcomed the Iranian dissidents who had taken refuge in their country. Sali Berisha, who had been the Prime Minister until only a few weeks earlier, was the one who had approved taking in the first group of 210 PMOI members to his country.

Mrs Rajavi's keynote address touched on the Mullahs' increased meddling in Iraq, the strategic impact of the crisis in Iraq and its impact on Iran, the developments in Syria, as well as the policies of the Mullahs' regime under the so-called moderate presidency of Hassan Rouhani.

34

Interviews with PMOI Refugees in Camp Liberty, September 2014

Ali Mohammad Sinaki

'I was born in Tehran in 1946 into a relatively rich and religious family. I finished elementary and high school in Tehran and in 1964 entered Tehran's National University, continuing my education in chemistry. In 1968 I received my first degree in chemistry. From 1969 to 1971, I worked in the Ministry of Education as a chemistry teacher. From 1971 to 1975, I worked in the Ministry of Commerce as a sugar-cube industry expert in Iran's sugar-cube factories. In 1975, I was accepted by the Massachusetts Institute of Technology (MIT) in the US to study nuclear engineering for a master's degree, and by using my scholarship from the Atomic Energy Organisation Iran (AEOI) I moved with my family, including my daughter, to the US and continued my studies until I received my master's degree from MIT. It was during this period that I became acquainted with the PMOI, choosing to become a supporter afterwards.

Finishing my studies in MIT in May of 1977, I went to the University of Michigan to continue my studies and get my PhD. Many developments and demonstrations against the Shah had begun in Iran during this period that I was a PMOI supporter, and I saw that in such changing times it wouldn't be right to continue my education in the US. Therefore, in January of 1978 I put my PhD on hold and returned to Iran, and began working in the AEOI as a nuclear fuel expert. This was while I was secretly working as a supporter for the PMOI, and during the 1979 revolution in Iran I was active in the demonstrations. Following the revolution's victory I realised that my expectations of freedom and democracy were not to be fulfilled under the framework of the Khomeini regime. I saw the PMOI as the only dignified organisation in pursuit of the cause of freedom, and so I started becoming active in the PMOI's employee section.

These overt activities continued until September 1981, when I was arrested on charges of supporting the PMOI. As a result I spent seven and a half years in jail in Evin and Ghezel Hesar prisons. During this period, in addition to the fact that I was tortured myself, I also witnessed other inmates being tortured. I also witnessed the 1988 massacre of political prisoners under orders of Khomeini himself. I have a few memoirs from that period, entitled *Memoirs of the Massacre of Political Prisoners*. I was released in November 1988 after seven and a half years behind bars. However, this release was not pleasant for me at all, because I entered a closed society under the shadow of a religious dictator. With my professional expertise I could have gone on with my ordinary life. But the faces of the martyrs and especially those PMOI inmates massacred in 1988 always passed before my eyes, making me feel a sense of responsibility.

Therefore, I was looking to join the PMOI. However, after being released from prison I was banned from leaving Iran, and during this period all I was thinking about was finding a way to get out of the country and join the PMOI to continue my struggle. In October 1989 I was finally able to pass through the border into Pakistan, and then with the help of my PMOI friends, in January 1990 I was able to go to Camp Ashraf. I was in Ashraf until February 2012 and then relocated to Liberty, and I have been in Liberty ever since.'

35

Washington D.C.

The first time I went to Washington D.C. on behalf of the PMOI was in July 2006. I had to address a major Congressional briefing on Capitol Hill on Tuesday 25 July on 'Women: Key to Establishing Democracy in the Middle East'. Congresswoman Sheila Jackson Lee chaired the event. I recall one of the speakers at the event was a young Iranian lady from California who had been imprisoned in Evin Prison in Tehran for being a supporter of the PMOI. She told us in graphic detail of the tortures she had endured before her release and escape to the West. She wept as she described how her bare feet had been whipped with electric cables until the flesh peeled off. She told us how a pregnant woman had miscarried after being tortured, and the guards had kicked the foetus across the floor of the cell. You could have heard a pin drop in the Caucus Room where the meeting was held. People in the audience were weeping. It was a profoundly moving experience.

The following morning, I had arranged to meet Will Schirano of the Heritage Foundation on Massachusetts Avenue. Like most Heritage Foundation acolytes, Schirano was a young, fresh-faced college graduate who left you in no doubt that he knew it all and was not about to be steered off his chosen right-wing Republican path in life. I explained that I had been previously to the Heritage Foundation before I was elected as an MEP and had lectured a large audience on devolved government for Scotland. I said, however, I wished to take this opportunity to brief the Heritage Foundation, as one of America's most influential think-tanks, on the need to remove the PMOI from the US Foreign Terrorist Organisations list.

As I spoke, Schirano became increasingly agitated and fidgety, twiddling his thumbs and on occasion 'harrumphing' audibly. When I had finished, he launched into a tirade, describing the PMOI as a Marxist Islamic cult, which had carried out terrorist operations and was guilty of killing Americans. I started to rebut his arguments, but he was deaf to all my explanations. He handed me a Heritage Foundation tie and bade me farewell. I was somewhat taken aback by his naked hostility. If this is what we are up against in government circles in the US, then God help us, I thought.

That evening I had dinner with one of the great American supporters of the PMOI, Professor Raymond Tanter. He roared with laughter when I told him about Schirano. 'These are just kids,' he said, 'they know nothing.' Raymond is a professor of political science at Georgetown University and an adjunct scholar of the Washington Institute, researching US policy options toward Iran. In the early eighties Dr Tanter served on the National Security Council staff and was personal representative of the Secretary of Defence to the 1983-1984 arms control talks held in Madrid, Helsinki, Stockholm, and Vienna. He has written many books on Iran and the Middle East. He is a great guy.

On Thursday 27 July I addressed a second Congressional Briefing on Capitol Hill, this time on the subject of 'EU and US: Options to Promote Femocracy in Iran'. Members of the United States Congress had sponsored the event and I joined a panel of members of the European Parliament, members of the UK House of Commons and House of Lords, Congressmen and women and Iran Policy Committee experts like Professor Tanter. The panel provided an opportunity for an intercontinental parliamentary exchange of views about Iran policy, as well as an opportunity for Washington policy-makers to hear European voices on the sensitive issue of Iran.

Mrs Rajavi asked me if I could go to Washington D.C. again in February 2009, just as President Obama took office to begin his first term as America's first-ever black President. It was an exciting time. Back in late 2008, as President George W. Bush neared the end of his beleaguered presidency, it was certain that neither Barack Obama nor John McCain would thank him for the legacy of conflict one or the other would inherit in the Middle East. Both candidates had named Iran as a key policy issue, but both from dramatically different perspectives. Obama wanted to sit down and negotiate with President Ahmadinejad, the crazed leader of Iran, who had repeatedly told the world that he wanted to wipe Israel off the map and was busily building the nuclear weapons that would enable him to do so. McCain ominously said that he would use all the power at his disposal, if he became President, to stop Iran developing a nuclear weapon. The choice between appeasement and military intervention loomed large.

Indeed in September 2008, the European Parliament sent me as an observer to attend the GOP Convention in Minneapolis St Paul, where McCain and Sarah Palin made their keynote speeches. I had some high-level meetings set up with Mitt Romney, Larry Eagleburger and Henry Kissinger. I asked Larry Eagleburger, former US Secretary of State under George Bush Sr., and now security and defence advisor to John McCain, what he would do about Iran if McCain became President. I was horrified to hear Eagleburger state that if we failed to deal with the nuclear weapons issue in Iran now, then for certain a nuclear weapon would be fired in anger during the next decade. When pressed by me whether he believed military intervention was the only answer, he replied, 'Yes!'

I met Richard S. Williamson, former US Ambassador to the United Nations and at that time special US envoy in Sudan. He was a key foreign policy adviser to John McCain and I discussed Darfur, Iran, Russia and a whole range of strategic issues with him. He said that advising John McCain on foreign policy was like coaching Tiger Woods on golf! But he said that the biggest problem facing the next US President was certainly going to be a nuclear-armed Iran. He reckoned the ascendancy of Iran in the Middle East had been linked directly to the war in Iraq and that the Mullahs' support for Hezbollah and Hamas and their determination to 'accentuate the Shiia–Sunni split,' has marked them out as a dangerous enemy of freedom and democracy.

When I visited Washington D.C. in February 2009, the American capital was frozen solid and covered in a thick blanket of snow. In an apparent attempt to regain the initiative in Washington, the Iranian Mullahs had sponsored some strident calls in the media, often in cyberspace, opposing the delisting of the PMOI. They did this by using subterfuge and deception. Of course their agents who expressed these views could provide no hard facts or evidence for keeping the PMOI on the list, so they resorted to insults and innuendo, claiming that the

PMOI was a cult-like group, which had no popular support in Iran. Apart from their absurdity, such claims had nothing to do with anti-terrorism law. However, they did serve to reveal the fingerprints of the Iranian regime, which always hides behind various cover names like the so-called 'Green Movement',[1] to spread its propaganda in an attempt to vilify their most feared opposition, the PMOI.

I met Ambassador Dennis B. Ross in the State Department. Ross had served as the Director of Policy Planning in the State Department under President George H. W. Bush and was special Middle East coordinator under President Bill Clinton. On the day I met him, he had just taken up his new role of special advisor to Secretary of State Hillary Clinton for the Persian Gulf and Southwest Asia (which included Iran). I was able to give him a comprehensive overview of the EU's position on Iran and Iraq, vigorously attacking the policy of appeasement and urging Ambassador Ross to give State Department support to the ordinary citizens of Iran who were desperate for regime change. I also filled him in on the need to delist the PMOI from the US list of Foreign Terrorist Organisations. He promised to do his best.

Despite Ambassador Ross's best efforts, it wasn't until 28 September 2012 that the US State Department finally formally removed the PMOI/MEK from its official list of foreign terrorist organizations, beating by days a 1 October deadline set by the US courts. Secretary of State Hillary Clinton said in a statement the decision was made because the PMOI/MEK had renounced violence and had cooperated in closing their Iraqi paramilitary base. This statement, as she knew, was risible. Had she not delisted the MEK/PMOI, the courts would have done it for her. Her hand had been forced and our campaign of many years had at last succeeded.

In all my high-level meetings in Congress and the Senate during my 2009 visit to Washington I explained the fact that there was not even one shred of evidence supporting the group's terrorist designation. I

1. The Iranian Green Movement was a political movement that arose following the fraudulent 2009 Iranian presidential election, in which protesters demanded the removal of Mahmoud Ahmadinejad from office. Green was initially used as the symbol of Mir-Hossein Mousavi Khameneh's campaign, but after the election it became the symbol of unity and hope for those demanding the annulment of the election result.

explained that the PMOI terror tag did not have any factual or legal basis and the group did not meet the legal criteria of a terrorist organization. Justice, law and fairness demanded their immediate removal from the list.

With the argument for keeping the MEK on the FTO list losing ground rapidly, lobbyists for the regime were now hysterically claiming that their delisting would 'embolden Iran's hardliners to intensify their repression of the Green Movement,' or even that, 'it would trigger a huge loss of US soft power in Iran,' and 'damage Iran's democratic progress'. The reality was obvious and deeply sinister. These strident voices did not come from the Opposition; they came directly from the Iranian Ministry of Intelligence and Security (MOIS). This was another typical disinformation manoeuvre to try to keep the fading embers of the failed appeasement policy alight in Washington. But, I argued on Capitol Hill, US citizens had to be clear, there was no realistic alternative to the Mullahs inside Iran. Mir-Hossein Mousavi Khameneh became the figurehead leader of the Green Movement as the default opposition to Ahmadinejad, following the blatantly swindled election of 2009. But when it counted the most, this spineless extremist of the 1980s, under whose premiership tens of thousands of political prisoners were executed, betrayed even his own supporters in order to save his own neck.

Many distinguished former members of the US administration during the Clinton, Bush and Obama era, including the former Secretary of Homeland Security, Tom Ridge and the former Attorney General until 2009, Michael Mukasey, stepped forward to support the delisting of the PMOI. They urged Secretary of State Hillary Clinton to heed the warnings from the Court of Appeals for the District of Columbia to delist the PMOI or the court would intercede and do it themselves.

On 24 February 2009, I spoke in the US Congress in Washington D.C. to a large audience of congressmen and women and staffers. Some journalists also attended. I said:

> I am here today to deliver two messages to the Honourable Members of this distinguished House. Firstly, delist the PMOI from the US terror list and secondly, protect the residents of

198

Camp Ashraf. By doing so, you will send the strongest possible signal to the fascist Mullahs that the policy of appeasement is over; that the West will not stand idly by and watch while they put the finishing touches to their nuclear missiles. By dealing with the Mullahs from a position of strength, rather than a position of weakness, we will be far more likely to gain their rapt attention.

Following my speech, I met with many of the PMOI's supporters in the US, a formidable collection of political leaders including two former CIA Directors, James Woolsey and Porter Goss, the former mayor of New York City, Rudy Giuliani, the former Governor of Vermont and former Chairman of the Democratic National Committee, Howard Dean, the former FBI Director, Louis Freeh, and the former US Ambassador to the UN, John Bolton. Democrats and Republicans alike had come out in open support of delisting the PMOI. These were brave politicians willing to put their own reputations on the line in the name of American justice.

I was back in Washington in January 2010 and this time delivered a lecture on Capitol Hill entitled 'Winning Hearts and Minds in the War on Terror', in which I said:

The PMOI was delisted in Europe and justice at long last prevailed. But the whole saga revealed the shocking lengths Western governments were prepared to go to please the fascist regime in Tehran, even to the extent of illegally fabricating false accusations of terrorism against innocent people in exchange for empty pledges from the Mullahs.

Sadly, this tragic state of affairs is still being maintained in the US, where the inability of the State Department to alter course in the face of overwhelming evidence, makes the passage of the Titanic towards the iceberg appear surefooted!

Of course promises by the Mullahs that they would cease their nuclear enrichment programme were never fulfilled and recent intelligence revealed to the West by the PMOI, including the revelation of the underground nuclear bunkers near the holy city of Qom, proves that work is continuing apace on the construction, not only of nuclear warheads, but also of the delivery systems to launch them and the trigger mechanisms necessary for their detonation.

It was PMOI supporters inside Iran, at huge risk to themselves, who first revealed to the West the existence of the Mullahs' nuclear programme in 2002. They continue to provide the West with up-to-date intelligence almost on a daily basis. It is time the West reciprocated by offering some help to the PMOI. These are not terrorists, they are allies in the war on terror. It is time for the State Department to wake up and smell the coffee!

Europe's feeble response in the face of the Mullahs' continuing intransigence has simply convinced the Mullahs that we are weak and encouraged them on their chosen path to Middle East domination. The current situation has placed the West in front of a fateful dilemma on Iran. We must either accept the emergence of a nuclear-armed, radical Jihadist theocracy, potentially the world's first 'suicide state', and its dominating role in the most sensitive region of the world, or we must adopt a firm and resolute policy to confront the Mullahs' ambitions. The critical situation in Iraq and Iran's well-advanced nuclear programme mean that the West has only a limited amount of time to make this crucial decision.

In January 2013 the Pentagon and the Library of Congress published a report entitled 'Iran's Ministry of Intelligence and Security: A Profile'. This was a fascinating if rather alarming document. It was based on exhaustive research undertaken by the Pentagon and the US Federal Research Division, Library of Congress, and it contained striking revelations about the extent of the activities of the Iranian Ministry of Intelligence and Security (MOIS) against dissidents, and in particular efforts to discredit the main opposition People's Mojahedin Organisation of Iran (PMOI/MEK).

The report stressed that the Iranian regime's MOIS uses all means at its disposal to protect the Islamic Revolution of Iran, utilising such methods as infiltrating internal opposition groups, monitoring domestic threats and expatriate dissent, arresting alleged spies and dissidents, exposing conspiracies deemed threatening and maintaining liaison with other foreign intelligence agencies, as well as with organisations that protect the Islamic Republic's interests around the world.

It continued:

According to Iran's constitution, all organizations must share information with the Ministry of Intelligence and Security. The ministry oversees all covert operations. It usually executes internal operations itself, but the Qods Force of the Islamic Revolutionary Guards Corps for the most part handles extraterritorial operations such as sabotage, assassinations, and espionage. Although the Qods Force operates independently, it shares the information it collects with MOIS.

The Iranian government considers the Mojahedin-e-Khalq to be the organization that most threatens the Islamic Republic of Iran. One of the main responsibilities of the Ministry of Intelligence and Security is to conduct covert operations against the Mojahedin-e-Khalq and to identify and eliminate its members. Other Iranian dissidents also fall under the ministry's jurisdiction. The ministry has a Department of Disinformation, which is in charge of creating and waging psychological warfare against the enemies of the Islamic Republic.

In other parts of the report it was stressed that:

The MOIS recruited former members of the MEK in Europe and used them to launch a disinformation campaign against MEK. After the 1991 Persian Gulf War against Iraq, the MOIS made anti-MEK psychological warfare one of its main objectives, but the MEK nonetheless has remained a viable organization.

The report also identified two MOIS agents operating from abroad, and explained how they were recruited and trained by the MOIS in Tehran to run a demonisation campaign, including launching a PMOI-defamatory website, iran-interlink.org.

The recruitment of a British subject, Anne Singleton, and her Iranian husband, Massoud Khodabandeh, provides a relevant example of how MOIS coerces non-Iranians to cooperate. She worked with the MEK in the late 1980s. Massoud Khodabandeh and his brother Ibrahim were both members of the MEK at the time. In 1996 Massoud Khodabandeh decided to leave the organisation. Later, he married Anne Singleton. Soon after their marriage, MOIS forced them to cooperate by threatening to confiscate Khodabandeh's mother's extensive property in Tehran. Singleton and Khodabandeh then agreed to work for MOIS and spy on the MEK. In 2002 Singleton met in Tehran with MOIS agents who were interested in her background. She agreed to cooperate with MOIS to save her brother-in-law's life – he was still a member of the MEK at the time. During her stay in Tehran, she received training from the MOIS. After her return to England, she launched the iran-interlink.org website in the winter of 2002. After she made many trips to Iran and Singapore – the country where the agency contacts its foreign agents – the MEK became doubtful of Singleton and Khodabandeh's loyalty to the organisation. In 2004 Singleton finally met her brother-in-law, Ibrahim, who was sent from Syria to Iran after the Syrians arrested him (it appears that Syrians closely cooperate with the MOIS). Eventually, the MOIS forced him to cooperate as well.

The Pentagon report proved immediately that the claim that the PMOI/MEK was an irrelevant group or had no support within Iran was clearly a myth. It demonstrated that the PMOI had always been and remained the most serious threat to the Iranian regime, and therefore the suppression of the PMOI had always been and remained a priority for the Iranian intelligence services. The report also underlined what we already knew, that the Iranian regime was the source of all disinformation against the PMOI. Indeed by actually naming Anne Singleton and her Iranian husband, Massoud Khodabandeh, as trained MOIS agents, it reinforced the findings of the British courts years earlier when they demanded the delisting of the PMOI, claiming that their blacklisting based on supposedly classified evidence supplied by these two spies as 'perverse'. Sadly, it was this self-same classified evidence which had been passed to the US State Department by the UK Foreign Secretary, Jack Straw, and which had been used to justify the continued terror listing of the PMOI in America.

Alarmingly, the Pentagon report also showed that Iran's known agents had enjoyed freedom of activity in Europe for years. The report made it clear that the Qods Force and the Islamic Revolutionary Guard Corps, together with the MOIS who control their activities, were involved in conspiracies to murder citizens and residents of the EU. It was perfectly possible that Alejo Vidal-Quadras, Paulo Casaca and myself were targets for 'extraterritorial operations such as sabotage, assassinations, and espionage.'

Similar reports have been made by some European intelligence services. The German Interior Ministry's Annual Report in 2013 on the Protection of the Constitution stated:

1.2 Target areas and focus of information gathering.
Priority task of the Iranian intelligence service apparatus is espionage and to combat opposition movements at home and abroad. Moreover, in the West, information from the fields of politics, economics and science to be procured. In the actions against Germany in particular from the MOIS, special focus is placed on the 'People's Mojahedin of Iran Organization' (MEK) and its political arm, the 'National Council of Resistance of Iran' (NCRI).

And the intelligence services of the Netherlands, AIVD, 2012 report, page 37, states:

AIVD has realized that the government of Iran is constantly active against the resistance movement PMOI. The Iranian Ministry of Intelligence (MOIS) controls a network in Europe, which is also active in the Netherlands. Members of this network are former members of the PMOI who have been recruited by the MOIS. Their mission is to impose a negative impact on public opinion about the PMOI by lobbying, making publications and organizing anti-PMOI rallies. These people also gather information about the PMOI and its members for the MOIS.

36

Interviews with PMOI Refugees in Camp Liberty, September 2014

Hassan Nezam

'My name is Hassan Nezam. I was born in Tehran in 1954 to a middle-class family. My father was a businessman. In 1972, upon completing my high school in Alawi School, I enrolled at the University of Tehran school of economics. I finished my studies, but before graduating I was arrested and taken to prison. When I was studying at the University of Tehran, I used to teach in schools in the southern and eastern parts of Tehran and at the same time I used to help my father with his business.

At Alawi High School the atmosphere was anti-Shah and some of the teachers were associated with the PMOI; that is where I was exposed to politics. When I enrolled in university in 1972, I continued my activities at the Students' Association where I established contacts with the PMOI for the first time. I was in contact with the PMOI from the beginning of my activities in 1972 till 1976, when I was arrested. My activities included distributing leaflets and taking part in anti-Shah demonstrations. At that time, the Shah's regime was regarded as an "island of stability", and through the use and intimidation of his secret police, "SAVAK", no one dared to oppose him publicly. This is where the student associations came in and tried to organise protests from the universities. For example, one of these demonstrations that was organised by the student association in 1978 turned into a widespread protest, and set the stage for the Shah's downfall. These demonstrations organized by the PMOI had started in 1975; it was the first time the slogan, "Death to the Shah" was taken up by the masses. In 1975, during the Ramadan celebrations in Tehran's Bazar, Tehran University students started chanting anti-regime slogans. Subsequently, other demonstrations on the campus occurred that spilled over onto the streets and marked the prelude to mass demonstrations and nationwide unrest.

In the summer of 1976 I was arrested by the SAVAK. I was tortured for three months and then was given a fifteen-year prison sentence. I spent my time in Qasr and Evin prisons. I was released after the popular uprisings in 1979. I was in contact with the PMOI and started my activities in the Azerbaijan region. During the political phase after the revolution, the thugs and hoodlums associated with the Islamic Republic party used to attack our centres and newsstands in the universities. To continue our political activities we were forced to pay a price on a daily basis by enduring violent attacks. This went on till 20 June 1981, when the PMOI's peaceful demonstrations were suppressed violently by the mullah regime's forces. This was a turning-point, and from this point on we had to continue our struggle in a clandestine manner.

In September 1982 I travelled to the Kurdistan region of Iran and stayed in Kurdistan till 1983. From Kurdistan I travelled to Iraq and joined the PMOI there. When Camp Ashraf was established I moved to Ashraf. When I was in Iran I was in contact with some of the resistance cells that were active in Iran. Upon arriving in Ashraf I kept up contact with these cells. Our activities focused on exposing the Khomeini regime's warmongering policies and supporting the patriotic personnel in the armed forces. During the Iran-Iraq war, through propaganda, the Khomeini regime used to send hundreds of thousands of students to their deaths in the front lines. They used to put a key around the students' necks and tell them that this is the key to heaven. Continuing the war was the best cover for the ongoing suppression inside Iran. Our goal was to put a stop to this war at any price. Many of the military personnel who were in contact with us were arrested, tortured and executed. Many others managed to come to Iraq and join the National Liberation Army, and some others managed to leave Iran and expose the warmongering policies of the regime internationally. These activities, along with the blows dealt to the regime by the National Liberation Army, forced Khomeini's regime to accept a ceasefire.

I lost most of my hearing during a terrorist attack by the regime's agents in Iraq and on top of that I witnessed the massacre of 52 of my friends at Camp Ashraf on 1 September 2013. Over a 10-year period I have witnessed the Iranian regime's terrorist operations in

Iraq against the PMOI. In 1999 an explosion ripped into a bus carrying PMOI members that resulted in 6 deaths and 21 wounded. In another incident in Habib Camp in Basra, a truck that was loaded with 1½ tons of TNT exploded, killing 6 and wounding 54 PMOI members. Three of our brothers were killed on Mohammed Ghassem Street in Baghdad in July 1995. I have had many interviews about the role of the Iranian intelligence forces under the direction of the Iranian regime's National Security Council.'

37

Dr Tariq al-Hashemi

I had been in touch with the deposed former Vice President of Iraq, Dr Tariq al-Hashemi for many months. He had fled to Turkey after his thirteen bodyguards had been arrested and tortured, one of them dying under torture. On the basis of bogus confessions made under duress, the twelve surviving bodyguards had each been sentenced to death and Dr al-Hashemi, the most senior Sunni in Iraqi political circles, had entered the *Guinness Book of Records* for having no fewer than five death sentences imposed upon him *in absentia*, allegedly for terrorist offences, which was Maliki's preferred charge for Sunnis he wanted to get rid of.

Shiia militias affiliated to the Iranian regime and Maliki's government had assassinated two of his brothers and one sister. He was perhaps the first and only senior Iraqi official to reveal the barbaric tortures that were taking place in Iraqi prisons. He visited the prisons and then showed films of the torture victims, which infuriated Maliki. He was also a strong supporter of the rights of Ashraf residents and had repeatedly said that they were refugees and Protected Persons under the Fourth Geneva Convention and their rights had to be respected.

I decided that the truth of Maliki's vicious repression of the Sunnis in Iraq could be best described in person by Dr al-Hashemi, and I invited him to address a special conference in the European Parliament in Brussels on 16 October 2013. The fact that Dr al-Hashemi was on Iraq's 'Most Wanted' list was of course a concern. Nevertheless we checked with Interpol and were assured that, as a political figure, he was not on their Red List, which would have meant instant detention and deportation back to Iraq, where he would have been executed within hours.

It was obviously a huge personal risk for Dr al-Hashemi to fly to Europe. He negotiated a visa with the Belgian authorities, which issued it based on the fact that he had received a formal invitation from me to address a meeting in the European Parliament. We organised a large attendance of leading ex-pat Iraqis and key political figures from the Middle East. Alejo Vidal-Quadras, the Vice President of the European Parliament, arranged with the Parliament's protocol services for a VIP greeting for Dr al-Hashemi when he arrived in the early afternoon of 16 October.

In fact, I was walking towards the VIP entrance to prepare to meet Dr al-Hashemi when my mobile phone rang. It was a senior official from the office of the Parliament's President, Martin Schulz. I immediately asked that my thanks should be conveyed to President Schulz for agreeing to the VIP reception for Dr al-Hashemi. 'In fact that is the very reason I have been asked to call you by President Schulz,' said the official. 'The President has decided that Dr al-Hashemi should not be allowed to enter the premises of the European Parliament and he has informed security to stop him from entering the building.'

I was stunned. 'This is the former Vice President of Iraq', I spluttered. 'What possible reason has President Schulz given for this ban?'

'I cannot answer that question,' said the official, 'you'll need to take it up with the President.'

'Put me through to the President straight away,' I said, but the official told me that the President was not available. Clearly, having landed this bombshell, he had made himself scarce, unwilling to have to confront me with his arguments for the ban.

I immediately called Alejo Vidal-Quadras. He was outraged and said that he would try to track down Schulz. We decided to rearrange the conference in another venue in central Brussels. We asked al-Hashemi to remain in his hotel until we could come back with new arrangements.

Dr al-Hashemi was staying in a suite at the Steigenberger Grand Hotel in Avenue Louise. I immediately jumped in a parliamentary car and headed down to see him. When I arrived there were several bodyguards posted in the corridor outside his suite. They ushered me in.

Dr al-Hashemi was pleased to see me, but clearly deeply concerned by this turn of events. 'How can the President of your Parliament do this to me?' he asked. I told him that it didn't surprise me in the slightest. I had no doubt that the Iraqi ambassador to the EU had informed Maliki, and Maliki had got directly in touch with Schulz, denouncing Dr al-Hashemi as a terrorist and pointing out that he was under sentence of death. This would be enough to panic the German socialist Schulz, who was ever keen to avoid any diplomatic incident that might have dented his own reputation. Rather than question the veracity of Maliki's claims, Schulz had simply taken the easy way out and instructed that Dr al-Hashemi should not be allowed to enter the European Parliament. It was a great betrayal of the European Parliament's claim always to fight for justice.

Just as we discussed this, there came a loud knock on the door and al-Hashemi's Belgian lawyer was ushered into the room. He had a message from the Ministry of Foreign Affairs and the Ministry of the Interior, because of the unfortunate situation that had arisen over Schulz's decision to ban Dr al-Hashemi from entering the European Parliament. As the visa for al-Hashemi had been issued on the basis that he was formally invited to the European Parliament, it now seemed that his visa was no longer valid. We asked him to explain what he meant by this and he said, 'Basically, if you no longer have a valid visa, you could be arrested and deported to Iraq at any moment.' He explained that the Belgian government simply wanted to inform al-Hashemi about this, but did not intend to take any action against him.

This was shocking news for Dr al-Hashemi and for all of us. I had invited him to Brussels in good faith and he had come on the understanding that he would be safe from arrest and deportation. Now, because of Schulz, it seemed that he could be arrested and deported at any minute and sent back to face the gallows in Baghdad. This had suddenly become a life or death issue. Nevertheless Dr al-Hashemi remained calm and continued to discuss the matter in an unruffled manner.

Dr al-Hashemi was pondering whether to head straight back to the airport in Brussels to catch the next available flight to Istanbul, but we cautioned against this, as it seemed possible that he might be stopped at border control, although we argued that it was quite unlikely that the Belgian government would create any serious problem for Dr al-Hashemi. Just then, a famous French politician, Bernard

Kouchner, former Minister of Foreign Affairs in the government of Nicolas Sarkozy and founder of Médecins Sans Frontières, joined us in the increasingly crowded room. Kouchner and al-Hashemi were old friends and they hugged each other warmly.

All of us now began a discussion about what to do next. I explained that we had managed to rearrange the conference in a large hall in the centre of Brussels. I said that whatever Dr al-Hashemi decided to do, he should at least take the opportunity of addressing the conference and the media, otherwise we would be seen as handing complete victory to Maliki. The lawyers meanwhile were in discussion by telephone with the Minister of the Interior. They explained that Dr al-Hashemi was a political target of Maliki's and was not on the Interpol Red List. Here we had to solve two problems: firstly, to ensure the security and safe return of Dr al-Hashemi, and secondly to prevent Maliki from making any political gains by cancelling our conference. With the help of the lawyers and our Belgian friends, we successfully neutralised the threat to Dr al-Hashemi's safe return to Turkey. To ensure that the conference went ahead, we changed the venue from the European Parliament to the Residence Palace. I chaired that conference. The keynote speaker was Dr al-Hashemi and several distinguished politicians also spoke, such as Sid Ahmad Ghozali, the former prime minister of Algeria, Yves Bonnet, former Director of the French DST (French Intelligence Service), Lord Maginnis of Drumglass from the UK, Tahar Boumedra, Paulo Casaca, Professor Tanter and Colonel Wes Martin. The conference was a resounding success.

As I sat in an anteroom with the former Iraqi Vice President waiting to make our entrance, we could suddenly hear shouting and noise from the main chamber. This went on for several minutes and we were informed that agents of the Iraqi and Iranian regimes had tried to infiltrate the meeting to cause trouble, and had shouted and become violent when the Residence Palace security guards forcibly ejected them.

Calm having been restored, we entered the room to a standing ovation from the audience. I introduced Dr Tariq al-Hashemi, and he then spoke eloquently about the deteriorating situation in Iraq, citing specific cases of human rights abuse and explaining how the judiciary had become corrupted by Maliki and did his bidding. He also provided an in-depth report on the problems that thousands of innocent Iraqis are facing resulting from false reports that led to their arrests, with their cases remaining in limbo for years. He showed a short film of his visits to many of these prisons and his pledge to the inmates to help. He explained how many of these inmates had been tortured and threatened to make them deliver forged confessions on TV. Dr al-Hashemi said most of those arrested were innocent, while the real criminals were roaming free with the security organs being fully aware of what was going on.

Dr al-Hashemi told the conference how Nouri al-Maliki seemed determined to carve out a role for himself as Saddam Hussein's worthy successor. Angered by critics in the press who had highlighted the spiralling violence and human rights abuses in Iraq, Maliki had banned Al-Jazeera and nine Iraqi TV channels, eight of which were Sunni. Without licences, news crews from the banned channels would be arrested if they attempted to operate in Iraq.

Iraq's descent into another sectarian civil war, prompted by Maliki's determined efforts to marginalise the Sunni population, had become an embarrassment to the US, who regarded the Iraqi Prime Minister as their adopted son. US State Department assertions that they were leaving behind a 'functioning democracy', following the withdrawal of American troops from Iraq, now had a hollow ring.

Dr al-Hashemi said that mass demonstrations against Maliki had been going on in six of Iraq's provinces and most of the major cities for the past four months. Hundreds of thousands of protesters were pouring onto the streets, particularly following Friday prayers, to demand an end to sectarian oppression, human rights abuses and arbitrary executions. Maliki had tried to stem the protests by offering talks, bribes and concessions, but all to no avail. In desperation, he turned to his real sponsors, the Mullahs in Iran, who willingly dispatched their menacing Minister of Intelligence, Heydar Moslehi, who was more than happy to advise Maliki on how Iran deals with street protests and demonstrations.

I thanked Dr al-Hashemi for his presentation and reminded the audience that Maliki runs one of the world's most corrupt regimes. Despite the restoration of oil production to an all-time high with an estimated $8 billion in earnings in the previous year alone, much of this money simply disappears. The infrastructure, devastated during the US invasion and the insurgency, has never been restored. There are only around four hours of electricity a day in Baghdad and most major cities. Many people do not have access to fresh running water. Sewerage systems have broken down. Pollution is rife. Baghdad is one of the world's filthiest capitals. And to cap it all, youth unemployment is running at around 30%. An entire generation has lost faith in the corrupt and oppressive Maliki government.

I then chaired a press conference for Dr al-Hashemi, where he presented documents and video clips showing the involvement of Maliki and his office in torture and flagrant human rights violations. In the press conference Dr al-Hashemi said he was ready to return immediately to Iraq and appear before a fair court, if a true opportunity was provided for him to prove his innocence and the innocence of his bodyguards who had been brutally tortured.

Following the press conference we set off for the airport. I was extremely nervous. If the Ministry of the Interior had given orders for Dr al-Hashemi to be arrested and deported to Iraq, his fate would be my direct responsibility. I had invited him to Brussels. His deportation and execution in Iraq would be a devastating blow for which I would hold myself responsible. At the airport I went with him to passport control at Terminal B. As we approached the border control officer with Dr al-Hashemi at the front, followed closely by bodyguards, his lawyers and me, we were becoming somewhat conspicuous. Other travellers were stopping to stare at our strange procession.

The border control officer examined Dr al-Hashemi's passport and boarding pass. He then looked at me and said, in English, 'What are you doing here?'

I replied, 'I am with Dr al-Hashemi, simply to wish him bon voyage.'

'Then please step back out of the way,' said the officer, rather abruptly. He stamped Dr al-Hashemi's passport and he was through. One of his lawyers accompanied him to Istanbul to ensure that there were no problems, but it seemed that everything was OK. I shouted my great thanks and best wishes to Dr al-Hashemi and headed back out of the airport. It had been a tense time.

Several hours later I was informed that Dr al-Hashemi had arrived safely in Istanbul and I breathed a great sigh of relief. It had been a difficult and nerve-racking experience, but we had demonstrated that we were able to stand up to Maliki and provide a platform to his most important opposition figure. The news of Dr al-Hashemi's trip sparked a hugely positive reaction in the Arab media and an angry one from Maliki's government!

38

Interviews with PMOI Refugees in Camp Liberty, September 2014

Nasser Khademi

'My name is Nasser Khademi. I was born in Tehran in 1981. I was a first year student of Physics at Tehran University when I left my studies and joined the PMOI. I can say that I have known the PMOI ever since I remember. My father was Hamid Khademi and my mother Fereshteh Azhadi, both leading members of the PMOI.

After the 1979 revolution, Khomeini started suppressing the freedom movement in Iran. The PMOI clandestinely managed to continue its political activities in exposing the Mullahs' plans for over two years. On 20 June 1981, when the last possibilities of political activity had been denied, the PMOI had to resort to underground operations. I was five months old at that time. My Mum, Dad and I used to live in the Sattar Khan district in a second storey apartment. When I was a year and a half old, my grandmother moved in with us. I don't recall any of the events and what I know is the result of what I have heard and the research that I have done. Because of my Mum's busy schedule my grandma was the person who took care of me.

On 2 May 1982 Khomeini's Revolutionary Guards found our home. Our house was surrounded at 9 am. Back then, just like now, the crime of being a Mojahed was execution, so the Revolutionary Guards without hesitation started firing at our house. Our home was under attack for several hours. The guards started firing using light weapons. With my Mum and Dad firing back, they realized they couldn't enter the house and they started using rocket launchers and then brought in a helicopter to continue firing on the house. It wasn't important to them that the house was in a residential and densely populated area of Tehran. They left the house in ruins. My Mum and Dad along with my grandmother were killed in the attack. My Mum had hidden me to avoid me getting hurt. The only eye-witness was

214

a woman who had posed as a Khomeini supporter and had entered the house with the Guards. She said when she entered the house the whole house was destroyed by fire and the bodies of the martyrs were scattered all over. She had noticed that one of the Guards had taken out a child who was barely alive; I was that child.

As a result of the rocket attacks on the house I was wounded in my legs, stomach and head and was rendered unconscious. To cover up their crime they had put me in the ambulance with the rest of the bodies and transferred me to a hospital nearby to remove the shrapnel from my body. I still carry some of the shrapnel in my body and the scars on my face and body are still visible. They transferred my Mum, Dad and Grandma's bodies to Evin Prison and placed them for display in front of the prisoners, and that same night they broadcast the images of their dead bodies from state-controlled television. They then buried the bodies in a shallow mass grave outside Tehran.

After months of following up by my remaining grandparents the Guards had told them they had buried the bodies in Khavaran Cemetery. This was the place where the martyrs of the 1988 massacre were also later buried. No one really knows the exact location where my Mum and Dad have been buried. I once heard that when my other grandmother had gone to visit the site and while looking for my father's body had reached under the soil and found part of the shirt that my Dad was wearing when he was killed. I am not sure of the authenticity of this occurrence. I never saw the shirt and no one was willing to talk about this issue. Maybe the trauma of the situation had made it impossible to pursue.

Upon hearing that I was still alive, my other grandma and relatives had started looking for me and after a month found me in one of the hospitals. My stay in hospital has a story of its own. When they were done with the surgeries, the Guards wanted to transfer me to Evin Prison. This was their usual practice whenever they attacked one of the Mojahedin's homes, and if they found any children alive they would transfer them to Evin Prison Women's Ward and have the female prisoners raise the child. On the day that our house was attacked, the news had spread all over Tehran. The neighbours used to tell me that when they heard the sound of the bullets they were filled with sadness, because they could not bear to see the martyrdom of people who had risen up for their freedom. The doctors and the nurses at the hospital felt the same way, and they had not permitted the Guards to transfer me to Evin Prison. They had told them that my situation was not stable and I had to be under constant medical supervision. My grandma found me at the hospital, and with the help of the doctors and nurses I was given to her care.

As a child, whenever I looked in the mirror and saw the scars on my face, I would remember the ordeal I had endured. The first question my friends used to ask me was, when did I find out that my Mum and Dad had been martyred, and what was it all about? I used to tell them that ever since I remember I knew about it. In the beginning my relatives tried to hide the facts from me and tried to introduce my Aunt as my Mum to me, but it was not possible. Whenever I would meet the prisoners who had been set free or the families of those who were martyred, they couldn't control their emotions and they would cry and hug me. They used to tell me, you are a remembrance from Fereshteh and Hamid! They used to show me the pictures they had of them in their homes. My other relatives would share the memories they had of my Dad whenever they saw me. Our neighbours used to point me out to one another and say, this is Khademi's son.

I remember when I was two years old, for my birthday they had made a cake with the number two written on it and designed with swans on the cake. There was a picture of my Mum and Dad in a picture frame next to the cake. I couldn't make out what was going on. I knew everyone has a Mum and Dad, but I really didn't know who mine were. Now I had my Aunt as a Mum and the person in the picture frame! All I can say is it was a confusing time for me. The martyrdom of my Mum and Dad was so important that all our friends, acquaintances and the neighbours knew about it and paid their respects on a regular basis. My Dad had two engineering degrees and was a political prisoner under the Shah. My Mum was studying Health at the university and was also a political prisoner under the Shah; they wanted to overthrow Khomeini's dictatorship and sacrificed their lives in the process.

My father was a parliamentary candidate after the 1979 revolution in his hometown of Golpaiegan, but he was prevented from standing due to vote rigging by the authorities. Wherever I went in

216

Golpaiegan people used to approach me and reminisce about my father. Even the supporters of the clerical regime used to talk about my father with respect. Having experienced thousands of encounters with people about the Mojahedin, even if I had not seen and felt the oppression by Khomeini's regime, I could easily tell that the Mojahedin are in the hearts and minds of the people. It was obvious that all the emotions expressed weren't for a young child, but it was towards the deeds of the Mojahedin who had sacrificed their lives for their people. This is how I came to know the Mojahedin. The Mojahedin fought against Khomeini and for their people.

The extent of oppression and injustice was very apparent to me as a child. I could see first hand the rise of addiction and prostitution among the people I knew. I had seen the rise in public hangings, poverty and widening income gaps. I watched poor children who were forced to sell flowers on the streets. I always pondered the solution to this mess and thought what could be done? Why should the clerics live in luxury when there are so many hungry children? Why should the clerics get away with stealing millions of dollars, while a man who steals to feed his hungry child has his fingers cut off? Why can't the young people wear the clothes they like and listen to music of their choice? Why should a young man be thrown off of a high-rise building in Tehran for participating in a party? How long should we live like this?

I felt like someone had their foot on my throat and was pushing harder every day making it more and more difficult for me to breathe. I had just enrolled at the university, and the older I got the more aware I became of the social facts and situation and the more I felt the pressure. It became unbearable. My brain could not handle all the questions and pressures. Even though we were relatively well-off financially, I still couldn't deal with all the shortcomings I was exposed to. I couldn't get any pleasure from going on trips or having fun; even getting 'A's from my maths teacher didn't satisfy me any longer. The world had become black and white. Even listening to my favourite music didn't feel like it used to. I felt that I had to take action and take part in the change.

I had reached a point that I had to make a decision. I either had to continue my education with the hope of becoming an inventor or something like that, or change the course of my life. The difference that I felt with the rest of my friends was that besides being a witness to the injustices, I knew the solution.

Finding a way to get there was not so easy. The oppression by the clerical regime had made it very difficult. A single mistake could lead to imprisonment and even execution. I tried a few different ways to contact the PMOI to no avail. Those days the Internet was not as widespread as it is today and the regime had complete control over it. It took a few months to prepare for the trip and then I set off for Syria and eventually Ashraf.'

39
Kurdistan

I believe that the task of every parliamentarian is to work for the respect of human rights and for the veneration and dignity of human life; these are core European values. This task is even more important in areas of the world in which, for one reason or another, tensions prevail over conciliation, misunderstandings over dialogue, fighting over peace.

In my role as President of the Delegation for Relations with Iraq in the European Parliament, I felt it was my duty to find the truth about what was happening in that country. This search for the truth was never intended to hamper dialogue with Iraq. On the contrary, it was meant to improve the quality of EU-Iraqi relations, especially following the ratification of the EU's Partnership and Cooperation Agreement, which was supposed to be the catalyst to promote the birth of an inclusive, pluralistic and anti-sectarian political force in Iraq, efficiently contributing to the abolition of the system of 'mu-hasasa', which saw the distribution of the country's wealth and powerful governmental positions to clans, tribes, sects, faiths and other closed circles, generating jealousy, inefficiency and corruption. I had long advocated that there should be no financial assistance to Iraq until we saw signs of good governance.

I had become a strong critic of Nouri al-Maliki and his sectarian approach to government. He had turned into a dictator, even waging genocidal campaigns against the Sunni population in many Iraqi provinces. It was imperative that I investigated this deteriorating situation on the ground. With this in mind I set out once again to Iraq on 22 November 2013. The European Parliament's security people had prohibited any visit to Baghdad, as it was deemed too dangerous. I therefore flew to Erbil in northern Iraq. Delavar Ajgeiy, the Head of the KRG Mission to the EU, met me at the new international airport. He had organised four hefty security guards and a fleet of armoured, black Toyota Landcruisers to stay with me throughout my visit. The security guards all had ominous bulges under their jackets, where they were certainly packing pistols.

I had let it be widely known that I was coming to Iraq and had invited key political and religious leaders to travel to Erbil in Kurdistan to meet me. I met with the Kurdistan Regional Government's President Massoud Barzani, and the Prime Minister of Kurdistan, Nechirvan Barzani. I also met leading Christian bishops, the Grand Mufti of Iraq and some members of the Iraqi Parliament, including the Chairman of the Human Rights Committee as well as leaders of the recent popular uprisings in six Sunni provinces.

I was invited to address a major conference in Erbil organised by the Chaldean Syriac Assyrian Christians. The conference debated the gradual erosion of Iraq's ancient Christian community. The 'Friends of Bartalla' conference took place in Erbil on 23 November 2013. Over 850 people, including the First Lady of Iraq, Hêro Ahmed Ibrahim Talabani, attended. I was called to the main stage in the auditorium and said:

> Prior to the Gulf War in 1991, there were more than one and a half million Christians in Iraq. They lived in absolute peace with their Muslim neighbours. Some estimates say there are now less than three hundred thousand. One of the oldest Christian communities in the world is facing extinction.
>
> In September, I invited Humam Hammoudi, Chair of the Iraqi Council of Representatives' Foreign Relations Committee, to address the European Parliament's Delegation for Relations with Iraq. He read lengthy passages from the Iraqi Constitution and told us that the current government has tried to transcend religious differences. He said 'We defend a multi-faith society and enshrine this in our constitution.' He said, 'Religious rights extend to all individuals.' While I was still trying to absorb these amazing statements, he took my breath away by announcing that: 'Christians in Iraq are living through a golden age and if they leave now they will miss out on the opportunities provided by the Iraqi constitution.'
>
> Mr Hammoudi's performance in Brussels perhaps illustrated the yawning gap between hope and reality! It was a

sad reflection on how the current government has abrogated control to Nouri al-Maliki, so that now, lawlessness, terrorism, corruption and the systematic abuse of human rights are each a daily feature of life in Iraq.

The EU has no army, but we have massive economic power. Instead of friendship and cooperation agreements and pledges of inward investment, Europe should link any economic aid directly to good governance. There should be no further aid to Iraq without a clear sign of respect for human rights, women's rights, plurality and an end to sectarianism. The EU should divert all financial aid to the NGO community, to encourage literacy programmes and education. Crucially, we must stop referring to the ethnic communities as 'minorities' and start referring to them only as Iraqis. This is your country. It is your constitution. The government should be a government of all the people and not just a government of some of the people. Iraq must become a country where Shiias, Sunnis, Christians, Jews, Turkmen, Yezidis and all ethnic communities can live in freedom, peace and prosperity. This is the future we all hope and pray for.

For a moment or two after I finished speaking, there was stunned silence in the room. No one in Iraq had ever heard a speech so openly critical of the Prime Minister and his government. Suddenly the auditorium erupted in applause. They liked what I had to say. They were happy at my frankness. Many people came up to me at the end of the conference, slapping me on the back and saying, 'That was a courageous speech. It needed to be heard in Iraq.'

Later I organised meetings in my hotel suite with Sunni representatives of recent popular uprisings in Iraqi cities, some of whom had travelled great distances to meet with me. They told me that there were frequent attacks, by forces loyal to the government, on mosques in Fallujah and Mosul and parts of Baghdad and Diyala Province. There was constant harassment of the Sunnis and other groups by the Shiites. 90% of arrested people are Sunni. Mass executions are predominantly of Sunnis. Four out of ten Sunni women were raped in prison.

Fears about the inclusiveness of the upcoming 30 April elections were expressed, because apparently there was a big operation under way aimed at marginalising and discriminating against the Sunni electorate, using, among other means, incorrect police charges and files with false accusations against Sunni candidates. The underlying problem was that in all evidence al-Maliki's government considered the participants in recent Sunni popular uprisings in Samarra, Mosul, Anbar, Fallujah, Ramadi, Diyala and Kirkuk to be al-Qaeda terrorists, which was not true. Those uprisings took place following the highly discriminatory government approach towards Sunnis and are in their essence and means radically different from the Salafist al-Qaeda, which is totally extraneous to Iraqi Sunni culture, as had been widely demonstrated by the Sunni Awakening movements during the US-led 'surge' in the years 2007-2008. Among other things, I was told that all Sunni mosques in Baghdad had been closed and three imams were killed on average every Friday in bomb attacks; in the previous year 400 imams were killed; six leaders of the Sunni population were killed in Mosul and also many supportive journalists were killed in the current year.

The crackdown on leading Sunni politicians by the overtly Shiia al-Maliki seemed to follow a clear pattern. Each time Maliki visited Tehran he received instructions from his puppet-masters, the Islamic Shiia Mullahs. This always involved ordering the arrest of another Sunni political leader when he returned to Baghdad. He also almost invariably initiated a brutal military assault on the 3,000 PMOI refugees held in Camp Liberty. Ominously, and clearly acting on instructions from Tehran, Maliki had also allowed the free flow of Iranian and Hezbollah military personnel and equipment through Iraq to bolster the dictatorship of Bashar al-Assad in neighbouring Syria.

I was determined to see for myself what was being done to counter Maliki's malign influence in Iraq. I received a phone call from Sheik Dr Rafie Alrafaee, the Sunni Grand Mufti of Iraq. He said that he was driving to Erbil from Dohuk and that he would send a driver and a car to take me to a secret location on his arrival in around 90 minutes' time. He said the location had to remain secret for his own safety. When I explained this to my Kurdish security team they were aghast. How could I go to an undisclosed address in a car with an unknown driver? They said this breached every tenet of their security code. Nevertheless, it was important that I should meet the Grand Mufti, so I told them that I was prepared to take the risk.

In due course, the driver arrived and I squeezed into the rear of a small Volkswagen. We tore off down endless backstreets in Erbil, until finally we entered a cul-de-sac, at the end of which several turbaned imams were standing, mobile phones in hand. They waved my driver into a parking place and then led me up a flight of stairs to a small room, filled with around a dozen people, at the end of which stood the Grand Mufti. He greeted me warmly and thanked me for agreeing to meet him.

The Grand Mufti is deeply committed to peace and freedom. He condemned the bombings and killings that take place daily in Iraq. He admitted that al-Qaeda were certainly involved in these atrocities. On the other hand, he told me the West must also realize that al-Qaeda were not the only terrorists. He stated that al-Maliki's special militias, sponsored by Iran, were setting off car bombs and assassinating political opponents on a daily basis. According to him, the 'Mukhtar Army' was directly connected to this series of atrocities, and was controlled by al-Maliki. They apparently manufactured the car bombs, which were then exploded outside Sunni mosques in Baghdad and other cities. Al-Qaeda was blamed for these bombings and the West believed this simplified version of reality.

At the end of our meeting I shook the Grand Mufti's hand warmly and asked him if he would be prepared to come to the European Parliament in Brussels to give evidence about the oppression of the Sunni population by Maliki at a special human rights conference. He readily agreed.

I also met Dr Salim Abdullah al-Jabouri, Chair of the Human Rights Committee in the Parliament, who has now been appointed its President (Speaker). He informed me that 50,000 people were in government prison camps, and apparently even more in secret prisons. Another 3,000 people were being held in urban secret jails. He promised to send me a complete dossier of human rights abuse that he has uncovered. He said that he would also be willing to come to Brussels to address a meeting of the Delegation for Relations with Iraq to speak about the human rights situation in the country.

The meeting with President Massoud Barzani took place in the President's Palace in the mountains of Salahaddin, and discussion ensued about the demographic issues affecting the Christians in Bartalla. President Barzani stated that he would ask Baghdad to set up a special committee to find a solution to the Christian/Shabak problem, which he considers 'very sensitive'. Concerning Syrian refugees, President Barzani renewed the Kurdistan Regional Government engagement of offering much needed shelter and hospitality. I informed him of my recent letter to Baroness Ashton asking that EU aid should be directed to Erbil, where it was needed, rather than to Baghdad. President Barzani walked with me to the front steps of his palace as I was leaving. I took this opportunity to raise with him the appalling massacre of 52 PMOI refugees in Camp Ashraf and the taking of seven hostages. The President gripped my arm. 'This was a foul crime,' he said. 'I have protested to Maliki and demanded the release of the hostages. I will do everything in my power to secure their release.'

The KRG Prime Minister, Mr Nechirvan Barzani, gave me the impression of being a young, dynamic and highly intelligent politician; the Minister for Foreign Relations, Mr Falah Mustafa, accompanied him. The Prime Minister told me that one of the recent achievements of the KRG was to stop the so-called 'honour killings', courageously announcing that these were 'dis-honourable' and that anyone involved would be prosecuted for murder. I also raised with him the question of the massacre at Camp Ashraf. He said that he condemned such violence, but that he was reluctant to offer a refuge in Kurdistan for the 3,400 PMOI refugees in Camp Liberty.

I visited Kawergocek Refugee Camp, around 45 minutes from Erbil, and was introduced to Whycliffe Songwa, the UNHCR Senior Field Coordinator, and to the Mayor of Khabat District, Rzgar Mustafa. They described to me how the KRG opened the borders with Syria in August 2013 and were immediately flooded with Kurdish Syrian refugees fleeing the civil war from the Jazeera region of Syria and from Aleppo itself.

On my return to Brussels I wrote to Baroness Ashton recommending that the European Commission should send extra funding to Kurdistan for the 'winterisation programme' for Syrian refugees. The money should be sent directly to the NGOs who are actively helping the Syrian refugees in Iraq, I said. It was deeply impressive for me to have seen for myself the extent of the aid being provided to refugees by the Kurds. Little did we realise that their situation would become even more precarious in the months ahead with the sudden emergence of ISIS – the Islamic State.

In the European Parliament I suggested to my own officials that we should organise a Human Rights Conference on Iraq in February or March 2014, to which we could invite the Chair of the Human Rights Committee from the Council of Representatives, Mr al-Jabouri; the KRG Minister for Human Rights and Sheik Dr Rafie Alrafaee, the Grand Mufti, in order to highlight the dire situation in Iraq.

40

Interviews with PMOI Refugees in Camp Liberty, September 2014

Khadija Borhani

'My name is Khadija Borhani, I am 45 years old and I was born in Qazvin. During the Shah's time my whole family was opposed to the monarchical dictatorship, and that is how I became aware of politics from early childhood. I was introduced to the PMOI through my brother Mehdi in 1977; I was only ten years old. In 1981, at 13, I was arrested by the Revolutionary Guards and transferred to the medieval clerical regime's prisons. Qazvin being a small city, the news of my arrest at such a young age spread through the city like wildfire. The prosecutor's lack of evidence and pressure from my parents led to my release.

My older brother Seyed Mehdi Borhani, after entering university in April of 1975 was arrested by the Shah's SAVAK. He was sentenced to seven years in prison. Due to the popular uprising by the people he was released in December of 1978. Upon his release he actively helped organise and took part in anti-Shah demonstrations in Qazvin. After the overthrow of the Shah he worked full time with the Mojahedin National Movement.

In August of 1982, during the attacks on the Mojahedin's bases, he was wounded and arrested by the Revolutionary Guards and transferred to Evin Prison, where he was subjected to the worst possible medieval tortures. After a week of torture they executed him. He was only 27 years old at the time of his execution. I was not aware of his death until my brother Hassan and I were trying to leave the country, three years later, where he gave me the news of his martyrdom. I was only 16 years old and was hoping when I crossed the border I would be able to see my brother Mehdi once again, so the news was very shocking to me.

My second brother, Seyed Mohammad Ali Borhani, was a student of geology at Shahrood Mining University. One afternoon in August of 1981 when the Revolutionary Guards attacked our house, Ali, who had just returned from work, was arrested and taken to prison. When in prison he accepted all the responsibility and diverted the attention from the other brothers who had been arrested as well. So he managed to save the lives of his brothers. His body was burned with cigarettes and his arm broken during torture; he was executed on 9 September 1981.

Ali was the first member of my family to be martyred. When he was killed I was also in prison. The night before their execution they read a list of names of people and Ali's name was one of the names on the list. They immediately called me out of the Women's Ward, where I was being held. As soon as I stepped out I saw Ali standing behind the door smiling. I was so happy to see him and asked him how he was. I never thought that he was actually going to be executed. He told me that the judge had a few more questions so they were taking him back to court, but, he said, he would be back tomorrow. I even asked him if he could bring a few books back with him. "What kind of books do you want?" he asked. I gave him the names of a few books. He never so much as hinted that he knew he was going to his execution. When he was ready to leave he hugged me so hard that when he left, I felt like my heart had been squeezed out of my chest. It felt as though I will never see him again. I wanted to ask him if he is really coming back tomorrow, then why is he hugging me as though he may never see me again; but he was taken away. Even though I was worried, I didn't want to think about the possibility of his execution.

The next day at 11:00 am my name was called out through the loudspeakers in the Ward, and when I went out I saw the rest of my brothers were there as well (I was in prison along with four of my brothers: Ali, Ahmad, Hossein and Hassan). When I realised that Ali was not with them I broke into tears and realised why he had come to see me the night before. I was only 13 years old at the time. My brothers told me what an impact Ali had had on the other prisoners and his cellmates. Ali was 25 years old when he was executed.

My third brother, Seyed Mohammad Mofid Borhani, came to know the PMOI in 1974 and after the revolution started working

227

full time with the organisation. When the PMOI was outlawed he had to continue his activities in a clandestine fashion. After a while he managed to leave the country and join the National Liberation Army. During the Eternal Light operation he was the commander of one of the units and was martyred in the city of Islamabad. He was 29 years old.

My fourth brother, Seyed Ahmad Borhani, was arrested with Ali and me and transferred to prison. He was the kind of person who could not bear any kind of injustice. Anything the Guards would say to him he would immediately give them the response they deserved and for this reason he was tortured constantly. Due to the blows he had received to his head and back he had lost a lot of weight and was suffering from constant headaches and back pain. They tortured him through sleep deprivation and he became extremely weak. After a year and a half in prison he was released for a short time and during this time he managed to get himself connected to the organisation again. But the unit he was connected to was compromised and he was arrested along with my other brother and brought back to prison. They started torturing him immediately. For over a year we had no idea where he was and my Mum and Dad tried to locate him but to no avail. They searched every prison and holding cell in every city in our state, only to be told that they should try looking in other detention centres, and this in itself was a form of torture for my parents. His cellmates used to say he was defiant and full of energy till the end. He was executed during the 1988 massacre of political prisoners at the age of 27.

My fifth brother, Seyed Mohammad Hossein Borhani, was in middle school in 1976 when my oldest brother Mehdi was arrested by the Shah's SAVAK. When the SAVAK agents had come to our home he had tried stopping them from entering the house and they had pushed him out of the way, hitting his head in the process causing him to stutter for the rest of his life. Despite going to many doctors to get rid of his stutter it remained with him until his last day. After the revolution Mohammad Hossein joined the National Mojahedin Movement and was working as a full-time member distributing Mojahedin newspapers. One day when they had gone to set up a street exhibition they were all arrested and taken to prison. He was in prison for a year and a half, and upon being released joined resistance units. The unit he was in was compromised and he was arrested and taken to prison for the second time. Like Ahmad, for over a year, we had no idea what had happened to him and where he was being held, and all the efforts of my Mum and Dad to locate him failed. He was tortured for seven years and was executed during the massacre of political prisoners in 1988. He was only 25 years old. I recall when Ahmad and Hossein were in prison, my younger brother Hassan and I went to visit them; when we told them that we were going to join the National Liberation Army, their eyes lit up with joy, and they said "Give Massoud our regards and tell him not to worry about us. When we entered the organisation we pledged to stay until the end and we have held steadfast to that pledge."

My youngest brother, just like the rest of us, was raised in a family that was political and from the beginning saw the injustices committed by the Khomeini regime. He started working part-time with the Mojahedin National Movement by distributing PMOI publications. My oldest brother Mehdi always used to refer to him as our little heroic militia. On 20 June 1981 he was arrested along with a few of his friends trying to sell newspapers at one of the PMOI newsstands. When the Guards tried to arrest him he tried to run away, but fell and injured his knee. After his arrest, the Guards used to torture him by hitting him on the injured knee, which caused severe permanent damage. He was only 15 years old when he was arrested. Without conducting any trial they kept him in prison for three and a half years. Upon being released he tried to get connected again to the PMOI and on 29 November 1985 managed to leave Iran and join the National Liberation Army. He was martyred during the Chelcheragh Operation at the age of 21.

After the execution of my brother Ali in 1981 my Dad was summoned to the prosecutor's office. While he was climbing the stairs to go into the building, Vahdani, one of the head torturers, saw him and said, "Don't bother coming up the stairs. We just summoned you to tell you we have executed your son." My father suffered a heart attack on the spot. When he regained consciousness, he told Vahdani, 'Do you know whom you have killed? You did not just kill one person, you have killed a thousand generations after him as well.'

Vahdani said, "If he was a bad person he will go to hell and if he was good he will end up in heaven; it is done and we cannot reverse what is done." He continued by saying, "You have to bring a death certificate so we can give you his body."

Upon leaving the building my father again fell unconscious in the street. The people passing by thought he had been struck by a car; they tried to take him to hospital. My father regained consciousness and told the people, "I wish I had been struck by a car, I have no idea how to break the news to his mother." With the help of the people on the scene he managed to get the death certificate for my brother. When he took the death certificate to Vahdani, he referred him to the morgue. At the morgue they told him to check all the bodies to try to find his son. After checking many lifeless bodies of young people who had been alive a few days earlier he finally found Ali's body, and with the help of the people who found him unconscious on the street he managed to take Ali's body home from the morgue.

My mother had a very resilient demeanour and held her head high. She said no one should feel sorry for her, because her son was not dead, he was martyred, so she should be congratulated instead.

The henchmen did everything to make life unbearable for my parents. They used to send them to other cities under the pretext of telling them their children had been transferred to another prison, just to make life miserable for them. Often the regime's agents used to attack them on the streets. In one incident one of the agents hit my Mum on the leg with a metal bar and she wasn't able to walk for months.

When my brother Hassan was released from prison we left the country, and through Pakistan managed to reach Camp Ashraf.'

41

Can Iraq Rise from the Ashes?

The Iraqi elections were held on 30 April 2013, and it was widely believed that the results of the election were a sham. Few people accepted that Maliki's 'State of Law' Party could have won 92 seats – three more than last time – following years of violence, venal corruption, repression and economic failure. There was also considerable scepticism about the alleged 62% turnout at the elections, given the background of rising aggression in Iraq and the genocidal campaign being waged against the Sunni population of Anbar Province. Considering the vicious shelling and barrel bomb attacks on schools, hospitals and civilian targets in Fallujah and Ramadi, and more than 6,000 deaths by the early summer of 2014 in Iraq, many political leaders agreed that the 62% voter turnout was a fiction.

Politicians in Iraq also expressed their dismay at widespread vote rigging during the elections. Ayad Allawi, leader of al-Iraqiya, claimed that two million ballot papers were missing, raising deep suspicions that major electoral fraud took place. News that all Iraqi police and army personnel were issued with two ballot papers each, one in their camps and the other sent to their homes, compounded fears that the election was rigged.

Nevertheless, the official election results showed Maliki winning the largest bloc, with a total of 168 seats won by Shiite parties, in a parliament of 328 seats. The Sunnis won 43 seats, the Kurds 62, with 24 seats going to secular parties, 8 seats allocated to minorities and 23 seats won by independents and others.

Although there is an actual Shiite majority in the Iraqi Parliament, it was no guarantee of Maliki's ability to form a coalition. Many of the Shiia factions vowed not to work with Maliki again, and intensive negotiations began in the weeks following the election as he attempted to buy or bribe different factions to join him. The Iranian regime, which regarded Maliki as their pliable puppet, was

231

also putting pressure on different political factions to support him for a third term as prime minister.

For the Mullahs in Tehran, a non-sectarian, fully democratic government in Baghdad would be anathema, and they were pressing ahead with their determination to secure another four years of authoritarian Shiite domination of Iraq, with the strings being pulled by Tehran. The presence of Iranian militias in the bloody campaign in Fallujah and Ramadi were visible signs of this interference.

The conclusion was that this election, the first to take place in Iraq since the withdrawal of American troops, had been significantly corrupted to the point where the result was almost certainly fraudulent. There seemed little doubt that hundreds of thousands of people were deprived of their right to participate in the 30 April elections due to violence and intimidation, rendering this the most undemocratic election of the post-Saddam era.

To begin with, as was their usual practice, the UN, the US and the EU stood back and watched developments from the sidelines. Despite the fact that the people of Iraq had suffered enough and were crying out for a non-sectarian government of national salvation, that could stabilise the current situation and allow all Iraqis a fair share of wealth and power, the West was content to act only as an interested observer. It was becoming abundantly clear to many, however, that another four years of corrupt dictatorship by Maliki could destroy Iraq.

Lawlessness, terrorism, corruption and the systematic abuse of human rights are each a daily feature of life in Iraq. The World Bank lists Iraq as having one of the worst qualities of governance in the world. Transparency International lists Iraq as one of the world's most corrupt countries. It has a dreadful human rights record and now is in third place after only China and neighbouring Iran in the number of people it executes. In spite of vast oil revenues, per capita income is only $1,000 per year, making it one of the world's poorest countries.

The situation for women in Iraq is dire. Women are subject to rape, attack and violence. Maliki's genocidal attacks in al-Anbar on the spurious pretext of war against terror had left 250,000 people homeless, mostly women and children, because they are the only ones who are allowed to leave the cities. Five or six provinces in Iraq were subjected to this kind of abuse. It even became impossible to travel from Baghdad to al-Anbar to deliver aid. The suffering of the displaced women and children went far beyond the sheer loss of their homes. They lost everything, including access to health care, education, everything.

Forcing people to move in this way was creating a new situation where a new identity was being artificially manufactured for vast swathes of the Iraqi population, splitting them up into sectarian divisions. This was something that had never been experienced even under Saddam. Iraqi women grew up next to Shiia, Sunni, Christians and Turkmen, and nobody cared what religion anyone was. But now Iraq was fracturing. Extreme levels of trauma, fear, anxiety and post-traumatic stress were being experienced by tens of thousands of Iraqis. Women were fighting for basic survival. Iraq has five million widows and five million orphans, but only 120,000 receive state aid. A widow's average benefit is in any case only £55 ($85) per month and average rent is £130 ($200) per month.

Only 2% of women are in the Iraqi civil service. Despite billions of dollars of oil income annually, Iraq is suffering from endemic corruption. The death penalty is not just for men. Iraq has become a slaughterhouse. It is barbaric. Children of men and women who have been executed on charges of terrorism, will grow up to become terrorists themselves, to take their revenge.

Education has suffered too. 92% of children have impediments to their schooling. Schools suffer from poor and dilapidated buildings; many schools even for 500 children have no toilets and often appallingly difficult transport links. Meanwhile the killing of teachers, scientists and academics, many of them women, goes on apace. Middle-class people are leaving the country by the tens of thousands.

Following my successful meetings in Erbil in November 2013, I had invited key speakers from Iraq to address a major human rights conference in the European Parliament, Brussels, on 19 February 2014. The speakers included some of the most prominent political and religious leaders in Iraq, including Sheik Dr Rafie Alrafaee, Grand Mufti of Iraq, Salim Abdullah al-Jabouri, Chair of the Human Rights Committee in the Council of Representatives, Haidar

Mulla, Member of the Iraqi Council of Representatives, Minister Falah Mustafa Bakir, KRG Head of Department of Foreign Relations and Yonadam Kanna, Chair of the Labour and Social Affairs Committee in the Iraqi Council of Representatives. I chaired the conference and drew attention to a highly critical report on Iraq by the European Parliament's Directorate-General for External Policies, entitled 'Iraq's deadly spiral towards a civil war'. I told the conference that a resolution condemning the ongoing violence and abuse of human rights in Iraq was also under preparation in the European Parliament and would be debated the following week in Strasbourg.

In my opening remarks I said:

> Last November, I was in Iraq. I met with many leading politicians, religious leaders and with courageous men and women who had led popular uprisings and protests in al-Anbar and six provinces of Iraq and in many Iraqi cities. The message from all of them was identical. They told me that lawlessness, terrorism, corruption and the systematic abuse of human rights are each a daily feature of life in Iraq. They told me that Prime Minister Nouri al-Maliki is rapidly becoming another Saddam Hussein, and that modern Iraq is a dust-bowl of violence and bloodshed.

In his address to the conference, Dr Rafie Alrafaee, the Grand Mufti of Iraq, said:

> Maliki is following a heinous policy of indiscriminate bombings of innocent people. The people of al-Anbar did not start the war. We did everything to reach a peaceful settlement. Maliki's forces attacked these peaceful rallies. They have bombarded the houses of innocent people. My own brother was killed last week in the bombardment and was not from al Qaeda or from Daesh [ISIS]. When Maliki launched his so-called war against terrorists in the desert in Anbar province, not a single combatant of al-Qaeda was killed. The only people killed were innocent shepherds. What is happening in Fallujah is genocide. 1,000 civilians have been injured. Events

234

in Iraq have taken a very dangerous turn. It could lead to a civil war in which all Iraqi people will lose. The European Parliament should deal with this matter. We've been handed on a golden platter to the Iranian government.

Salim Abdullah al-Jabouri, Chair of the Human Rights Committee in the Council of Representatives and now President of the Iraqi Parliament said:

We called on the international community to come to our rescue, but we were faced with just talk and no action. Now the tears of Iraqi women have dried up. We're sick of unfulfilled promises. But all of this has not put an end to bloodshed in Iraq. All of the violations are serious, all are important. They are issues of international governance and international law. We Iraqis are the ones who suffer. Investigators use torture to obtain confessions. We need to adopt legislation that will put a stop to violations of prisoners. A person can be detained for years on false accusations. But human rights violations will not lead to the eradication of terrorism. Our committee has managed to get many women released from prison. Iraq is rich in diversity, but the killing still goes on. There are around ten car bombs every day. The Iraqi media should be given more freedom to report the truth. Tens of thousands of civilians have been displaced in al-Anbar Province. A generation has lost all of its rights.

Haidar Mulla, Member of the Iraqi Council of Representatives, said:

Mr Stevenson has increased the influence of the EU in Iraq and, in particular, he has increased the importance of human rights. We had hoped that Iraq would become a democracy after the fall of the previous regime. But our human rights record is not something we should be proud of. Our task is difficult and complex. We have to pave the way for a culture that respects human rights. The Government of Iraq has not implemented Article 19 on human rights. This is not a gift to the people. It is their right. Currently there is a ratio of one military personnel to 27 civilians and even so we cannot live peacefully. We have a political crisis and we have to deal with it politically.

Minister Falah Mustafa Bakir, KRG Head of Department of Foreign Relations, said:

Human rights is not a privilege. It is a basic right. We care about human rights because as Kurds we have a long experience of suffering.

The conference was judged to be a great success, but again the subsequent media reports caused a furious backlash from Baghdad, with Maliki once again condemning me for only backing the Sunnis, which was quite untrue, and for giving a one-sided picture of what was happening in Iraq!

Many of Iraq's wounds are self-inflicted, resulting from failed political leadership. Nouri al-Maliki focused all of his efforts on remaining in power, steadily becoming more authoritarian and repressive and implementing sectarian policies that led directly to ethnic polarisation. By tightly controlling the military and security forces from his own office, he guaranteed that the very forces that could have ensured stability and an end to conflict contributed to the exact opposite. He used those forces, with direct assistance from the fascist Iranian regime, repeatedly to attack, kidnap and murder the innocent and defenceless refugees in Camps Ashraf and Liberty, committing crimes against humanity for which he must be held accountable in the international courts.

Maliki also marginalised or openly discriminated against all non-Shiia minorities, despite the fact they were supposed to be protected and have equal rights under the Iraqi constitution. The Christian population of Iraq has shrunk to fewer than 300,000 and many have been forced to flee from the Islamic State (IS), faced with an ultimatum to convert to Islam, pay a special non-Islamic tax, or die. Soon, some people think that one of the oldest Christian communities in the world may become extinct. But they are not the only minority facing ethnic cleansing.

The Yezidis, whose Zoroastrian religion pre-dates Christianity by a thousand years, are regarded as devil-worshippers by the jihadists of IS, who have massacred them in their hundreds and driven them from their homes. It was the plight of thousands of Yezidis facing starvation, dehydration and death on Mount Sinjar that drew Obama and Cameron back into the Iraqi conflict, both promising military and humanitarian aid.

It was the US and the UK – George W. Bush and Tony Blair – who invaded Iraq and overthrew Saddam, declaring: 'Mission accomplished'. This created the ethnic melting pot that the Iranians exploited and that Nouri al-Maliki debased. The predictable result was violent reaction by the oppressed minorities, notably the Sunnis, and the alienation and growing disillusion of the Kurds. Maliki's genocidal campaign against the Sunni population of al-Anbar province raged on for many months, inevitably sucking in elements of ISIS from the Syrian civil war, which capitalised on the fear and loathing of Maliki among the Sunni population. The escalating violence finally exploded into a civil conflict equal to, or worse than, the sectarian civil war that broke out during the US occupation. ISIS made rapid territorial gains in both the south and north of Iraq, capturing entire cities like Mosul and driving tens of thousands of Christians, Yezidis and other ethnic minorities to flee for their lives.

In the face of this onslaught the Iraqi military collapsed. The astute use of social media by ISIS ensured that ghastly films and photographs of mass slaughter and beheadings of captured Iraqi soldiers spread panic in the ranks. Thousands of Iraqi military personnel tore off their uniforms, dropped their weapons and fled. ISIS captured hundreds of tonnes of new weaponry, tanks, Humvees, rocket launchers and small arms. More importantly, they took control of rich oilfields and banks, and became one of the wealthiest terrorist organisations in the world.

Success bred success, and more and more jihadists flooded into Iraq from Syria to join the war. Such were their territorial gains that they ditched the name ISIS and re-named themselves the Islamic State (IS). Their leader, Abu Bakr al-Baghdadi, declared himself Caliph, or head of state of the new Caliphate. The US State Department has designated al-Baghdadi as a Global Terrorist and offered a $10 million 'dead or alive' reward for his capture or death. Undeterred, in July 2014, al-Baghdadi made a speech from the Great Mosque of al-Nuri in Mosul, northern Iraq, in which he declared himself the world leader of all Muslims. He announced that the Islamic State would march on Rome and conquer the whole of Europe and the Middle East. His declaration of a Caliphate caused great consternation amongst many Middle East governments and religious leaders, who claimed such a pronouncement was void under Sharia law.

The expansion of ISIS inside Iraq took the world by surprise. Suddenly even the Kurdish Peshmerga were being forced to retreat as Islamic State jihadists moved relentlessly towards Erbil, the KRG capital. Maliki exploited the worsening crisis for his own ends, pleading with the West and neighbouring Iran for military assistance, and repeatedly stating that he was the only person who could resolve the crisis. Western leaders, however, began to realise what many others and I had been arguing for years – that Maliki was the problem, not the solution. Only his removal from office and replacement by a non-sectarian government of national salvation could reunite the country and lead the fightback against the IS terrorists.

It rapidly became apparent that Maliki no longer had majority support, even amongst his own Shiia political factions. Obama and John Kerry were by now openly calling for his removal, and as the Islamic State began even to threaten the borders of Iran, the Mullahs saw the writing on the wall and threw their long-time puppet to the encircling wolves. When the newly appointed Iraqi President, Fuad Masum, ignored Maliki's entreaties and invited Haider al-Abadi to form a government, Maliki reacted furiously, stating that he would report the President to the judiciary for breaching the constitution. As leader of the main Shiite political faction that had won most seats in the election, Maliki argued that it was his constitutional right to remain in charge as Prime Minister. This was a great irony coming from Maliki, a past master at breaching the Iraqi constitution. Nevertheless, bolstered by growing international support, even from the Iranian Mullahs, President Masum ignored Maliki's threats and gave the job to Haider al-Abadi.

238

Realising the game was up, Maliki finally agreed to stand aside, and the Manchester University-educated Haider al-Abadi began active negotiations to form a new, inclusive government, involving Shiias, Sunnis, Kurds and all ethnic minorities and political factions. The prospects for a government of national salvation and an end to sectarian strife began to grow.

There is no doubt that the disruption and mistakes made by the US following the 2003 invasion contributed to Iraq's current predicament and its years of failed governance. Constant interference and manipulation by Iran has exacerbated this situation and helped to divide the nation further. It was intolerable that the Western powers said nothing in the face of such tyranny and corruption. Iraq's progress always depended on the willingness of its leaders to turn away from a narrow focus on their own power, wealth, ethnicity and faction. If, with Maliki now gone, they do not move forward, Iraq will face civil war and disintegration. It will become a failed state.

After five years as President of the European Parliament's Delegation for Relations with Iraq from 2009 to 2014, and many visits to the country and discussions with its political leaders, I cannot now simply wash my hands and walk away. It is for this reason that I decided to set up the European Iraqi Freedom Association, whose main motivation is to work towards the restoration of democracy, freedom and justice in that beleaguered country. The people of Iraq have been tortured, beaten, abused and robbed of their heritage and livelihoods by a long succession of corrupt and dictatorial leaders. They deserve a better future, and the European Iraqi Freedom Association will be their voice in Europe.

Many distinguished politicians and notable leaders who share these objectives have joined me in this task, including my longstanding friend and collaborator Alejo Vidal-Quadras, Vice President of the European Parliament from 1999 to 2014, Paulo Casaca, MEP from 1999 to 2009, Geir Haarde, former Prime Minister of Iceland, Sid Ahmed Ghozali, former Prime Minister of Algeria, His Excellency Tariq Al-Hashemi, former Vice President of Iraq, Lord Carlile, former National Security Advisor to the UK government, and Giulio Terzi, former Foreign Minister of Italy. I anticipate many other distinguished political colleagues will join.

Our objective is to see a non-sectarian government of national salvation that can unite the Shiias and the Sunnis in Iraq and bring together the many other diverse ethnic factions. The first imperative if this goal is to be achieved is for the eviction of the Iranian regime from Iraq. They relentlessly built up their influence and internal meddling in Iraq during the eight years of Maliki's dictatorship, and progress towards national unity cannot happen until they are forced out.

We have achieved one of our first objectives by seeing the departure of Nouri al-Maliki, a corrupt and brutal sociopath. We must now place our faith in Haider al-Abadi, the new Prime Minister, and trust that he will not repeat the mistakes of his predecessor. If he unites the Shiias, Sunnis and Kurds in Iraq and offers the hand of friendship to the many ethnic minorities and ejects the agents of the Iranian regime and its criminal militias from the political scene, he will be able to revive the tribes and lead a successful fight against the Islamic State terrorists, driving them back to Syria.

It will be a mountainous task for al-Abadi. First he has to set up an inclusive cabinet, clear of the influence of foreign powers, particularly the Iranian regime. Then he must order the immediate release of all political prisoners, especially the women who have been imprisoned by Maliki under bogus terrorist charges. Next he must demonstrate that he will welcome the participation of all parts of Iraqi society, particularly the Sunnis and Kurds, in power-sharing, recognising the people's rights in Sunni provinces and entering into dialogue with the tribal leaders and Sunni revolutionaries.

He must begin rounding up the savage militias associated with the Iranian regime, such as Badr, Asaib and Kataib terrorists, as well as other criminal gangs that have played a significant role in Maliki's rule and instigated the sectarian war in Iraq. He must purge the army of Iranian mercenaries and all those that Maliki has recruited under his sectarian policy, restoring patriotic officers and turning it into a professional and national army. Only such an army, supported by the tribes and the people, will be able to confront extremist and terrorist groups like the Islamic State.

The new Prime Minister should also disclose to the Iraqi people the names of those who carried out the executions, massacres, bombardment and rocket attacks against innocent people, and those responsible for poverty and state corruption; all should be held accountable in the courts. He must re-establish the independence of the judiciary, dismissing those who have turned Iraq's justice system into a political tool wielded by Maliki. He must also arrest and hold to account the perpetrators of the six massacres at Camps Ashraf and Liberty, as well as lifting the inhuman siege against Iranian refugees at Liberty and guaranteeing their rights and security and their right to ownership of their property at Liberty and Ashraf.

The new government should prepare the ground for an early free and fair democratic election under UN supervision to restore true sovereignty to the people's representatives.

I certainly hope that Dr al-Abadi will take rapid steps towards implementing these measures to fulfil the wishes of all the people of Iraq. This way, he will enjoy the full support of the world community and particularly the EU. He now has in his hands the historic role of saving Iraq, or presiding over its total disintegration.

42

Interviews with PMOI Refugees in Camp Liberty, September 2014

Bahar Abehesht

My name is Bahar Abehesht. I was born in Tehran on 14 March 1982. I was a math major in high school and from early childhood studied and competed in martial arts. Upon joining the PMOI and after the US attack on Iraq, which led to voluntary disarmament of the NLA, I continued my education online in the field of computer programming and software.

I came to know the PMOI from the time I was very young. My Mum and Dad were both members of the PMOI. When Khomeini returned to Iran and the suppression of the PMOI began, both my parents were forced to go into hiding. In 1982 when my Mum was pregnant, my Dad was arrested by the Revolutionary Guards in northern Iran in one of the PMOI's bases. He was tortured severely, and after he had refused to repent he was executed. He never saw me. When my Mum went to hospital to give birth to me, the hospital was surrounded by Revolutionary Guards looking for PMOI members and supporters. One of the doctors was a member of the Fedayeen guerrillas and knew my Mum was with the PMOI; he transferred her to a special ward at the hospital to be safe from the Guards. Immediately after she gave birth she was put in a car and discreetly transferred out of the hospital to a safe house on Majidieh Street.

After a few hours the Revolutionary Guards had entered the hospital and arrested the doctor who had helped my Mum and took him to prison. He was later executed. My Mum lived with a few other PMOI members in a safe house in Tehran's Pars district. On 2 May 1982, the regime launched a widespread attack on PMOI bases and safe houses across Tehran, and my Mum and I were arrested and taken to Evin Prison. I was only a few weeks old at the time. Despite my grandparents trying to secure my release from prison and raise me

242

in their home, the regime did not permit it and I was in Evin Prison till I was two years old. In Evin Prison my Mum was under constant torture and long interrogations, so she was not able to take care of me, and I was cared for by other female prisoners.

At the age of two my grandparents managed to get custody of me and take me home with them. If I want to describe how I came to know the PMOI I have to say that since I opened my eyes to this world I was surrounded by the PMOI. All I saw of the Khomeini regime was torture and execution, and from the PMOI, paying the price of freedom. I was raised in a family where my Dad and uncles, along with five other members of my family, were all executed by the regime for being members of the PMOI. I was raised hearing the name of Massoud Rajavi. It is customary in Iran that when a child is born they recite verses of the Koran in their ears, but they told me when I was born that they had whispered "Death to Khomeini, Long Live Rajavi" in my ears.

Seeing my Mum and uncles in jail and then seeing their pictures set up on our fireplace, I used to ask my grandparents, "Why is my Mum in prison? Why did they kill my Dad and uncles?" When I was little they would refrain from replying and change the subject, but when I was five years old, one day my grandfather told me about the Mojahedin. He said that they fought for freedom and sacrificed their lives to free the people of Iran. Every night at 8 p.m. my grandfather would try to listen to the PMOI radio programme, sifting through the static. This is how I spent my childhood, and this was a glimpse into how I came to know the PMOI.

In our home we knew Massoud Rajavi as our leader. They used to show his picture to us and tell us, "This is uncle Massoud, one day he will return to Iran and call all the children whose fathers have been executed to join him." So as someone who had lost her father, I felt an intense relationship with the leader of the resistance. When I grew up I always wanted to see him and always thought about him. Since I was raised in a family who were PMOI supporters, I came to know the meaning of injustice and freedom early on. My Mum spent ten years in Khomeini's jails. The signs of savage torture are still visible on her body. My older uncle spent seven years in the Shah and Khomeini's prisons. My younger uncle was severely tortured for five years; his cellmates had even documented the tortures he endured and I still have a copy of their report with me. The Khomeini regime executed him after five years of torture. Since I was a child I learned from the Mojahedin that you have to pay a price for freedom.

In 1988, I was taken to my mother in prison. Under Khomeini's regime, if a child needs to be with her mother and the mother happens to be in prison then she has to go to prison to join her mother. So I accepted the terms and joined my Mum and the rest of the PMOI women in prison. 1988 coincided with the massacre of PMOI prisoners. I will never forget the events that transpired that year. I witnessed first hand the transfer of prisoners for mass executions. I saw their mutilated bodies when they returned from the torture chamber. The torturers used to whip the prisoners using cables to a point that most could hardly stand on their feet. Most of the PMOI could not eat the prison rations and had bleeding ulcers. Many had problems with their kidneys because of the lashes they received; some of them had to go through dialysis because their kidneys were not functioning.

Some experienced constant headaches and migraine from being hit in the head and most suffered from poor eyesight. I saw with my own eyes the bodies of the women who were tortured; their torn backs, feet and hands. I have seen the correctional cells with only a small window for air, in which they would place many people at the same time. I have talked through those small windows to the prisoners and exchanged information. They were all my friends, and despite all the tortures they endured they were all upbeat and energetic. Even though I was in prison with them, as long as I was amongst them I had a good feeling. They use to sing and read poetry and tell me about their resistance under torture. They told me: "You have to leave the prison and tell everyone what is happening in here." Most of them knew that they would soon be executed, but they never lost their passion for life. Most of the people who were in prison with me were executed in the 1988 massacre of political prisoners, including Mozhgan Sorbi, 26, Azadeh Tabib, 25, Mahin Ghoreishi, Fereshteh Hamidi, and others . . .

Azadeh Tabib was a champion in resistance under torture. My Mum and Azadeh were suspended from the ceiling for long periods of time. The pressure on their arms and wrists was so much that they weren't able to move their wrists and they were transferred to hospital for surgery. Mahin Ghoreishi, whose husband was executed, had a seven-year-old boy named Mohammad. Mahin was executed because of her belief in freedom and her membership of the PMOI. My Mum had taught me a poem with revolutionary innuendos and when the regime's Guards heard me sing it, they took my Mum to the interrogation rooms and severely tortured her; when she returned she looked victorious and started telling her friends about the episode. I have a lot of facts from the torture methods applied and the resistance of the Mojahedin at Evin Prison; when the time comes to put the officials of the regime on trial I will testify and present them to an international tribunal responsible for their trial.

Once when the prisoners were led to the yard for fresh air, I was about five and a half. A few of my Mum's friends started talking to the Guards, keeping them busy while my Mum and a few others took me to the corner of the yard and had me stand on top of the shoulders of one of the tallest female prisoners. They told me to start calling the names of some prisoners. I could hardly see the other side of the wall, all I could see was one of the cells buried in the ground with the bars peeking through. I started calling the names they told me. As soon as I started calling their names they started lining up behind the bars at the window of the cell. They were my Mum's friends who were defiant prisoners sent to the underground cells as punishment. I relayed the information my Mum and her friends gave me; it was so exciting. When I was done with relaying the information, they used to ask me to recite them this poem:

> The star was torn to pieces, but never fell out of the sky,
> Star, O Star, this is how it is,
> Whoever has a star, will end up at the gallows.

From their tiny cells they used to clap their hands and give me the sign of victory. Then they would recite a poem to me as well; unfortunately I don't remember the words. All I remember is that it was a poem about resistance and freedom. In 1988 everyone who was in the correctional cells was executed.

Martyred Mojahed Mahin Ghoreishi once called me and asked me, "Do you know the tale of the little black fish?" I told her that I had the book and I had read it, and she told me, "You have to become like the little black fish and start swimming till you reach the ocean." She was executed for being a member of the PMOI and she left me a scarf with the embroidery of a little black fish on its corner.

When the mass executions began and they were executing people in waves, the prison officials started removing the children from the prison wards. They had started the executions and they sent me to my grandma and grandfather's house in Karaj. During the mass executions, most of the people I had come to know were executed. My Mum was supposed to be executed as well, but through the intense efforts of my grandfather and his friends who were the heads of some banks in Tehran, they managed to rescue her from death row.

When I turned 15, I felt that I could not live in a society which was oppressed by the Mullahs. Despite the fact that I lived in an affluent family, there was always something inside me that made me rebel against the poverty and injustice around me. I did not want a life of oppression under the Mullahs in Iran. I always thought of Massoud Rajavi and wanted to fight for a free Iran alongside him. When I turned 17, I told my Mum that I didn't want to stay there any longer and I wanted to go where Massoud Rajavi was and become a freedom fighter. My Mum was always under surveillance, so I had to flee Iran illegally to the Iraqi border in order to join the Mojahedin. I managed to go through the Salmas mountains in north-west Iran and entered a village in Turkey. Trying to reach Turkey through the mountains while I was waist-deep in snow took 20 hours. I thought I might be arrested at the border trying to reach Ashraf.

When I reached Turkey I took refuge in a home at the first village I came to. I told them that I had run away from Iran. Both my legs had turned blue from walking in the snow. When I got to the villagers' home I could not walk or stand on my feet any longer. With the help of the villagers I recuperated, and when I felt better I got myself to the Iraqi border. When I finally made it to Baghdad, I was so exhausted I could hardly stand up. Finally I made it to the first Mojahedin base, and was greeted warmly by my brothers and sisters; it was as though after years of searching I had finally found my ultimate destination. I was part of the third generation after the revolution to join Ashraf.

In 2003, after the war in Iraq, we had to turn in our weapons to the Americans, and in return we were supposed to be protected; but what transpired was the betrayal of that promise by the United States. In Ashraf I started taking online courses in computer software and programming. Upon completing the courses, I worked towards updating the computer systems in Ashraf. On 28 and 29 July 2009, when the Iraqi forces attacked us I was hit with metal bars and bats. They used high-pressure water cannons on us, which caused the loss of hearing in my right ear. It had damaged the mastoid bone in my ear and the effects are irreversible.

During the 8 April 2011 attack on Ashraf, the Iraqi forces attacked us using loaders and armoured vehicles. One of the Iraqi soldiers put his gun to my chest and said, "If you don't move I am going to shoot you." They kept hitting us with clubs and bats. The bullets kept passing through the air very close to me and struck a friend who was filming the assault. My friend and I were picked up by the loader and thrown off a considerable height and half of my body was caught under the loader. I was pulled out and taken to hospital, where I was told that my right kidney had been damaged and was bleeding.

Oppression in my country is savage and criminal. Being a witness to the massacre of 30,000 political prisoners at the age of six has been extremely traumatic. Daily executions of young people, cutting off hands, and suppression of freedom of speech in the twenty-first century are catastrophic. My country is one of the richest countries in the world and you have no idea the degree of poverty I have witnessed in Iran. The Mullahs' prisons are filled with political prisoners. Believe me, I always wished I could have seen my father who was a PMOI member. I had heard so much about him and his bravery, but these Mullahs took him away and made me and many other children orphans.

I feel that, amongst the many people who are born, there are only a few who will leave a lasting mark on this world; this is the destiny of human beings. I found my destiny in my struggle, and I know that believing in freedom has its own challenges and hardships. The Iranian regime and their Iraqi and Western allies have challenged us in

247

so many different ways through these years; but they cannot destroy us. We represent an ideology and a belief system that cannot be simply destroyed. The struggle is not part of my life; it is all of my life. We are in this to the end.'

43

I Am Ashrafi

How easily the West allows itself to be repeatedly duped by the fascist rulers of Iran. Past-masters at the art of deception, they have defied world opinion for the preceding decade in their race to build nuclear weapons, but after eight tortuous years of confrontation with the unstable Ahmadinejad at the helm, Supreme Leader Ali Khamenei finally realised that the only way to buy more time was to convince the West that a moderate had emerged as the new president of Iran.

The arrival of the cleric Hassan Rouhani, following the presidential elections in Iran, seemingly ticked all of the boxes. The Western press crowed that this new 'moderate' president, who had attended university in Glasgow, Scotland, would be open to dialogue on stopping the nuclear programme and would be a harbinger of positive change for the repressed masses in Iran. Sadly, nothing could be further from the truth.

Firstly, the role of president in Iran is virtually ceremonial. Total power under the Iranian constitution lies with the unelected 'Supreme Leader' Ayatollah Ali Khamenei, who succeeded the late Ayatollah Ruhollah Khomeini, founder of the Islamic Republic. The Supreme Leader is supposed to take his instructions directly from God, and as such can overrule acts of parliament and can even choose which candidates can stand for election.

Under article 110 of the constitution, the Supreme Leader can dismiss the president and appoint or remove commanders of the Revolutionary Guards and the army, the chief justice, and the head of state-run radio and television, among many others. On top of that, he has the power to issue a 'state decree' which overrides all decisions made by any person or institution in the country. Decisions on sensitive issues such as the war in Syria or the nuclear programme are entirely in the domain of the Supreme Leader, not the president.

249

Elections in Iran are not a contest between the governing party and the opposition. At best, they are a shuffle within the ruling clique, and even then women are excluded, denying half the population their right to representation. The real opposition has been systematically arrested, tortured and executed. The so-called Council of Guardians, whose members are handpicked by the Supreme Leader, can easily disqualify candidates in any election.

Hassan Rouhani emerged from a list of eight hand-picked candidates, who were variously advisers, aides or representatives of Khamenei. Rouhani has been part of the fascist establishment for three decades. He held the position of Secretary of the Supreme National Security Council for 16 years and was appointed by Khamenei as a member of the powerful Expediency Council. He was also chief nuclear negotiator with the European Troika, where he later proudly declared that he had successfully bought time to advance Iran's nuclear weapons technology while he deceived EU leaders who were busy negotiating with him.

Rouhani's approval by the Guardian Council, while former President Ali-Akbar Hashemi Rafsanjani was disqualified, was yet another sign of his slavish subservience to the Supreme Leader. Rouhani's role was now mainly to buy time for the Mullahs' nuclear goals, something that he had successfully done in the past. Indeed in his book, *National Security and Nuclear Diplomacy*, he laboriously complains about the PMOI's nuclear revelations in 2002. He makes it quite clear that the regime's problems began after the PMOI exposed Iran's two major nuclear sites in Natanz and Arak.

Rouhani was also faced with three major issues that had to be resolved if the Mullahs' regime was to survive. The first was the nuclear issue, second the war in Syria and Iraq and the inexorable rise of the Islamic State (ISIS or ISIL), and third was the toll of sanctions on Iran's devastated economy. The regime was facing a dire situation due to the impact of sanctions, as well as the downturn in the cost of oil and widespread youth unemployment. There are currently an estimated five million unemployed youths in Iran.

The entire survival of the regime is based on the notion of the absolute rule of the clergy, and any deviation from this principle will inevitably lead to a rupture of the environment of fear and terror and result in its fall. It is for this very reason that Khamenei has resisted any form of political manoeuvring, let alone serious political reform. Internal reform is unlikely to happen regardless of who holds the presidency. A free Iran will be one with no Mullahs in power.

To date, over a year into Rouhani's allegedly 'moderate' presidency, more than 1,000 people, many of them political prisoners, have been executed. On average, a prisoner has been hanged in public or in prisons in various cities in Iran every seven hours. The executed include women and teenagers, and often people who were under the age of 15 when they were first arrested. Large numbers of prisoners are now executed collectively in groups of 21, 11 and 6 persons. This is while thousands of prisoners in various prisons in the country are on death row.

Meanwhile IRGC Brigadier General Mohammad Reza Naghdi, commander of the merciless Basij force, has announced the formation of a 'Council of Promotion of Virtue and Prevention of Vice'. The mission of this institution is the suppression of youth, particularly young women and girls, under the Mullahs' pretext of 'mal-veiling'. Organised gangs affiliated with the Mullahs' regime have been splashing acid on the faces of a large number of young women in Esfahan and other cities to punish them for 'mal-veiling'. The clerical regime has resorted to a wave of executions and suppressive measures in order to heighten the atmosphere of intimidation in society and to prevent an outbreak of protests.

And yet, despite the danger he poses, the West has fallen head-over-heels in love with the broadly smiling Hassan Rouhani. Indeed Rouhani is no longer smiling, he is laughing, literally all the way to the bank! His tactics of deception have fooled the West into reducing sanctions and effectively removing any threat of military intervention, and as a result, the national currency, the rial, is doing quite well, while the Tehran stock exchange has staged a remarkable rally.

Meanwhile the West, crowing about our success in achieving meaningful dialogue with Iran, has blunted the only remaining tool with which we could have held the Mullahs to account, because our main weapon in dealing with Iran is economic. In the spring of 2014, over 100 European businessmen visited Tehran to explore new, lucrative contracts; the Iranians even held a major energy conference in London in the summer of 2014, when leading oil companies from the West were encouraged to reopen contracts for oil and gas exploitation in Iran. This renewed surge of interest in commercial profits despite violations of basic human rights in Iran, has rescued the evil Mullah regime when it was on the brink of collapse.

And what has the West won in return? Of course there are some good things in the nuclear agreement, but it is a temporary stopgap. It has actually achieved very little. It only dealt with the enrichment question. What about the Iranian military machine? What about their missile delivery systems? What about the estimated 19,000 centrifuges? Why didn't we demand the dismantling of 14,000 of these machines? We have capped the accumulation of enriched uranium, but failed to stop research and development into more advanced centrifuge technology. This does little to stop the threat of a future nuclear-armed Iran.

Indeed in a wide-ranging interview Dr Ali Akbar Salehi, Iran's Nuclear Chief, claimed that, 'The entire nuclear activity of Iran is going on . . . Iran can reverse its nuclear concessions [made in the joint plan of action] in a few hours.'

The horrific events in Gaza in July and August 2014 brought international condemnation against Israel. For one country in the Middle East, this was exactly the outcome they had sought. Iran has supplied missiles and munitions and other sophisticated weaponry to Hamas for years. They have provided money and training for the Hamas fighters. Their objective was to provoke Israel into a ground war, and the bloody result, with gruesome photos of dead children on TV screens and newspapers around the world, is the best possible recruiting sergeant for fundamentalist Islam and the Iranian Mullahs' vision of a global Islamist movement united against the West and its apostate, secular supporters. They did the same in Lebanon during the July 2006 war between Hezbollah and Israel.

The fascist regime in Tehran is the main sponsor of war and terror in the Middle East, and the tragic outcome in Gaza is exactly what Tehran wanted. It distracts domestic attention in Iran from the economic crisis caused by the downturn in the price of oil, and distracts international attention from the Mullahs' rush to produce a nuclear weapon. Iran's foreign policy objective is to become the dominant regional power in the Middle East. They want to unite the Islamic world in submission to their own austere and disturbing vision of a totalitarian and fundamentalist Islamic brotherhood, where human rights, women's rights and freedom of speech are ground into the dust. Shamefully, the West has done nothing to confront or expose Iranian aggression. Faced with mounting evidence of the Mullahs' sponsorship of terror, the West has gone out of its way to appease Tehran.

Iran is like a poisonous spider, sitting at the centre of a deadly web that seeks to extend its malign influence across the entire Middle East. The Mullahs export terror. They support the murderous Assad regime in Syria and they fund and arm Hezbollah in Lebanon and Hamas in Gaza. They relentlessly spread their toxic dominion across Iraq, using Nouri al-Maliki in the past as their willing puppet, until their ruthless sectarian policies led to civil war and the virtual breakup of Iraq. The revolutionary uprising by the Sunni tribes quickly destabilised the country and provided an ideal opportunity for the Islamic State to exploit. They poured over the border from Syria, seizing many Iraqi cities and rapidly advancing to within 50 miles of Baghdad.

But, such was the West's enthusiastic love affair with the so-called moderate Iranian President Rouhani, that the EU's almost entirely useless High Representative for Foreign Affairs, Baroness Ashton, even decided to pay an official visit to Tehran in the spring of 2014. Her visit coincided with Israel's interception of a ship from Iran carrying dozens of long-range surface-to-surface rockets, assault weapons and hundreds of thousands of bullets, destined for Palestinian militants in Gaza. Iran is the world's leading exporter and bankroller of terrorists, and their cat-and-mouse attempts to persuade Baroness Ashton and others that they have no intention of producing nuclear weapons is a farce.

Ironically, Baroness Ashton landed in Tehran on Saturday 8 March – International Women's Day! Iran's repression of women is globally renowned. In fact, on 4 March, the regime had hanged a 25-year-old woman who had been held in prison since she was a teenager. Her name was Farzaneh Moradi, and she had a ten-year-old daughter.

As already noted, Iran has hanged at least 1,000 people, many in public, since Rouhani came to power. Many women have been victims of organised acid attacks for mal-veiling. Just before Ashton's ill-judged visit, there was a shocking public execution of a 26-year-old young man in the city of Karaj, where the hangmen even deprived the condemned man from seeing his mother who was present at the scene, causing a great public outcry. In addition, the Mullahs' Supreme Court approved a sentence to blind a man and cut off his ear and nose. Ashton, of course, in her fawning supplication to the fascist Mullahs, failed to condemn any of these barbarities during her visit, and inevitably, her presence in Tehran was exploited as a propaganda tool by the regime.

Nor did Ashton's visit to Tehran stop the Mullahs from piling pressure on Iraq to kill or hand over the Iranian dissidents in Camp Liberty. It is time the West woke up. We have seen countless initiatives to stop the nuclear programme. All have failed. We have seen the appointment of Special Envoys like Dan Fried, Jean de Ruyt and more recently Jane Holl Lute, tasked with resolving the Ashraf crisis. All have failed. We have seen the cack-handed efforts by the UN Secretary General's Special Representative in Iraq, Martin Kobler, pave the way for the death, destruction and incarceration of innocent men and women.

We cannot continue with the policy of appeasement toward Iran, nor can we countenance military intervention. But we can show support for the vast majority of Iranian citizens who long for freedom and who pray for the fall of the fascist regime. The most tangible way to show our support for the Iranian people is to support the biggest, best-organised and legitimate opposition – the PMOI. To do so would be to send a clear message to the Mullahs in Tehran that we are no longer prepared to stand idly by while they spread terror and death across the Middle East and the wider world.

In tandem, we must rescue the unarmed refugees trapped in Camp Liberty in Iraq. Since their protection was handed to the Iraqis by the US military, they have suffered 26 separate attacks resulting in 116 dead, 1,300 injured, 7 hostages (6 of whom are women) who are still unaccounted for, and 24 dead because of the inhuman medical siege. All of this has been done wilfully under the direct instructions of Nouri al-Maliki and with the active connivance and encouragement of the Iranian regime. Maliki has stepped aside as Prime Minister in Iraq and his immunity from prosecution, which came with that job, has now vanished. He must immediately be indicted for crimes against humanity and brought before the international courts for trial.

In the meantime, rather than allowing ourselves to slide into the depths of depression at the failure of our politicians, let us remember the words of Victor Hugo:

> Nations, like stars, are entitled to eclipse. All is well, provided the light returns and the eclipse does not become endless night. Dawn and resurrection are synonymous. The reappearance of the light is the same as the survival of the soul.

Iran has suffered a long period of darkness. The light of liberty has truly been eclipsed. But the Mullahs' days are numbered. The reappearance of the light is imminent; in fact we can see the first faint glimmers of dawn breaking through the blackness and the torchbearers are the PMOI in Camp Liberty and their supporters around the world. I count myself privileged to say I am with them every step of the way. I pray that one day soon I will walk hand-in-hand with them through the streets of a liberated Tehran.

I am Ashrafi.

More than two centuries ago the famous Scottish poet Robert Burns wrote verses of praise for King Robert The Bruce of Scotland, which could become the PMOI battle cry for their campaign for freedom and justice in Iran.

> By Oppression's woes and pains!
> By your sons in servile chains!
> We will drain our dearest veins,
> But they shall be free!
> Lay the proud usurpers low!
> Tyrants fall in every foe!
> LIBERTY'S in every blow!
> Let us do – or die!

255

Postscript

At the time of going to press there are still some 2,700 Iranian refugees, including 700 women, being held under unbearable conditions in Camp Liberty, near Baghdad Airport. The siege by the Iraqi government has continued, denying access to the camp for basic commodities such as food, water, fuel and medical supplies. The lack of fuel meant that subsequently all of the camp's electricity generators stopped working. Air-conditioning immediately ceased to function and with outside temperatures soaring above 48°C in the blazing summer heat, many of the residents quickly became seriously dehydrated, requiring urgent medical attention which was also denied. In addition, water pumps stopped working, the contents of fridges and freezers began to rot and septic tanks overflowed with polluted sewerage. Liberty was rapidly becoming hell on earth.

UNAMI, who signed the Memorandum of Understanding with the government of Iraq against the wishes of the Iranian refugees, has now abandoned those men and women to their fate. Despite having repeatedly guaranteed their safety and security when they coaxed and cajoled the residents into deserting their long-term home at Camp Ashraf and moving to the tiny Liberty concentration camp, UNAMI has now stopped visiting Liberty altogether, concerned for the safety of their own personnel against the background of rising violence in Iraq. Similarly, UNHCR, which interviewed every one of the residents and provided each with formal refugee status, has also abandoned them to their fate, having failed to operate the promised 'revolving door' policy that would have seen them interviewed, registered and immediately re-settled to countries of safety.

The government of Nouri al-Maliki, in its dying days, used this hiatus to apply maximum suffering on the beleaguered refugees, and this is still going on. I and others had warned about this looming crisis in numerous letters, statements and communications to the US Government, the United Nations Secretary General and the EU's High Representative, but as usual, our pleas were ignored. The United States has particular responsibility, since the residents' current situation is a direct result of the US-led invasion of Iraq in 2003 when senior American officials gave written assurances to each of the residents that their safety and security would be guaranteed. But so far over a hundred residents have been murdered in repeated brutal attacks by Maliki's forces and more have died due to the inhuman medical restrictions imposed by the Iraqi government. Countless residents have been maimed and wounded in the recurring attacks and violence.

This shocking betrayal of innocent, unarmed men and women by the leading global institutions and governments of the UN, the EU and the US must rank alongside some of the worst duplicity in history. Having forcibly herded these men and women into a tiny killing ground, they then walked away, knowing that the inevitable outcome would be bloodshed and death.

I am deeply grateful to all those senior politicians, judges, generals and journalists who have put their own personal reputations on the line by exposing this perfidy and demanding action. Sadly, our collective cries have been ignored. It is a shameful chapter in human history and I can only hope that someone in office, somewhere, reading this account, will cry 'enough' and ride courageously to the rescue of these besieged refugees. In the meantime, our efforts to save the 2,700 will continue, as will our determination to bring to justice those who murdered and maimed the innocents.

As the Irish statesman Edmund Burke famously said: 'The only thing necessary for the triumph of evil is for good men to do nothing.'

Struan Stevenson
March 2015

Books and Publications Consulted

Lincoln P. Bloomfield Jr, *The Mujahedin-E Khalq, MEK, Shackled by a Twisted History* (University of Baltimore, 2013).

Friends of a Free Iran, *People's Mojahedin of Iran – Mission Report.*

The Mujahedin-e-Khalq, report by the British Foreign Office (March, 2001).

Ervand Abrahamian, *The Iranian Mojahedin* (Yale University Press, 1992).

Mohammad Mohaddessin, *Enemies of the Ayatollahs* (Pluto Press, 2004).

National Council of Resistance of Iran, *Meet the NCRI* (June, 2014).

Tahar Boumedra, *The United Nations and Human Rights in Iraq – The Untold Story of Camp Ashraf* (New Generation Publishing, 2013).

Hengameh Haj Hassan, *Face to Face with the Beast – Iranian Women in Mullahs' Prisons* (Homa Association, 2013).

William R. Polk, *Understanding Iraq* (I. B. Taurus, 2006).

Christopher de Bellaigue, *Patriot of Persia – Muhammad Mossadegh and a Very British Coup* (Bodley Head, 2012).

Patrick Cockburn, *Muqtada al-Sadr and the Fall of Iraq* (Faber and Faber, 2008).

Index

Notes: Arabic names with the prefix 'al-' are indexed under the main part of the name, e.g. Nouri al-Maliki is indexed under 'Maliki'. However, organisations and places beginning with al-, such as al-Qaeda, are indexed under 'al-'.